POLITICAL HUMOR

POLITICAL HUMOR

From Aristophanes
to Sam Ervin

Charles E. Schutz

RUTHERFORD ● MADISON ● TEANECK
FAIRLEIGH DICKINSON UNIVERSITY PRESS
LONDON: ASSOCIATED UNIVERSITY PRESSES

79998

Associated University Presses, Inc.
Cranbury, New Jersey 08512

Associated University Presses
Magdalen House
136-148 Tooley Street
London SE1 2TT, England

Library of Congress Cataloging in Publication Data

Schutz, Charles E
  Political humor.

  Bibliography: p.
  Includes index.
  1. Political satire—History and criticism.
I. Title.
PN6149.P64S3   320′.02′07   74-197
ISBN 0-8386-1536-8

Contents

79998

Preface

A Map of the Maze

I have been collecting political humor for almost twenty years. As a teacher of politics, I have found it to be useful for illustrative purposes. As a citizen and student of politics, I have also found political humor to be a release for my own confusions and frustrations. And, as an occasional participant in politics, I have observed that political witticisms can lighten the load of sober speech-making for audiences and also serve as a symbolic means of the candidates' socializing with them.

Yet, I never thought systematically about the uses of political humor; the sobriety and pretentiousness of modern scholarship seemed to militate against it. Some time ago I was asked to speak on current politics before a men's group. Because partisan emotions were running high at the time and I was in no mood for the hassles that would follow upon any analysis, I sought the traditional escape from anticipated hostility; I resorted to political humor. Utilizing my file of humor and supplementing it with the current

7

political jokes, I gave the group a lecture studded with jokes and padded with a cursory analysis of them. I found the humor to have certain recurring forms and a common anti-political bias. The reception of the talk was enthusiastic, and my vanity prodded me into further exploration of the material.

I went over the humor that I had collected and began to think about its nature. I then repaired to the library for articles and books on political humor; there was nothing except anthologies and incidental commentaries. Moreover, in a large literature on the psychology of laughter and humor, and on the dramatic criticism of comedy, there were no independent analyses of political humor. Yet political humor, with its targets of power and social authority, may be exemplary of all humor.

Because political humor is often a reaction to the greatest concentration of power in society, it exemplifies humor as a sublimation of aggression, a safe release for aggressiveness against superior force. Because government is the authoritative institution that enforces society's taboos, we use political humor against it to vent our resultant frustrations on it in a form that allows us some release for the suppressed urges.

But politics itself is a kind of sublimation of force, for it substitutes rhetoric and compromise for weapons and victory in social decision-making. Humor provides a socially acceptable release of the repressed emotions of our primitive aggressiveness. Politics as a war of words is then an arena in which humor is indispensable for limiting the war to words. And, because wordplay is the essence of much humor, the political arena will be the natural abode of the bon mot, particularly as comic invective.

Above all, political humor is often a highly rational project. Though its origins may lie in sublimation, its effectiveness depends upon its rational development. Modern psychology has contributed greatly to the understanding of humor, but its literature mostly overlooks the rational element in it. But political humor to be effective must communicate, primarily through the medium of words, and its target is an external object of common perception. Of necessity, political humor becomes objectified, and a rational project of man.

The original approach to this study lies in the failure of the literature on humor to deal with its rational and purposeful communication. Humor in politics is the most telling example of that failure, and this study seeks to remedy the ignorance. Humor in politics is a significant phenomenon, both for understanding politics and for understanding humor in its most social role. The first aim of this study is a systematic analysis of political humor to further that understanding.

In reviewing theories of humor to assess their relevance to politics, I found little that was directly related to politics, but I did derive a general orientation. I also found that the consideration of humor was philosophically respectable; many of the greats have deigned to comment on the lowly pursuit. However, in relation to political humor, I found that Aristotle, Freud, and Koestler have provided the most needful elements for understanding it.

This, then, is a theoretical study of political humor. It adapts several theories of humor to politics, but it is not a study of theories of political humor. I found none. Rather, this study examines political humor in its several varieties, presents that humor, analyzes it, and draws theoretical conclusions from it.

The selection of the political humor has been guided by my own tastes and my appreciation of its political utility. But my political tastes are formed by our democratic culture and my professional study of it. Second, most of the humor presented has stood the tests of time and publication. It does have political appeal.

Further, the tentative theory that I have formulated is a conclusion of the study of political humor. Of course I had theoretical predispositions, but several conclusions that are central to my understanding would initially have been strongly rejected. I now consider comic political invective to be the most natural political humor, and, despite any radicalism of political humor, I hold that it is essentially conservative in thought and in impact.

I would argue that the conclusions that enter into this theoretical prolegomenon (a big word for bet-hedging) make sense in relation to what is known of the psychology of humor and the politics of democracy. It may be said that the conventional wisdom was the a priori point of view from which I approached political humor, and I got what I gave. There is truth in that. Political science is no science—I am not even sure that science is—and the psychology of humor is humorless.

This study begins with the most current political jokes and stories, because they are of immediate interest and serve as a bridge to the analysis of perennial humor. After this humor is classified under broad headings, it is explained in accordance with the political functions it serves.

A warning is in order, without apology. The current humor includes "dirty" political jokes. They are necessarily a part of the popular political culture, and vulgar and blasphemous humor is quintessentially a part of democratic politics. Incidentally, I like dirty political jokes, and, along with many others, I laugh at and repeat them. In fact, the virginal avoidance or priggish discussion of obscene humor in most of the literature distresses me.

The previous scholarly avoidance of dirty political humor led me into an analysis of Aristophanes' political comedies. Because his work is classical, it is a respectable subject of scholarship if properly euphemized. Scholars have also felt compelled to apologize for his bawdy genius without seeking to come to terms with its democratic vitality. The vulgarity of Aristophanic comedy is supremely typical of democratic humor, and Aristophanes is the comic genius of political criticism. He is the citizen critic who employs comic satire to reform the politics of his time. His dramatic satire, with its classical originality, depth, and vulgarity, is a model for all subsequent satire.

The study of Aristophanes opened a new vista in Plato for me. In reading the literature on Aristophanes, I ran across Lane Cooper's *Aristotelian Theory of Comedy*, and I became aware of a tradition that was cognizant of the comedy in the Platonic dialogues. I was also brought to understand that Aristotle's characterization of Socrates as an ironic man is a labeling of him as a kind of comic figure. This, in combination with Aristophanes' satirizing of Socrates in the *Clouds*, impelled me toward a reexamination of the humor of the Platonic Socrates.

Consequently, the Socrates of the *Symposium* and *Republic* emerged as another basic model for the political humorist. Socrates is Aristophanes' comic antagonist of politics. In studies of Green dramas, it is possible to view them in ritual opposition as the impostor (*alazon*) versus the ironic man (*eiron*). In the *Clouds*, Aristophanes is the ironist and Socrates the impostor. In the *Symposium*, Plato reverses their roles, though he drops a one-to-one relationship. In the *Republic*, Plato enshrines Socrates for posterity as the supreme political ironist.

However, for me, Socrates is the wise fool criticizing politics ultra-politically; Aristophanes is the comical wise man whose comic criticism is eminently political. Socrates condemns politics from his otherworldly vision. Alcibiades' description of Socrates in the *Symposium* as a kind of satyr led me to the chapter 3 title of sage satyr, a divine fool whose otherworldly wisdom gives him the appearance of an earthly clown.

The joyous comedy of the *Symposium* characterizes Socrates, but Socrates scales the highest peak of divine comedy in the *Republic* as he plumbs the depths of man's earthbound contradictoriness. The *Republic*, Plato's greatest political dialogue, is here given special consideration, because it is a form of divine comedy. James K. Feibleman in his *In Praise of Comedy* defines divine comedy as

comedy which takes the largest field that comedy can take for criticism and remain comedy, i.e., not lose all of its criticism through diffusion and become pure joy. The criticism of divine comedy is directed at nothing less than the whole field of the finite predicament: the glorious effort and partial failure of that which is limited as it strives to comprehend (and thus partially to transcend) its limitations.

Feibleman, in commenting on Dante's *The Divine Comedy*, catches the comic spirit of the *Republic* perfectly. He states that "the divine comedy consists in the fact that in their [men's] efforts to raise themselves above their limitations and to contemplate this actual world *sub specie aeternitatis*, they remain human after all and that necessarily 'a trace of earthly weakness and worldly levity clings to them' (Karl Vossler, *Mediaeval Culture*)."[1]

I therefore argue that the contradiction between man's transcendent impulses and his existential limitations is at the very heart of politics. In turn, Plato's *Republic* as the political philosophy of the contradictoriness of the human condition is the highest expression of divine comedy. In it, the divine vision of the Platonic Socrates, faced with man's earthly intransigence, is transformed into the profoundly anti-political irony of divine comedy.

Thus, I find contradiction to be the deepest root of political humor (and, possibly, of humor in general). I understand politics in this study in the Aristotelian sense as the activities of civilized and free men in their self-governance, using persuasion and compromise to achieve agreement on matters of social action. I find politics in this democratic sense to be the most contradictory of all men's social endeavors—it aspires to the best in man as it constantly comes to terms with the worst in him.

After I had come to feel and think the comic Aristophanes and Socrates, my third model of political humorist was predetermined. I am steeped in American political humor, and I unashamedly idealize Abraham Lincoln. To appreciate American political humor is to love America's greatest humorist-politician, Abraham Lincoln. Moreover,

1. James K. Feibleman, *In Praise of Comedy* (New York: Horizon Press, 1939, 1970), pp. 212-13, 48-49.

to discover the contradictory nature of political humor is to be introduced to the living contradiction of Lincoln. I rank Lincoln as the greatest of political humorists, for he is fully the democratic politician who lives his humor and uses it politically. For him, humor becomes a form of political reasoning and a means of democratic communication.

I shall argue that Lincoln's humor is intrinsic to his political genius. Yet, that raises the question of how he avoided the curse of Corwin's Law of the political success of solemn asses.* The answer lies in an American contribution to political humor at which Lincoln excelled—the comical political story. The storytelling tradition of small groups under the primitive conditions of frontier life was combined with democratic humor to create the political story. This development took place under the good offices of another American institution—the comic sages of common sense.

The comic sage of common sense is my fourth and final model of political humorist. There does remain a general type, shared by all the humorists and practised by most politically conscious people. It can be dubbed the comic vituperator, the practitioner of comic political invective. The practice is explicated in chapter 7, on comic political warfare.

The humor of the comic sages is not that of clowns but of earthy wisemen who coat their political pills with the sugar of buffoonery. They also cloak political wisdom in Socratic irony, but without divine attribution. With the partial exception of Abraham Lincoln, the comic sages are strongly anti-political. They merge into today's journalist-political satirists, with, however, a radical change of style.

The myth persists that political humor is the kiss of death in politics, despite the outstanding electoral success of several comic sages. I come down to the earth of everyday democratic politics to dispel this misapprehension of political humor. Again in chapter 7, "American Politics: Comic Warfare," I posit the naturalness of humor to politics. Politics is a highly civilized substitution of persuasion and par-

*See chapter 1.

ticipation for force and rank in governing men. It parallels humor in sublimating man's aggressions into peaceful wordplay. Thereby, comic invective is the natural and necessary accompaniment of politics in the abdication of force.

Political humor may have certain universal elements because of its very political nature. But a country's political humor will also reflect its particular history and circumstances. The obscene political humor of Aristophanes was presented as staged dramatic comedy, a very unlikely medium for American democracy. The dramatic comedy of ancient Greece was derived from the *komos*, a phallic religious festival in celebration of fertility, at once popular and permissible.[2]

I have been selective in my presentation of American political humor, but I have selected it widely. Wherever I have looked, and whatever the political humor at which I have looked, I have found it to be deeply anti-political. In sum, our political humor is a negative criticism of democratic politics. As comic ridicule, it extends from government through to the sovereign people themselves. Yet, I love politics and I love political humor. They are not incompatible. Therein lies my final understanding of political humor, for without it politics would be intolerable, in fact would be less than politics. That is what is meant in the concluding chapter by the *positive* negativity of political humor; its very nay-saying maintains and strengthens politics.

Beyond that, humor and politics merge in a manner in which politics itself can be seen as a kind of comic drama, realistically ridiculous and divinely ludicrous. By the drama of politics is meant society's staging of political action in its purposeful self-governance. The citizens are assigned roles as actors, and the game is played according to certain rules and conventions, resembling a script. Yet, in the political drama, things keep falling apart. Life constantly exceeds the bounds of the script, and the drama is burlesqued. As long

2. F. M. Cornford, *The Origins of Attic Comedy* (New York: Doubleday and Co., Anchor Book, 1914, 1961).

as it remains political, though, it is comical. For politics, in comparison with any alternative means of governance, has a minimal happiness to it.

Nevertheless, the premises for the political drama are as "unreal" as the purposes of it are idealistically impossible. And both man's realism and his idealism constantly exploit the comic elements of the drama. Only his sense of humor maintains the balance between the two and the tenuous survival of politics.

This, then, is the sketch and intention of my inquiry into political humor. In extracting the approach and the argument, I have deserted the humor. I apologize and will make amends with ample recompense in the work itself.

Charles E. Schutz
Albion College

Acknowledgments

I wish to thank the following publishers for having given me permission to quote from published works:

A. S. Barnes and Company, Inc., for permission to quote from Arthur P. Dudden, ed., *The Assault of Laughter*.

Beacon Press, for permission to quote from Herbert Marcuse, *An Essay on Liberation*.

Brandt & Brandt, from *Nineteen Eighty-Four* by George Orwell, copyright, 1949, by Harcourt, Brace & Jovanovich, Inc. Reprinted by permission of Brandt & Brandt.

Columbia University Press, for permission to quote from Jennette Tandy, *Crackerbox Philosopher in American Humor and Satire*, copyright 1925.

The *Detroit News*, for permission to quote from Arthur Hoppe, "Our Man Hoppe," published in The *Detroit News*, August 26, 1963.

Dial Press, for permission to quote from Leonard C. Lewin, ed., *A Treasury of American Political Humor*, copyright © 1964.

Doubleday and Company, Inc., for permission to quote from James Russell Lowell, "What Mr. Robinson Thinks" and from Kenneth S. Lynn, *The Comic Tradition in America*.

E. P. Dutton & Co., Inc., from *The Symposium* by Plato. Translation by Michael Joyce. Published by the Bollingen Foundation. Everyman's Library Edition. Reprinted by permission of the publishers, E. P. Dutton & Co., Inc.

Simon & Schuster, Inc., for permission to quote excerpts from *Presidents Who Have Known Me* by George Allen.

The Tudor Publishing Company, for permission to quote from Aristophanes, *The Eleven Comedies,* published by Tudor Publishing Company 1912, 1936.

POLITICAL HUMOR

1

The Sense of Political Humor

Wherein our sensing is made sensible

Introduction

In Herbert Muller's *Adlai Stevenson: A Study in Values*, the author writes of Stevenson, "Many voters questioned his integrity because of his wittiness, or violation of what he called the 'Republican law of gravity.' " Muller adds that Stevenson's humor was violating a national tradition, for "Americans have traditionally preferred to keep their politics solemn or stuffy."[1]

Leon Harris, author of *The Fine Art of Political Wit*, writes that American politicians have become more pious and less witty. He thinks that this tendency has increased because of television, for which the experts have advised the same banality and conformity for politicians as for commercials.[2] Richard Strout, the well-known TRB (*New Republic* columnist) of political journalism, writes:

1. Herbert J. Muller, *Adlai Stevenson: A Study in Values* (New York: Harper and Row, 1967), p. 9.
2. Leon A. Harris, *The Fine Art of Political Wit* (New York: Dutton and Co., 1964), p. 13.

Even on the lower planes of politics humor is a dangerous tool. American voters are an apathetic lot, and the first job of any politician is to get them aroused enough to go to the polls. But how do you excite an audience if it is waiting all the time for a quip?

Strout theorizes that humor indicates a sense of proportion that is antipathetic to the zeal of reformers and ambitious politicians. Moreover, he continues that the politicians must motivate the voters by inducing them to believe in the current panaceas and absolutes. In short, the humorous is not conducive to the grim earnestness of political campaigning. Strout concludes, "When an American politician is wooing the public or making his eternal vows to the electorate, a mood of reverent solemnity is the tradition."[3]

The above-named authors, and most other on American humor, cite the advice of Senator Thomas Corwin of Ohio to President Garfield in the nineteenth century, "Never make people laugh. If you would succeed in life, you must be solemn, solemn as an ass. All great monuments are built over solemn asses." This solemnity has become known as Corwin's Law of American politics.

Yet, there is a countertradition in American politics, and one well worth exploring for the light it throws on our political thought and prejudices. In campaigning, politicians may seldom be comical, but that is a narrow strip on the stage of political comedy. The broad stage is occupied by the people themselves and by the politicians conversing with each other. The humor may originate popularly, professionally, or among the politicians, but any politically aware person can testify to its never-ending proliferation.

Political humor takes the form of jokes and witticisms, anecdotes, satires, dramatic comedy, cartoons and caricatures, and perhaps the most common form, political invective. In fact, the pervasiveness of the latter may prove to be of particular significance for democratic politics.

3. Richard Strout, "Foe of the Bon Mot: Politics," *New York Times* Magazine, April 22, 1956.

For instance, at the completion of the 1972 Democratic Presidential Convention, a television commentator said that a delegate had summed up the character of the new presidential nominee, George McGovern, as a "humble, self-effacing egomaniac." Again, a Democratic staff man wrote that former Governor Endicott Peabody of Massachusetts was the only man ever to seek the Vice-Presidential candidacy who had four towns named after him: Endicott, Peabody, Marblehead, and Athol.

Political inventive is often crude and cruel, but if it is comical, its impact is not only tolerable but pleasurable. This study will contend that comic aggression, most apparent in political invective but discernible in most political humor, is peculiarly appropriate to politics. More generally, the politically humorous performs an invaluable function for democratic politics. Finally, humor is natural to politics, which can be understood as a kind of comic drama staged by society to aid in its governance.

Several caveats are in order before attempting this humorous speculation. First, the primary emphasis will be on the political functions and relationships of humor. Second, this work is not an anthology of humor, but it will use examples of political humor whenever possible. Humor is like Louis Armstrong's remark on jazz, that if you don't feel it, there's no use explaining it. The examples will include bawdy and obscene jokes, partisan ones and ones with personal references, but they are the actual humor and, thereby, objective date of American politics. Their victims cover the political spectrum, and their victimization is comical, not vicious. As former President Truman said of politics, "If you can't stand the heat, stay out of the kitchen."

Third, much political humor is public property, of unknown or multiple origins, reworked and applied to new situations and personages again and again. There is the story of the politician who said that his rival would either die of hanging or a dread disease and received the reply from the rival that the outcome would depend upon whether he embraced the first politician's principles or his mistress. It is attributed to both Disraeli in the nineteenth century and John Wilkes in the seventeenth.

The defection of Mayor John Lindsay of New York from the Republican to the Democratic Party and his subsequent running in the 1972 Democratic presidential primaries occasioned another old standby. A Democratic party leader said that it reminded him of the story of the small-town minister who said that if the town whore reformed and repented, he would certainly let her join the church, but he wouldn't let her lead the choir. The same anecdote is attributed to Senator Jim Watson of Indiana, commenting on former Democrat Wendell Wilkie's Republican presidential candidacy in 1940.

Political humor has something of a folk nature, and the same story will appear in different guises with different characters but the same point over the years. It is a testimony to certain enduring features of politics that they continue to be objects of ridicule or aggressive humor. As we proceed, I will note these recurring targets, for they yield insights into the problems of man's governance.[4]

Childhood and Comedy

Aristotle holds that man is a political animal, but that the young lack the experience necessary to political wisdom. In like manner, Montaigne's statement that man is the only animal who laughs can be qualified with the observation that children are essentially humorless. Nevertheless, the comic potential, like the potential for politics, is in the child. He possesses an incipient rationality whereby he glimpses incongruity and contradiction; he learns through imitation, and he must already sublimate much of his aggressiveness. With the deepening and developing of the child's reason, these sources of humor will extend and be-

---

4. Most political humor has a kind of folk quality, passed on by word of mouth and constantly being readapted. Therefore, unless there is a specific attribution to the humor, or the source is necessary to the gist of it, this essay will not cite authorship.

come conscious in him, even permitting him to create humor.

Freud says that the child's recognition of incongruity in the awkward movements of the clown or the abnormal behavior or appearance of his fellows is drawn from an application of a standard of normality, subjectively derived. The child knows what he himself is capable of; the failure in another to achieve it gives him pleasure, for he thereby feels superior—and probably more secure. The same sense of superiority occasions the child's laughter at another's mishap. It is indirectly aggressive, for he has imaginatively triumphed over the other, another evidence of his superiority that enhances his security.[5]

Freud's theory is somewhat simplistic, but we need not be concerned initially with whether the roots of humor are subjective or objective. The rational recognition of incongruity is an element of common sense and, certainly, or humor. Later, the recognition develops into an awareness of contradiction, irrelevance, absurdity, the ridiculous—all of them founded on a perception of the disparity of things and an intuition of unity behind them. A sense of humor does include an implicit rationality, a standard of what is proper, consistent, coherent, or sensible. The enjoyment of humor includes a kind of knowledge—a perception of some disparity. Perplexity over some joke or witticism is not enjoyable to the hearer.

Even the mimetic origins of comedy yield to this interpretation. At the infantile level, the child finds it funny to imitate someone or something. In doing so, he demonstrates a physical competence and, in duplicating the other's actions, a kind of mastery over him. He thereby gains a sense of superiority, but he has also recognized and responded positively to a part of reality. He has performed a rational action.

Henri Bergson in his *Laughter* gives another explanation,

---

5. Sigmund Freud, *Wit and Its Relation to the Unconscious*, in *The Basic Writings of Sigmund Freud*, ed. and trans. A. A. Brill (New York: The Modern Library, Random House, 1938).

which Freud views favorably. To imitate someone or something else is to duplicate it, to mechanize it. The essence or impulse of life is founded upon variability—*vive la différence*. In mimetic behavior we sense the incongruity between the mechanical sameness and the living variability. Bergson believes that often we laugh at or joke about anything resembling the mechanical counterfeit of life in a social response that will punish rigidity or inflexibility, for it would interfere with the life impulse of adaptability to change. It may be added that we laugh because, when we perceive the artificiality of the mechanical counterfeit, we are relieved to discover its make-believe nature. Laughter releases the tension we build in expectation of a threat to our life impulse.

One could say that caricatures and satires have their roots in childish mimesis. Pure imitation of someone or something is in the adult replaced by selective interpretation of certain of its features. The thing in itself is intentionally distorted through emphasis upon, or subtraction from, characteristics of it. Primarily and technically, the devices are comical, intending to ridicule something and to cause humor in others present. However, selective mimesis is both sublimated aggression and an appeal to a common standard of right. Humor is far more than funny, even with children.

The child's and the adult's laughter is believed by most authorities to be a physiological release of energy that was pent up in the first place to contend with an expected action. The humor lies in the reversal of expectation. Some unanticipated alternative to it occurs and effects a relief of tension. Laughter results as a release of energy built up for the original expectation. Most important, the humorous alternative to the originally expected action is a verbal or symbolic substitute for an anticipated aggressive situation. Humor sublimates aggression; peace is restored and relief results. If politics can be understood as the substitution of persuasion for sheer power, then humor is a kind of political response to a possibly disruptive social situation.

The unanticipated alternative to an originally expected

action can be understood as the collision within us of two incompatible chains of reasoning. External stimuli of some sort cause us to think and prepare ourselves for the customary logic of their circumstances. Suddenly, while reasoning according to the logic of the initially promised events, a counterpremise or event intrudes, totally disrupting the previously rational expectations, and mentally forcing in us a startling reversal of conclusions. This collision of two incompatible matrices of reasoning that leads to the shock of an unconventional conclusion is Arthur Koestler's explanation of the creative potential of humor in his *The Act of Creation*.

However, the collision of alternative logics occurs most naturally in children's thought, which is why it so often seems comical to adults. The child's rational processes are not fully socialized. He sees events oftentimes from a more "natural" perspective. He has not acquired the logic of convention or the social premises for "correctly" interpreting the vents.

Professional humorists consciously continue this conflict of the "natural" with the conventional logic of events. Jules Feiffer, the political cartoonist-writer, expresses this childlike perspective. When he was referred to as a writer of adult cartoons, he replied that there was nothing adult about his cartoons, that he wrote for children. He said, "The questions I seek to raise are always questions a young, not very bright, child might ask. Questions like 'what is good and what is bad? Is good always good? Is bad always bad?' A child would answer 'Yes.' "[6]

Feiffer often adapts a children's fable to drive home a political moral. In one written in the midst of the Vietnamese escalation in 1966, Feiffer's drawings show a little boy in various postures reading a book. The story line for each panel is as follows:

One day a little boy went to see the Emperor on parade and saw riding, grinning, and waving in a bubble domed carriage a giant of a man who was stark naked.

6. Susan M. Black, "Sokolsky, Meet Feiffer," *The New Republic* (June 6, 1960), pp. 17-18.

"Why," exclaimed the little boy, "The Emperor has no clothes!"

To which a wise man replied, "While it is just criticism to quarrel with the Emperor in his *taste* in clothes, it is *irresponsible* criticism to say he is naked because that approach fails to offer an alternative."

"Besides," said a second wise man, "How can you be so sure that the Emperor doesn't have access to material that we don't have? What you're *really* objecting to is *style*."

To this a third wise man added, "Whether or not the Emperor should have gone into the street without clothes is now merely a debator's point. The fact is that he is there, and we are committed."

Whereupon the wise men called for unity in the face of divisiveness while reminding themselves of the importance of tolerating the little boy's dissent.

Or, as the Emperor who had taped the dialogue was to later put it, "Only in an atmosphere of free debate can we determine the facts."

In the last panel of the cartoon, the little boy stares directly ahead and thoughtfully states, "Moral: The Emperor has clothes, you better believe it."

The child's innocent perception of the bare reality conflicts with the sophisticated reasonings of the socially responsible adults. In the conclusion, the boy cynically accepts the conventional contradiction of reality, but he states his acceptance in a way that startlingly emphasizes its absurdity. The child's logic is not presented in the story line, but it is implicit between the realistic premise and the absurd conclusion. The reader is drawn into participation by supplying it for himself and then is shocked by the reverse conclusion. Freud terms this comic technique "economy of expenditure in thought."

A classical capsule illustration of the conflict of logics leading to the shock of an absurd conclusion is contained in the comment of the venerable U.S. Senator Langer in 1956 upon the second-term nomination of President Eisenhower for the Republican candidacy. Eisenhower had had intestinal surgery and a heart attack in his first term and was already in his late sixties. Langer said, "I deserve the nomination more than Eisenhower does. I'm older. I'm sicker. And I need the rest more than he does!" The conflict between the popular opinion about Eisenhower's qualifications for the presidency and the unclothed reality of his competence is starkly presented in Langer's recital of his absurdly superior qualifications over Eisenhower's.

Neither Feiffer nor Langer is exercising rationality alone. Both comic ventures have an aggressive intent. Their authors have sublimated aggressions, relieved some tensions, gained social acceptability for their onslaught on authority, and managed to convey a rational message to a possibly hostile audience.

As the child is socialized, he must learn to repress much of his aggressiveness. Society cannot permit most aggressive actions among its members. As the child learns that particular types of aggressiveness will be punished, he tends to repress thoughts that would trigger prohibited actions. An aggressive thought is pushed back into the unconscious; therein it sometimes makes strange associations (resembling dream creation), seemingly disparate from its realistic referents. The formerly aggressive thought then emerges disguised as a humorous expression. The aggressiveness has been sublimated, though it continues to lurk beneath the surface.

Here is the Freudian model for humorous thought as it takes place in the child and later in the adult. The pleasure in such humor is in the feeling of release from the tensions of repressing the impulse to be aggressive, and also in a sense of superiority at the successful exercise of a prohibited aggression, albeit in a comic transfiguration. The laughter and pleasure of the audience are two-fold: first, from a sympathetic participation in the sublimated aggression, and, second, from a sense of personal superiority at having successfully perceived or learned the reality within the comic disguise.

The notion of humor as an expression of sublimated aggression is of importance to politics. Politics as a peaceful means of settling social conflicts requires of its citizens that they forgo direct action or aggressiveness in pressing their claims. They must behave according to highly structured social conventions and repress more primitive impulses. Aggressive humor allows the citizens to peacefully exercise their aggressions and gain a harmless release of some of the tensions occasioned in civilized living. Thereby humor facilitates politics, but, paradoxically, politics that requires the repression becomes a prime target for aggressive humor.

In sum, the childhood roots of political humor mirror an ancient issue of political philosophy—the conflict between nature and convention. The child discerns the artificiality of the conventional without recognizing the necessity and naturalness of all human conventions. But he thereby posits a standard in opposition to all social reality. He serves as a kind of preview revolutionary and gives us a glimpse of the critically realistic function of comedy.

Phallic Humor and Democratic Politics

Much of children's humor is scatological, and Freud, in line with his psychology, places it within what he calls the cloaca (common chamber) of sex. Sex-related humor is the most popular, continuous, and probably most ancient of comic forms. Its pervasiveness can then be expected, but its significance is generally overlooked. Political humor results in part from sublimated aggressions. Civilized sex, like politics, requires an enormous repression of primal behavior and aggressions. Their partnership in humor is bound to be a winning combination.

The dirty political joke ranges all the way from the vaguely suggestive to the outright obscene. Yet, most of the genre is denied existence in the literature of humor. Even Freud treats it and examples of it with Victorian priggishness. However, the pervasiveness and popularity of phallic political humor suggests a possible relationship between its vulgarity and democracy; the *vulgus* is the *demos*.

Only slightly suggestive in its sexual allusion is the quip of General Grant in respect to President Lincoln's critics: "For the President to answer all the charges the opposition would bring against him would be like setting a maiden to work to prove her chastity." The metaphor is clever in its ridicule of political opposition, but it is stimulating in its adroit use of two terms that interest and intrigue all men.

A more complex and phallic example of political humor is drawn from a daily newspaper column. As the columnist recounts, "A woman recently read an advertisement for the new feminine hygiene spray that stated it was for the most important part of you, so she sprayed her head. It worked too. She turned into a Republican." Here there is no overt obscenity. The audience engages in the implied reasoning and supplies its own sex. But for added attraction, there is a double punch line and a puzzle. The double shock doubles the humor, for there is initial relaxation, then new tension, and, this time, a puzzle to solve before release of tension—why a Republican?

A splendid example of simply phallic humor is the slogan of the youth demonstrators against the Vietnamese war at the 1968 Democratic presidential convention: "Dump the Hump!" Explicitly calling for the rejection of Senator Humphrey as a presidential candidate, the slogan employs rhyme, pun, and double entendre, with the nickname "hump" serving both as a reference to physical deformity and as a slang word for fornication. However rude and aggressive the phrase, its comic brevity is genuinely amusing.

If sordidness is a measure of splendor in phallic humor, the prize recent example is the bumper sticker distributed by a Left-wing magazine. It reads, "Vote for Nixon in '72. Don't change Dicks in the middle of a screw." Aside from the offensiveness of an almost explicit sexual reference, there are again the rhyme, the pun on the nickname Dick, the dual meaning of screw; and, finally, the parody of the aphorism, "Don't change horses in the middle of the stream." Moreover, the sexual taboo is not only violated, but the obscene humor is aggressive against the highest political authority, the President, with flagrant irreverence.

If one can speak of comic overkill, the above jingle presents it. The prosaic campaign statement is followed by a shockingly obscene conclusion that accuses the president, through sexual metaphor, of defrauding the people. Yet the jingle remains uproariously funny, and even a partisan of the victim can find humor in its technical virtuousity. At least, the latter would not take arms against it, whereas a straightforward statement of the same message might cause violent reprisal.

Freud finds obscene humor to be disguised aggression for the purpose of avoiding violent reprisal. He also finds obscene humor to be a form of exhibitionism replacing more direct, but prohibited, sexual action. Yet, the conjunction of sex and politics in humor strains this subjectivist interpretation. The historical origins of the term *comedy* throw a different light on phallic humor. The history relates phallic humor much more directly to Freud's theories on taboo and on "civilization and its discontents."

It has been observed that obscene humor makes aggressive expressions and sexual allusions permissible and pleasurable. Otherwise, they might be considered offensive or call for reprisal. Comedy originated as a social institution that contained the same permissibility of the sexually prohibited. Most authorities believe that the term *comedy* is derived from the Greek *komos*, the phallic procession that took place as a part of the fertility rites of the ancient Greeks. In the festivities, the prohibited became permissible and the taboos were temporarily suspended.

Later, in the Golden Age of Greece, the term became affixed to the short plays that were staged at the close of the great tragedies. These plays were lighthearted parodies of the tragedies and were first known as satyr plays. Both the *komos* and the satyr plays were marked by obscenity, irreverence, and defiance of established authorities.

The great comic playwright of Athens was Aristophanes,

and in his plays one can easily discern the staples of the comic diet. The philosophic undertones and political intent are there too, but almost subversively. In the *Clouds* the then living Socrates is the butt of the comedy; he is satirized. In Aristophanes' mockery of Socrates, one immediately apprehends that most durable of comic popularizations, the ridiculing of the intellectual—from the barbs at ivory-tower professors to Governor Wallace's "pointy-headed intellectuals."

But there is serious political intent in the Greek comedies. They not only seek to amuse the audience with satire and ridicule; they also constitute a socially approved medium for criticizing social authorities and conventions. The criticism is negative; like almost all humor, it derides without advocating positive reforms or explicitly stating the applicable standards of judgment. But, as can be seen in Aristophanes and most satirical comedy, there are implied standards of politics. The comic ridicule, posited on the standards, is intended to motivate the audience toward particular reforms.

The origins of comic caricature employed in satire probably lie in mimicry. The art of the mime, developing out of childish imitation, reached high dramatic form in ancient Greece. Lane Cooper states, "To the mime, in which modern authorities find the other chief source of the genus (comedy), Aristotle alludes in connection with the Dialogues of Plato; we may suppose that he thought well of the mime, which was sometimes more decent than Aristophanes, sometimes far less."[7]

Mimicry is originally an imitation of some person or thing. Then an emphasis is placed upon a defect or ugliness in it in order to yield a comic effect. The emphasized characteristic is defective, but not seriously so, or it could be tragic. The pleasure is derived from our perception of the defect by way of our associating it with our sense of proportion (pp. 60-61). Thus comedy resembles real life

7. Lane Cooper, *An Aristotelian Theory of Comedy* (New York: Harcourt Brace and Co., 1922), p. 20.

with its normal defects and foibles. However, the implicit comparison in comic caricature relies upon our sensing what is right and proper. Comedy can exercise man's reason and develop in him a conscious knowledge of proportion. For Aristotle, learning is agreeable to naturally rational man. It follows that learning is most pleasurable through humor.

Ancient comedy was a subversive learning experience. Some authorities have characterized it as a popularizing of the philosophies of the day. Leo Strauss points out that Aristophanic comedy is founded upon a political morality.[8] Strauss calls *Lysistrata* "the most indecent and the most moral (most harmless or least revolutionary) of Aristophanes' plays" (p. 198).

Aristophanes, shamelessly utilizing sex and ridicule of the famous, could attract the widest audiences. Glossing over his sense of justice and morality with bawdy humor, he could expose the contradictions between the good and the actual. Speaking in obscenities and with coarse humor, Aristophanes could be a moralist for the common people of his time without boring them or antagonizing them with his superiority.

In political comedy there is an inverse relationship between *indecent* and *moral*. The indecent is most often shockingly unconventional, and is comic in good part because of it. The moral is not the customary, but some standard of right implicitly posed in defiance of it. Yet, the unconventional morality is seldom revolutionary, otherwise it wouldn't be popular comedy. It must exist in the traditions or deeper values of the people. Thus, the comic moral often utilizes an indecent medium. Neither Plato nor Aristotle approved of the indecency, and their recommended humor would have had its phallus and fangs removed, perhaps appropriately for an aristocratic or gentlemanly polity.[9]

---

8. Leo Strauss, *Socrates and Aristophanes* (New York: Basic Books, 1966), pp. 11-53. Strauss holds that Aristophanes' comedy may well be as radically critical as Aristophanes alleges Socrates' teachings to be. At the same time, Aristophanes remains deeply critical of Socrates.

9. Cooper, pp. 108-10. Plato, *Laws* 7. 816-17 and 11. 935-36.

Cooper cites Aristotle as stating that comedy originated in Megara when it became a democracy (p. 172). It is not known that Aristotle related comedy to democracy, but the permissiveness of public comedy would require a considerable measure of political freedom. Its moral laissez-faire is not in keeping with Plato or Aristotle's politics. However, this study will argue that the implicit morality and explicit effects of political humor and comedy are very much in keeping with democratic politics. Comedy is functional to politics, and democratic politics is a kind of comedy.

The sexual medium of comedy as a means of moralizing is suited to the larger, lower classes of a democracy. Phallic humor speaks in a universal language, and possibly the need to escape the restrictiveness of social taboos—at least, symbolically—is proportionally greater as the level of the citizenry descends.

This statement is, of course, a catharsis theory of comedy and humor, and many theoreticians have employed it, though not politically. Cooper believes that Aristotle's lost work on comedy may have contained it, since it was basic to his theory of tragedy. Yet, if it did, he rejected its institutionalization. Interestingly, Cooper quotes Proclus Diodochus, a fifth-century commentator on Plato whose criticism demonstrates an understanding of the political function of catharsis:

We must tell . . . secondly, why, in particular he [Plato] does not admit [into the ideal State] comedy and tragedy; and that, too, when they contribute to a purgation of those emotions which it is neither possible wholly to check in, nor yet safe to gratify completely, since they in fact require a movement, as it were, at the proper time, and this movement, being effected when we hear a recital of these emotions, renders us undisturbed by them for the rest of the time. (p. 84)

Plato and Aristotle saw politics and comedy in their original settings; they theorized about both, but they would have excluded all but the most innocuous comedy from politics. Their political morality blinded them to a moral of politics, that comedy can make tolerable the necessary repressions of the social order. Humor is not revolutionary; it is stabilizing, for that at which we laugh is being acted upon in a manner that no longer calls for direct aggression.

There is another political function performed by humor and comedy, which can be called the leveling function. The revolutionary slogan of John Ball's Peasant Rebellion in medieval England was deadly serious, but, at the same time, it is a comic calling-to-common-humanity of the high and mighty. It proclaimed, "where Adam delve and Eve span, no man was there a gentleman."[10]

Sexual and scatological humor that points to our common humanity is termed by Freud an "unmasking." In effect, humor that employs references to our basic biological drives and functions strips away cultural superficialities to reveal man's common and continuing animality. When phallic humor is employed against personages who have attained social eminence, it not only has the pleasure in it of permissibly expressing sex and flaunting its taboo, but it also levels the superiors to a common equality. They too are vulnerable, and thus inferior. Ergo, we are delightfully superior to our superiors.

A crude but effective leveling humor is demonstrated in the anecdote about then President Lyndon Johnson's visiting his home state of Texas and being taken on a tour of the oil fields by his protégé, the then Governor of Texas. The President delicately sniffs the air and inquires of the Governor if he smells something. The latter replies No. Again, the President sniffs the air, and this time insistently asks, "John, did you pass gas?" The Governor denies it, but obsequiously replies, "I will if you want me to."

The former governor, a very ambitious politician, became a key man in the Nixon administration. He is considered to be a very arrogant and aggressive public leader. In the joke he is vulgarly accused of an exceedingly accommodating

10. Norman Cohn, *The Pursuit of the Millennium* (New York:Harper Torchbook, 1957, 1961), p. 211.

sycophancy. The joke allows us to express aggression against the threat of his superiority, and the grossness of its exaggeration delights our sense of taboo violation.

There is another category of political humor that seems to belong within the genre of phallic humor, that is, comic blasphemy. Impious witticisms are violations of social taboos, and, to the extent in which religion is looked upon as a support of state and society, comic blasphemy can be viewed as aggressive political humor.

Possibly the suspension of sexual taboos in political humor is closely associated with a permissiveness in humor toward impiety. There may well be an overarching structure of what Wilmore Kendall has termed the public orthodoxy in society in which sexual restrictions, respect for authority, and proper piety interlock with one another. If so, political humor could be expected to associate the various taboos for heightened effect. For instance, if religion strengthens authority, political humor in attacking authority will be likely to ridicule its religious pretension.

Joe McGinnis in *The Selling of the President 1968* recounts that, on the day of Nixon's electoral success, the Reverend Billy Graham, fashionable evangelist and unofficial presidential chaplain, came sweeping into the lobby of the President-elect's suite:

"We did it," he said, grinning, his blond hair neatly waved. He went directly to President Nixon's room, without explaining whether "we" meant Billy Graham and Richard Nixon or Billy Graham and God or perhaps all three together.[11]

Comic woe is the certain lot of the high moralizers and the religiously righteous in politics. Gladstone, that most self-righteous of British statesmen, was continually being derided by his witty opponent, Disraeli. Once Disraeli said "it isn't only that Gladstone always acts as if he has an ace up his sleeve, but that he thinks God put it there."

11. Joe McGinnis, *The Selling of the President 1968* (New York: Trident Press, 1969), p. 163.

George Romney, ex-Governor of Michigan and presidential candidate in 1968, is well known as a very moralistic Mormon. Zoltan Ferency, once his gubernatorial opponent, said that what bothered him about Romney's presidential candidacy was that "it's an honorable thing to seek the Presidency, but I'm afraid he [Romney] just wants to use it as a stepping stone." And another wag wrote of Romney's presidential bid:

It is a worthy note of our times and politics that when Governor Romney of Michigan was trying to decide whether to run for Governor, he spent one month meditating with God. But when seeking advice on whether to run for the Presidency of the United States, he spends a week-end in New York, talking it over with New York political leaders.

Note that the first witticism derives humor from reducing the highest political office to a mere promotion toward Romney's ultimate aspiration. The audience fills in the office for itself, experiencing the enjoyment of participation and the shock of mild impiety. The second story ridicules religious politics by exposing a disproportion of values at the same time that it states a seeming fact about presidential politics. Comic cynicism is joined with a humorous impiety.

A political cartoon, which only lightly touches upon religion, shows two very conventional-looking, middle-aged angels standing in the clouds, with other angels in the background. One of the dour-faced angels says to the other, "What I can't stand about this place is that there are so damn many bleeding-heart liberals up here." In this one-liner, the heavenly setting adds the spice of taboo to the stock ingredients of incongruity and contradiction.

A newspaper (*Detroit Free Press*, June 9, 1967) reported a political debate in the Illinois House of Representatives that is itself classical comedy, but in the debate a religious reference is employed for added effect. Here is the story:

A bill to outlaw topless waitresses was amended in the Illinois House to cover topless waitresses of large proportions. The House voted to make another exception, then killed the bill. The original bill would have defined a topless waitress as obscene under the criminal code.

Rep. C. L. McCormick offered an amendment to exempt topless waitresses whose brassiere cup size was D or smaller.

"You know, obscenity is only in the mind," he said. "So I decided anything over a D cup was obscene."

"I think I know the story," House Speaker Ralph T. Smith interrupted. "And I wish the gentleman would attend to the fact that we have some of the younger generation in the galleries."

"But I'm just trying to make a couple of points, Mr. Speaker," McCormick replied.

In explaining his amendment, McCormick told a story of a woman going to church unclothed from the waist up. The minister met the woman at the door.

"You can't come in here like that," the minister said.

" 'But I have a divine right,' " the woman replied, McCormick told the House.

"The minister responded: 'I know it, madam. You also have a divine left, but you still can't come in here like that.' "

"That explains my amendment, and I move its adoption," McCormick said. Both amendments were adopted on voice vote. Then Rep. Thomas R. House offered an amendment to kill the bill. It was adopted.

Combining sex and religion for the purpose of comic ridicule doubles the effect of McCormick's attack on the bill, for there is serious intent behind his clowning. He opposes the morals legislation, but because of the moralistic leanings of many Americans toward sumptuary legislation, open opposition can be politically risky. In this case the comedy is not only sublimated aggression, but it is a tactical device to avoid the charge of immorality. Through ridicule, McCormick gently exposes the weakness of the proposed legislation. It resembles the wisecrack about the

nineteenth-century crusader for censorship, Anthony Com-
stock: "he would censor women's skirts on a windy day."

Senator Ervin of North Carolina has used comic impiety
with devastating effect in ridiculing the late Senator Joseph
McCarthy. Ervin was on a Senate committee that recommended censuring McCarthy for his demagogic behavior,
and McCarthy retaliated in typical fashion by trying to
smear the committee members. On the floor of the Senate,
Ervin responded by relating the following anecdote:

I now know that the lifting of statements out of context is a
typical McCarthy technique. The writer of Ecclesiastes as-
sures us that "there is no new thing under the sun." The
McCarthy technique of lifting statements out of context was
practised by a preacher in North Carolina about seventy-
five years ago. At that time, the women had a habit of
wearing their hair in topknots. The preacher deplored that
habit. As a consequence he preached a rip-snorting sermon
one Sunday on the text Topknot Come Down. At the conclusion of his sermon an irate woman, wearing a very pronounced topknot, told the preacher that no such text could
be found in the Bible. The preacher thereupon opened the
Scriptures to the seventeenth verse of the twenty-fourth
chapter of Matthew and pointed to the words: "Let him
which is upon the house top not come down to take anything out of his house."

No finer example of lying through selective quoting could
be given, and the good Book itself is used as the instrument
of deception. Aside from the uproarious humor of the contradiction and irreverence, Senator Ervin delivers a political
moral: Oftentimes in politics, moral crusades, like McCarthy's anti-communism, are rank deceptions serving crude
self-interest. In the Senate that day (November 15, 1954),
Ervin attacked McCarthy with a second anecdote:

Mr. President, many years ago there was a custom in my
section of the country, known as the South Mountains, to
hold religious meetings at which the oldest members of the
congregation were called upon to stand up and publicly tes-

tify to their religious experiences. On one such occasion they were holding such a meeting in one of the churches and old Ephraim Swink, a South Mountaineer whose body was all bent and distorted with arthritis was present. All the elder members of the congregation except Uncle Ephraim arose and gave testimony to their religious experiences. Uncle Ephraim kept his seat. Thereupon, the moderator said, "Brother Ephraim suppose you tell us what the Lord has done for you." Uncle Ephraim arose, with his bent and distorted body, and said, "Brother, he has mighty nigh ruint me." Mr. President, that is about what Senator McCarthy has done to the Senate.

Senator Ervin's second anecdote uses the comic twist on the conventional logic, and making the Lord the villain of the story adds to the shock of delight. The comic impiety may also carry another political truth; the highest morality in politics may not necessarily be all that it seems to be.

Aside from the technique of taboo violation, is there an underlying consistency to comic blasphemy in politics? Ridicule does appear to be a means of counterattack when religious and moral authority intrudes upon politics. Edmund Burke wrote, "politics and the pulpit are terms that have little agreement."[12] In democratic politics the intrusion of religion and high morality into public affairs can be very dangerous, because it impassions and enflames the tolerant attitudes required for the peaceful resolution of social issues. Yet, in the United States, with its puritanical legislative bent, moralistic politics appeals to many people. As the saying has it, all politicians have to be for God, mother, and country, and against sin.

Directly criticizing political moralizing or religious politics may be risky for a political career. Political humor, with its comic permissiveness toward taboo violations, can be resorted to as disguised aggression against moral and religious pretensions in politics. Moreover, comic blasphemy often

12. Edmund Burke and Thomas Paine, *Reflections on the Revolution in France* and *The Rights of Man* (New York: Doubleday and Co., Dolphin Books, 1961), p. 23.

makes the assumed moral superiority of some political pre-
tender the target for ridicule. Thereby, impiety becomes allied with the leveling urge of the people and their repressed aggressions against all authority.

The comic form can also disarm the partisanship of the
audience. Because the ostensible purpose of the attack is
humorous, they don't have to line up immediately with the
pro-morality forces to protect their self-images. Humor de-
fuses the emotional involvement, and, through the comic
gloss, the people can view more objectively the disparity
between the reality and the high moral claims.

In sum, sexual humor, and taboo humor in general, perform a worthy service for democratic politics. Taboo humor
provides a stabilizing outlet for repressed aggressions. Politics too requires a repression of aggressiveness in order to
peacefully settle social conflict. When political humor is
combined with taboo violation, its universal appeal accommodates popular rule.

Again, there is a moral benchmark implicit in all political
humor, however obscene or blasphemous. Personages and
politics are made comical in light of the disparity between
pretensions and actuality, between ideality and stark reality. Where there is universal franchise, phallic political
humor provides a universal moral medium of the lowest
common denominator. We all can take the moral message
when it is in a negative form, knocking down our social
superiors.

Religion provides a moral precondition for politics, but its
political interference can threaten the mutual tolerance
necessary to peaceful politics. Comic blasphemy undermines the popular moral appeal of religious politics by ally-
ing itself with other powerful popular motivations.

Last, phallic political humor in its sexual and scatological
explicitness becomes the great leveler that helps to maintain a semblance of equality among a free people. Comic
reminders of the incessant biological demands of our inescapable bodies serve to remind the populace and their

heroes that they remain fallibly mortal. As Montaigne put it, no matter how high the throne upon which a man sits, he still sits upon his ass.

Comic Invective in Politics

This study contends that humor is natural and pervasive in politics. No demonstration of that contention could be convincing without considering comic invective in politics. Invective is the abuse, ridiculing, or insulting of someone or something. In its comic or humorous guise, the aggressiveness of invective is cushioned by wordplay, metaphor, and analogical narrative. Yet, the direct insult is always close to the surface, and comic invective is the most aggressive of all humor.

Abraham Lincoln is generally considered to have been a gentle humorist, but, like all politicians, he could employ the comic insult devastatingly when necessary. In his early campaigning in Illinois, Lincoln was repeatedly interrupted by a young politician who fancied himself an orator. Finally, Lincoln retaliated:

"I don't object," said Lincoln, "to being interrupted with sensible questions, but I must say that my boisterous friend does not always make inquiries which properly come under that head. He says he is afflicted with headaches, at which I don't wonder, as it is a well-known fact that nature abhors a vacuum, and takes her own way of demonstrating it.

"This noisy friend reminds me of a certain steamboat that used to run on the Illinois river. It was an energetic boat, was always busy. When they built it, however, they made one serious mistake, this error being in the relative sizes of the boiler and the whistle. The latter was usually busy, too, and people were aware that it was in existence.

"This particular boiler to which I have reference was a six-foot one, and did all that was required of it in the way of pushing the boat along; but as the builders of the vessel had made the whistle a six-foot one, the consequence was that every time the whistle blew the boat had to stop."[13]

Much more savage, but still borderline political humor, is the invective resorted to by the late Governor Earl Long of Louisiana, the successor to his famed brother Huey's political dynasty. A. J. Liebling in his *The Earl of Louisiana* records one campaign speech of Earl Long. In it Long takes issue with Camille Gravel, a Democratic National Committeeman, for having the effrontery to question him:

"Mr. Gravel, I got nothing against you personally. Now you keep quiet and I won't mention your name. If you don't I'll have you removed as a common damn nuisance." He (Long) paused for an answer we couldn't hear and then bellowed:
"If you're so popular, why don't *you* run for Governor?"

Later in the speech Long refers to de Lesseps Morrison, Mayor of New Orleans:

"I see Dellasoupo has been elected one of the ten best-dressed men in America. He has fifty-dollar neckties and four-hundred dollar suits. A four-hundred dollar suit on old Uncle Earl would look like socks on a Rooster."

After this triumph for himself and the common man, Long touched upon a rival for the Governorship, William Dodd, the State Auditor:

"I hear Big Bad Bill Dodd has been talking about the inefficiency and waste in this administration. Ohyeah. Ohyeah. Well, let me tell you, Big Bad Bill has at least six streamlined deadheads on his payroll that couldn't even find Bill's office if they had to. But they can find that *Post Office* every month to get their salary check—Ohyeah."[14]

13. Alexander McClure, *Abe Lincoln's Yarns and Stories* (Chicago: The Educational Company, 1901), p. 78.
14. Leonard C. Lewin, ed., *A Treasury of American Political Humor* (New York: Delacorte Press Book, 1964), pp. 149-51.

Those writers who bewail the demise of political humor have ignored its most fertile source and its political spontaneity. Thus, a writer to "Letters to the Editor" in the *New York Times* in 1968:

To the Editor:
In regard to James Reston's statement (news analysis Aug. 8) that Richard Nixon's nomination was the greatest comeback since Lazarus, may we refer you to the Gospel of St. John, Chapter II, Verse 39: "Martha, the sister of him that was dead, saith unto him, 'Lord, by this time he stinketh.' "

From "Tricky Dick" (Richard Nixon) to "Oily Everett, the Wizard of Ooze" (the late Senator Everett Dirksen of Illinois), and the characterization of President Kennedy's ill-fated Bay of Pigs venture as "a choir boy's Budapest," contrasting it with the ruthlessly efficient Russian suppression of the Hungarian revolution, political invective pervades the realm of politics and is natural and necessary to it. Yet, the comic insult is not in itself political. It does not go after issues or the substance of politics. Often, the invective is directly personal, attacking characteristics or attributes of the politician or political party that are peripheral to the question at issue.

Robert Penn Warren in *All The King's Men* has his fictional Huey Long define the *argumentum ad hominem*: "If you use the right kind of *argumentum* you can always scare the *hominem* into a laundry bill he didn't expect." Political invective is *argumentum ad hominem*, but its causes and effects are highly political. Though much public argumentation takes place over issues, political decisions are seldom made on the simple merits of an issue at hand or on its ideological facets. Politicians, as representatives of special interests in society, represent those interests in their positions on issues. They are not directly affected by the particular merits of those issues.

To that extent, a personal comic insult is as appropriate

as a political argument. If the humor is successful, its reception and repetition may impair the personal standing of the victim and have some influence on the balance of political power. Regardless of that, the comic political invective relieves the tensions of competition under the conventional restraints of the political arena. And it does so in a socially approved and peaceful manner.

As personal as comic invective often is, its aggressiveness is less harmful than would be that of moral or ideological ridicule. Basic moral questions, which include the ideological premises of politics, are generally out of bounds in the democratic political arena. Otherwise, because of the passions they enflame and the deep differences among men that they stimulate, moral politics would rend the delicate web of understandings that permits peaceful compromise of day-to-day issues. Personal ridicule in politics is less disruptive than substantive aggressiveness, particularly when political invective is understood by the denizens of the arena to be their distinctive sport.

The political sport of comic insult is, like sports in general, a kind of mock warfare. Thus, the effects of political invective are deeply social. They effect a psychological release for the politician and citizen in the competitive aggressivenss of politics. But, above all, through the use of words, which are the prime medium of politics, the sport of comic insult allows the war of interests and ideas among men to be continued in peace. The mock warfare of political humor displaces and diffuses the real conflicts among men. Thereby, it facilitates their political reconciliation; real deeds from mock wars proceed.

2

Aristophanes, Satirical Sage

Wherein the clown becomes wise man

Introduction: Satire

Hail Satire! Hail, clear-eyed, sharp-tongued, hot-tempered, outwardly disillusioned and secretly idealistic Muse! Mother of Comedy, sister of Tragedy, defender and critic of Philosophy, hail! You are a difficult companion, a mistress sometimes elusive and tantalizing, sometimes harsh and repellent; but in your mercurial presence no one is ever bored. Stupidity, Self-satisfaction, Corruption, the Belief in Inevitable Progress—these and other intellectual monsters, produced spontaneously from the waste energy of the human mind, you have destroyed again and again. Still they are reborn, and still you arise to destroy them.—Gilbert Highet, *The Anatomy of Satire*

The word *satire* is of Latin origin and meant a melange or hotch-potch, something like a variety show. Gilbert Highet says that it has a multifarious subject matter, and generally its writing contains cruel and dirty words, trivial and comic words, and colloquial anti-literary words. The typical weapons of satire are irony, paradox, antithesis, parody, colloquialism, anticlimax, topicality, obscenity, violence, vividness, and exaggeration.[1]

Satire is a form of comedy, ranging from drama through poetry to prose narrative. It must be amusing or humorous, but satire is essentially an attack on someone or some social institution. It may ridicule, parody, or caricature its target, but the purpose of satire with its negative approach is positive change. The Roman satirist Horace understood satire to deal with important ethical and social problems in a simple manner and with earthy humor. He believed that satire, thereby, bridged the gulf between philosophy and the general public (p. 35).

The formal literary invention of satire is attributed to Horace, and his predecessor, Lucilius, but the essence of satire stems back to the Greeks. Horace says, "that satire in Lucilius entirely depends on the Old Comedy of Athens," and he is referring to Aristophanes' comedies. However, the dramatic comedy of the Greeks was succeeded by the prose satire of the Romans. Highet holds that there is no relation between the early comedies, called satyr plays, and the later Roman satire. He says that the two terms became related "largely so the scholars could explain the shocking coarseness of satire by saying that it was inspired by the funny obscene satyr-folk" (p. 232).

Despite this unrelatedness, there is a great similarity between Roman satire and the earlier Greek dramatic comedy. One classical authority has taken up the Platonic roots of the genre. C. W. Mendell finds that satire developed in ancient Rome as a means of presenting popularly the philosophic doctrines of the various Platonic schools: Stoic, Cynic, and Epicurean. He refers to the satirical techniques developed from conscious study of the Platonic dialogue, and he concludes, "parody was an established means of popularizing philosophy which Plato had not scorned."[2]

1. Gilbert Highet, *The Anatomy of Satire* (Princeton, N.J.: Princeton University Press, 1962), p. 18.
2. C. W. Mendell, "*Satire as Popular Philosophy*," *Classical Philology*, 5 (April 1920): 154-55.

Unfortunately, neither Mendell nor Highet takes up the comic element in satire. Yet, it may well be that it is the political function of comedy that made the satire an effective means of communication.

The question is how the comic element may bridge the gap between esoteric knowledge and popular philosophy. What are the political interrelationships of comedy, particularly when it is acknowledged that the moral intent of satire is social and political reform? Yet, these authors are to be thanked, for satire is now found to contain, albeit negatively, some philosophical or moral doctrine. Its comical use must be understood if the political import of comedy is to be appreciated. I shall identify Greek Old Comedy and the later satirical form, using the metaphor of the satyr as a personification of satire in analyzing satire as political comedy. Technical differences are acknowledged, but kinship is apparent. Hopefully, the analysis will support the assumption.

It is proposed here that Aristophanes, the greatest of all political satirists (though he didn't know he was satirizing), be studied as the sage or wise man using the comic form to present his philosophy. His three most political plays will be the examples considered. Next, Socrates will be viewed as the satyr or "divine fool," a man who comprehends reality from a vision of the "divine" or perfectly good in such an unusual manner that this thoughts and actions appear comical to his more conventional fellows. Aristophanes' *Clouds* suggests the noble appellation; Plato's *Symposium* confirms it. *The Republic* will be considered as the divine comedy of the divine fool.

Aristophanes

Aristophanes has seldom been studied or even mentioned in political thought, a most notable exception being Leo Strauss's *Socrates and Aristophanes*. Yet, it could be said that he is the true opponent of Platonic political philosophy and, in some ways the true defender of Athenian politics. He is not a systematic philosopher, nor does he even present a coherent doctrine, but his medium of satiric comedy is no more dramatic than Plato's dialogue. And, whereas the latter was and is suited to intellectual aristocrats, Aristophanes' comedy may be suited to the broader citizenry of Athens and elsewhere.

All of Aristophanes' extant eleven comedies have political significance, but three of them are most famous for their comic political message. *Knights* is Aristophanes' attack on the prevailing democracy of his day and its reigning demagogue, Cleon. *Clouds* is the classical satire of Socrates and of the political consequences of abstract intellectualism. In *Lysistrata* he enlists sex against the Pelopponesian war and ridicules the rule of men by envisioning a feminine political conspiracy.

In *Knights* the play's characters are personifications of the constituent elements of Athenian democracy. The People are characterized in Demos, a rich but confused and vacillating citizen land-owner. The demagogue is called the Paphlagonian, or the Tanner, and represents Cleon, the historic demagogue of the period. He is the overseer of Demos and panders to his appetites while managing his business.

Demos's two slaves, under Cleon, are Nicias and Demosthenes, who were actually admirals of the Athenian navy, and thus aristocrats. The hero of the satire is Agoracritus, Sausageman.[3] A citizen of the lowest origins, he comes to oppose Cleon and "politically" vie with him for the favors of Demos and the office of overseer. Lastly, the chorus is the Knights who represent the second highest order of Athenian citizens. They oppose Cleon and support the Sausage-seller as a means of restoring their aristocratic ways.

3. This interpretation of Sausageman as Aristophanes' hero is not the orthodox one. This will be explained but from the comic perspective. Strauss holds that Aristophanes speaks through Demosthenes and the Knights. Authorities cited in the translation used seem to hold that Aristophanes is ridiculing Agoracritus for his low political skills of democratic manipulation. Strauss is far more favorable to the character but stops short of making him a "comic" hero. However, from the satiric perspective, this essayist concludes that the comically negative characteristics given Agoracritus by Aristophanes convey a positive political truth of democratic leadership.

The satire begins with the two slaves (Athenian office holders) burlesquing their woes as a result of their master's weaknesses and of Cleon's pandering to them. Their master is described as Demos of Pnyx, that is, the People of the Public Assembly, and "a perfect glutton for beans." The latter phrase is a colloquialism for living off his salary as a judge—the people fatten themselves at the public larder. The slaves mock Cleon by representing him as saying, "Dear Demos, try a single case and you will have done enough; then take your bath, eat, swallow and devour; here are three obols (the salary paid to the citizen juries)."[4]

The slaves complain that while Cleon fawns upon Demos, he beats them, robs them of credit, and steals their sustenance. They decide that an end must be put to the intolerable situation. Yet, Demosthenes grieves,

none can escape the Paphlagonian, his eye is everywhere. And what a stride! He has one leg on Pylos and the other in the Assembly; his rump is exactly over the land of the Chaonians, his hands are with the Aetolians and his mind with the Clopidians. (p. 13)

The colloquialisms are literally translated as his rump gapes open, his hands beg, and his mind steals. Here is biting satire and pithy description of demagogy.

The slaves drink for inspiration and steal an oracle of Cleon's, which the intoxicated Demosthenes interprets. The oracle is a reference to the liking of the populace for favorable predictions, which Cleon divines from omens for them. Demosthenes finds that the oracle names the various popular rulers after the death of Pericles—an oakum-dealer, a sheep-dealer, and a leather-tanner (Cleon)—and each more of a scoundrel than the other. He says that the leather-seller will be succeeded by a sausage-seller of even baser craftiness, who is to be the aristocrat's weapon for the destruction of Cleon.

In comic miracle, Sausageman makes his appearance and is sold on the mission of overthrowing Cleon by gaining

4. Aristophanes, *The Eleven Comedies* (New York, Tudor Publishing Co., 1912, 1936), p. 12.

Demos's favor. He is told that he will be the greatest of men—the ruler of democracy—"because you are a sad rascal without shame, no better than a common market rogue." His bad parentage and lack of education are deemed the necessary traits for leadership. When he asks how he can be capable of governing, Demosthenes answers:

Nothing simpler. Continue your trade. Mix and knead together all the state business as you do for your sausages. To win the people, always cook them some savoury that pleases them. Besides, you possess all the attributes of a demagogue; a screeching, horrible voice, a perverse, cross-grained nature and the language of the market-place. In you all is united which is needful for governing. The oracles are in your favour, even including that of Delphi. Come, take a chaplet, offer a libation to the god of Stupidity and take care to fight vigorously. (pp. 21-22)

The craftsman's skill and knowledge as analogous to the art of governing are satirized into feeding the public cupidity, possessing low character, and ignorance.

The Sausageman, with the support of the slaves and the chorus of the Knights, stands firm when Cleon appears. The chorus attacks Cleon and accuses him of public malfeasance. Then, Sausageman and the leather-tanner begin an invective-laden shouting match against each other. Sausageman proves unworthily worthy in this first competition; he outshouts, outboasts, and outinsults Cleon. The chorus gloats:

But here is another man, who gives me pleasure, for he is a much greater rascal than you; he will overthrow you; 'tis easy to see, that he will beat you in roguery, in brazenness and in clever turns. Come, you, who have been brought up among the class which to-day gives us all our great men, show us that a liberal education is mere tomfoolery. (p. 27)

The dialogue is studded with coarse obscenities, accusations based on rumors of Cleon's peculations, and contempt for the people, who can always be fooled. Cleon says to his rival, "I do not fear you as long as there is a Senate and a people which stands like a fool, gaping in the air." And the chorus tells Cleon that: "to steal, perjure yourself and make a receiver of your rump are three essentials for climbing high" (pp. 31-32). Despite the comic drama, it is vicious ridicule of the people and their politicians.

Cleon retreats to the Senate to accuse Sausageman and expose the conspiracy against himself. The chorus sends the Sausage-seller after him to again out-trick him. He returns and regales the Knights with his second triumph. He recounts that when he heard Cleon lying to the Senate, he prayed:

"Come, gods of rascals and braggarts, gods of all fools, toad-eaters and braggarts and thou, market-place where I was bred from my earliest days, give me unbridled audacity, an untiring chatter and a shameless voice." No sooner had I ended this prayer than a lewd man broke wind on my right. (p. 41)

Sausageman recognizes a good omen, enters the Senate, and undermines Cleon by lies that promise the Senators anchovies and feasting. He also bribes them with seasonings for the foods. He leads the people's representatives by their bellies.

Cleon must resort to a new approach. After further mutual insults and accusations, the two rivals compete before Demos. Both profess their love of Demos, and he orders their appearance before him at Pnyx, the Public Assembly. Sausageman laments the choice of arenas, for he says "at home this old fellow is the most sensible of men, but the instant he is seated on those accursed stone seats, he is there with his mouth agape as if he were hanging up figs by their stems to dry" (pp. 45-46). A seemingly contradictory opinion of Demos has surfaced—his common sense is fully adequate for his daily and practical concerns, but as a public functionary he is a fool.

Both Cleon and Sausageman plead their love for Demos,

but the latter gains ground by caring for Demos's personal comforts, giving him a cushion and shoes. Cleon retaliates by boasting of the military victories he has won for the glory and imperial rule of Demos. He is accused of making war to conceal his rogueries and make Demos dependent on him while being deprived of the wealth of his own lands.

Demos begins to believe in the thievery of Cleon and Sausageman continues to make personal gifts to Demos. The personal nature of the gifts symbolizes his love of the people as individuals. When Cleon tries to do the same, Sausageman tells Demos that Cleon's gifts are poisoned and cause extreme flatulence among the citizens (Aristophanes' language is somewhat more ribald. For one thing, he has Sausageman charge, "Very well! it was Cleon who had caused the price to fall so low, so that all could eat it (silphium, a plant used for food flavoring) and the jurymen in the courts were almost poisoned with farting in each other's faces."

Demos is impressed with Sausageman and comments, "Faith! here is an excellent citizen indeed, such as has not been seen for a long time. 'Tis truly a man of the lowest scum!" Demos decides to give Sausageman Cleon's steward's ring, but Cleon gets another chance by competing at reading oracles.

Again, Sausageman excels at the oracles by his bitter predictions and his reinterpreting Cleon's divinations. Demos concludes that he will award the reins of state to the one who treats him best. And the chorus shouts:

> Demos, you are our all-powerful sovereign lord; all tremble before you, yet you are led by the nose. You love to be flattered and fooled; you listen to the orators with gaping mouth and your mind is led astray.

DEMOS: 'Tis rather you who have no brains, if you think me so foolish as all that; it is with a purpose that I play this idiot's role, for I love to drink the lifelong day, and so it pleases me to keep a

CHORUS:

DEMOS:

> thief for my minister. When he has thoroughly gorged himself, then I overthrow and crush him.
>
> CHORUS: What profound wisdom! If it be really so, why! all is for the best. Your ministers, then, are your victims, whom you nourish and feed up expressly in the Pnyx, so that, the day your dinner is ready, you may immolate the fattest and eat him.
>
> DEMOS: Look, see how I play with them, while all the time they think themselves such adepts at cheating me. I have my eye on them when they thieve, but I do not appear to be seeing them; then I thrust a judgment down their throat as it were a feather, and force them to vomit up all they have robbed from me. (pp. 51-52, 64-65)

Aristophanes, in the midst of his bitter satire on democracy, has again inserted a comic twist. Fat, appetitive, stupid Demos explains his choice and treatment of politicians. He does act according to his pleasures, but he is shrewd concerning the purveyors of them. He remains their master. And Aristophanes' revealing of Demos's earthy practicality opens up the possibility of the reform of his affairs.

The rivals for Demos's affections and political power shower luxurious foods, wines, and comforts on their apparently insatiable master. The contest ends when Sausageman steals by trickery a delight that Cleon has prepared for Demos. He presents it to Demos, boasts of its acquisition, and Demos accepts it even more heartily, telling Cleon "get you gone! My thanks are only for him who served it."*

---

*A contemporary story told by the late Senator Barkley expresses the same sense of democratic gratitude. Barkley, campaigning for reelection in Kentucky, stopped to shake hands with an old farmer and supporter of his. He asked the man if he would vote for Barkley. The farmer replied, "I dunno." Barkley expostulated, "Why, how can you say that? I've gotten you farm subsidies, helped to get you the dam built for irrigation, helped pass a special bill for flood relief for you, and sponsored your son through West Point!" The farmer answered, "Yep, I know, but what have you done for me lately?"

Sausageman's victory is sealed when Demos askes what is left in the baskets of gifts brought to him by each of the rivals. Sausageman's basket is empty, proving his devotion to all of the people. Cleon's basket reveals even more and better gifts remaining than had been bestowed on Demos. He serves Demos to better himself.

After Sausageman reveals his lowly origins, upbringing, and behavior (probably more boastful lies), Cleon concedes victory to him.* Sausageman then states that his name is Agoracritus ("to judge in the market-place") and says, "Demos, I will care for you to the best of my power, and all shall admit that no citizen is more devoted than I to this city of simpletons" (pp. 69-73).

The chorus, sharing the victory of their champion, call for revenge on their political enemies, and Demosthenes asks for office. Agoracritus rebukes the one, calling for holy silence, and telling the chorus to repair from politics to prayer. He ignores the office-seeker. And he then reintroduces Demos, whom he has remade in his Sausageman's kitchen. Agoracritus announces the reformed Demos:

He has once more become as he was in the days when he lived with Aristides and Miltiades. But you will judge for yourselves, for I hear the vestibule doors opening. Hail with your shouts of gladness the Athens of old, which now doth reappear to your gaze, admirable, worthy of the songs of the poets and the home of the illustrious Demos. (p. 75)

Demos thanks Agoracritus as his best friend—no longer his pandering subordinate. Agoracritus reminds him of his past political stupidity. Demos blushes in shame and

*Sausageman's willingness to boast of his lowly origins and behavior in courting Demos have comical parallels in the anecdote told about the late Representative Adam Clayton Powell. Powell was giving a street-corner speech in Harlem. He bombastically cited his congressional achievements for the blacks, his promises for their progress, and his general championship of the downtrodden.

A middle-class black, standing in the crowd, became extremely offended at the disparity between Powell's self-panegyric and his notoriously disreputable behavior, particularly because of his warm reception by the poor blacks. Turning to another onlooker, he cried out, "My God, he's always absent from Congress; he has white and black mistresses on his governmental payroll; he uses our tax money on his expense account for whoring, drinking, and traveling!" His companion replied, "Yeah man, ain't he cool."

thereby proves his new prudence toward politics. Agoracritus rewards his "political" wisdom with material comfort, thirty years of truces, and a place of retirement in the country. The satire represents the first two as (1) "accept this folding stool, and to carry it this well-grown, big-balled slave boy," and (2) the truces are "personified on the stage as pretty little *filles de joie*." Aristophanes has not suddenly become moralistic in his comic morality.

The final act of Agoracritus is one of mercy. He merely sentences Cleon to the occupation within the city that accords with his inner spirit. Agoracritus pronounces sentence:

'Twill not be over-terrible. I condemn him to follow my old trade; posted near the gates, he must sell sausages of asses' and dogs'-meat; perpetually drunk, he will exchange foul language with prostitutes and will drink nothing but the dirty water from the baths. (pp. 75-79)

Agoracritus does not visit unnatural cruelty on Cleon; rather, social function has been aligned with personal capacity. Though historic Athens did not so fare, the satirical ending is one of comic happiness; the state has been put right.

What is this doctrine of political rightness that Aristophanes conveys in his satire of democracy? First, the people are not the villain in the misuse of the state. Cleon and the demagogues are the villains, through their pandering to the basest of popular characteristics. And the demagogues are not of the people; the true representative of the people is he who is of the lowliest origin—Sausageman. Yet, the latter, in his "natural" love and understanding of Demos, guides him aright and restores him to his proper function, farming in the country.

Second, when the people are engaged in their proper activities, they are entitled to material necessities (shoes, cushion, cloak, food) and some comforts. In fact, ultimate sovereignty, not the practice of ruling, seems to be conceded to the people by Aristophanes. Demos passes judgment on Cleon and Agoracritus, and does so correctly. Despite the pandering to his appetites, he sees that Agoracritus cares for him for himself, whereas Cleon cares for him only to better Cleon.

Third, the aristocrats, as personified in the plotting slaves and the chorus of Knights, are not exactly characterized as fit rulers. Nicias is fearful. Demosthenes must think through drink and act through another person; with success, he immediately seeks office. The Knights are carping, and must be led; with success, they seek bloody revenge. Demos, on the contrary, with success, is reformed to correct proportions, is merciful to Cleon, is shameful of past behavior, and becomes a friend of Agoracritus.

Fourth, Athenian imperialism is satirized as a plot of the demagogues that confuses the people's politics and wastes their domestic resources for worthless vainglory. Clearly, for Aristophanes the wealth of a country need not be extended in war and conquest. It is for the material comforts of the people.

Other themes also are present: the monstrosity of jury payment, the bribing of the Senate, the superiority of a "natural" upbringing over the current "liberal arts tomfoolery," and the political nonsense of religious oracles. However, there is a final major theme remaining, and it is the one on which the burden of the satire turns, namely, the practical reform of a corrupted democracy.

The rivalry between Cleon and Agoracritus, or Sausageman, is at heart an *agon* over selfish versus public interest, bad versus good, the Unjust versus the Just Speech (*Clouds*). But in regard to the latter, the justice of the speeches in politics is not in their utterances, but in their speakers and their intent. In politics one must adopt the means relative to the situation and necessary to the end. Not all means, for Sausageman, when he can do so, uses the inherently good means, and as the situation changes, his means becomes cleansed. Moreover, the aristocrats' relief from Cleon begins when they adopt the democratic Sausageman as their means to reform democracy.

It is easy to paraphrase with "when in democracy, do as

the democrats do." Certainly the comedy is in exaggerating, in all of their vulgarity and coarseness, the undeniable vices of democracy. But the satire also reverses the aristocratic logic and displays democratic sensibleness and aristocratic degradation. The perennial democratic humor of leveling the rulers through ridicule and sexual unmasking is counterbalanced by exalting the lowest of the low as the superior man because of his uncorrupted inferiority.

The comic satire has been able to speak to the Athenian people and to criticize them and their political actions. But the comic message is not an anti-democratic diatribe, for even satire seldom adopts a polar extreme. Nor is it politically relativistic, an easy comic stance. Rather, the Demos has a place in government and is due political position and material returns from the state. Moreover, political leadership of a people requires popular techniques of communication and understanding (vaguely paralleling techniques of phallic comedy).[5] This political accommodation of the truth to popular weaknesses would be the essence of evil to the Platonic Socrates, but, as we will see, even to the Aristophanic Socrates of *Clouds*, the practical realities are a matter of unconcern. However, democratic leadership can be progressive, purifying the people of the failings that require a comic mimicry of demagogy."*

5. For leveling humor, sexual unmasking, and phallic comedy, see chapter 1, "Phallic Humor and Democratic Politics."

*The most notable "sausage-seller" in American politics was Huey Long, a Governor of Louisiana and later United States Senator. Huey Long was coarse and power-hungry, but he may well have partaken of the ethos of Agoracritus. As a governor, Long was not above parodying his democratic constituency to achieve his goal. For instance, he was one of the few Southern demagogues who did not appeal to racism against the blacks for his political popularity, but, if need arose, he was prepared to do so:

Long was once approached by some Negro leaders who pointed out that although a majority of the patients in the Charity Hospital were Negroes, there were no Negro nurses. Long promised to correct this, but warned the Negroes that they might not like this method. Some days later, Long announced he was making an inspection of the hospital, and drove out surrounded by police outriders with their motorcycles roaring and their sirens screaming. He was, as always, followed by reporters, for whom the Kingfish invariably provided good copy. After inspecting the hospital, when he was asked what he thought, Long exploded: "It's a Gawd-damn disgrace! That hospital's full of niggers being tended by nice white girls! It's a Gawd-damn disgrace, and I won't stand for it!" Needless to say the hospital soon rectified the disgrace.[6]

6. Leon A. Harris, pp. 17-18.

This essay does not intend to give a synoptic analysis of *Clouds* or *Lysistrata*. *The Knights* has yielded Aristophanes' diagnosis of democratic ills, his prescription for their cure, and the comic function attendant upon the two.

However, *Clouds* must be considered in the light of the issue posed by Aristophanes in *Knights*, namely, the prudential necessities of democratic reform and political stability. It will be maintained that Aristophanes is the comical philosopher contained by and devoted to an actual polity. In *Clouds* Aristophanes' charge against Socrates is that the latter is the philosopher come to the polis, but not of it. In effect, Socrates makes judgment upon the state from outside and above it—from a sky-suspended basket or, colloquially, from Cloud Eight.

But Aristophanes is not an undiluted conservative satirizing a subversive Socrates. Just as in *Knights*, his conservatism is critical and reformist, but it is founded on the bedrock of the political actualities of Athens and the ethical value of its existence.

Briefly, summarizing the plot of *Clouds*, Strepsiades, an Athenian citizen of rural vintage and conventional values, is burdened by debts to the point of ruination. His playboy son, Phidippides, spoiled by his snobbish mother and imbued with the new urbanism, has squandered his father's fortune on horse-racing and other worthless pastimes. Strepsiades, desperate for relief, conceives of sending his son to Socrates' sophistical school, which teaches a rhetoric of deceit whereby wrong can be made to look right. Thereby, Strepsiades can defraud his creditors, that is, can circumvent the laws.

Phidippides refuses to go to the school. He will have nothing to do with the weird-looking, laughable intellectuals. Strepsiades is driven to go the sophistical school himself. Despite his slow-wittedness, he is accepted by Socrates. He is confronted in the school by extremes of unconventional behavior and thinking (something resembling the present popular view of a hippie commune). Most important, he is confronted by a ragged, disreputable Socrates, suspended in a basket. Strepsiades asks for an explanation, and Socrates replies:

> I traverse the air and contemplate the sun.
>
> STREPSIADES: Thus, 'tis not on the solid ground, but from the height of this basket, that you slight the gods, if indeed—(hesitation to convey, if you believe at all).
>
> SOCRATES: I have to suspend my brain and mingle the subtle essence of my mind with this air,—'tis just the same with the water-cress.[7]

Thus, Aristophanes ridicules the ivory-tower philosopher with his seeming nonsense—reasoning. Yet, in comic metaphor, the issue is joined. If Socrates thought with his feet planted firm on the ground of earthly reality, mundane considerations would sap his mind of the basic truths that are "things of heaven." Satirical ridicule is not wholly inaccurate concerning the Platonic Socrates.

Strepsiades says that he wishes to learn "the truth of celestial matters" from Socrates in order to cheat his creditors of his debts. Heaven is to be used by men to deal fraudulently or, at least selfishly, with earthly matters. Nevertheless, Socrates accepts Strepsiades but insists that he renounce the traditional Olympian deities and accept as the real gods the Clouds, who constitute the play's chorus.

Socrates calls upon the Clouds to appear, and praises their power by which they carry in their "loins the thunder and lightning." Strepsiades renders obeisance as they appear, saying: Oh! adorable Clouds, I revere you and I too am going to let off my thunder, so greatly has your own affrighted me. Faith! whether permitted or not, I must, I must crap!" (pp. 313-14).

Air unto air, the new reverence is crowned with irrever-

7. Aristophanes, *Clouds*, p. 311.

ence, and the heavenly worship, verbally pledged, is simultaneously undermined by earthly importunities. In like manner, Socrates describes the new deities (and the effects of their worship or heavenly contemplation): "They are the Clouds of heaven, great goddesses for the lazy; to them we owe all, thoughts, speeches, trickery, roguery, boasting, lies, sagacity." Strepsiades replies, "Ah! that was why, as I listened to them, my mind spread out its wings; it burns to babble about trifles, to maintain worthless arguments, to voice its petty reasons, to contradict, to tease some opponent" (p. 315).

In some delightfully obscene and blasphemous passages, Aristophanes has Socrates prove that Zeus is not the powerful god and the Clouds are the chief divinities.[8] The Clouds then grant Strepsiades his wish to study under Socrates and they bless his dubious purpose.

Socrates quickly discovers Strepsiades' stupidity and vulgarity, but still takes him off-stage for instructions. In the intervening parabasis (an intermission in which the author speaks through the chorus to the audience), the Clouds, oddly enough, invoke the protection of Zeus, other gods, and, significantly, Athena, the patron goddess of Athens. Yet, in the play proper the clouds seek to replace Athena (the Clouds are not dependable—the epitome of flux?).

Socrates despairs of Strepsiades, who manages to learn only some simple rhetorical tricks. Having a comic common sense bordering on nonsense, Strepsiades is nevertheless impervious to Socrates' cosmic wisdom and abstractions. The Chorus counsels Strepsiades to send his son for instruction in his place. Phidippides reluctantly accedes, but warns his father that he will repent his demands.

Phidippides is first antagonistic to Socrates, but he yields to instruction. Socrates consigns him to the teaching of the Just and Unjust Discourses, staged personifications of speeches, respectively in praise and defense of justice and of injustice. The latter two proceed to debate the existence

8. See chapter 1 on comic blasphemy.

and utility of justice. The debate is invective-ridden and nonsensical, but each agrees to expound his doctrine and to allow Phidippides to choose between them.

Just Discourse argues the benefits of conventional values and the old education. Unjust Discourse uses the "new ideas and subtle fancies" to counter him. The first pleads his case on the grounds that the old ways are best because they are old, that is, they conform to the old values.

Unjust Discourse boasts of being able to win with weaker arguments, and he proceeds to confute his rival with exceptions, irrelevancies, and circumlocutions. Just Discourse proves to be stolidly enmired in conventional thought and incapable of exposing or countering the sophistries of his derider. When Just Discourse righteously reminds the latter that the chastity of Peleus earned him the hand of Thetis, Unjust Discourse taunts him:

who left him in the lurch, for he was not the most ardent; in those nocturnal sports between two sheets, which so please women, he possessed but little merit. Get you gone, you are but an old fool. But you, young man, just consider a little, what this temperance means and the delights of which it deprives you—young fellows, women, play, dainty dishes, wine, boisterous laughter. And what is life worth without these? Then, if you happen to commit one of these faults inherent in human weakness, some seduction or adultery, and you are caught in the act, you are lost, if you cannot speak. But follow my teaching and you will be able to satisfy your passions, to dance, to laugh, to blush at nothing. Are you surprised in adultery? Then up and tell the husband you are not guilty, and recall to him the example of Zeus, who allowed himself to be conquered by love and by women. Being but a mortal, can you be stronger than a god?[9]

Unjust Discourse forces Just Discourse to concede victory by using a verbal trick, a chain of associations leading to an absurd conclusion. After this, Socrates gives Phidippides

9. Aristophanes, pp. 355-56.

secret instruction in like sophistry. Socrates later returns and tells the proud father that his son is an accomplished cheat, and father and son go home.

Phidippides quickly demonstrates for his father his skill at legal chicanery, and Strepsiades is overjoyed at his seeming financial salvation. But the first creditor to appear is disposed of by the simple verbal gymnastics of the father, and so also the second creditor. Suddenly, the chorus reverses itself, speaking censoriously:

Whither does the passion of evil lead! here is a perverse old man, who wants to cheat his creditors; but some mishap, which will speedily punish this rogue for his shameful schemings, cannot fail to overtake him from today. For a long time he has been burning to have his son know how to fight against all justice and right and to gain even the most iniquitous causes against his adversaries every one. I think this wish is going to be fulfilled. But mayhap, mayhap, he will soon wish his son were dumb rather! (p. 368)

And the prediction is fulfilled. Phidippides begins to beat his father, and when Strepsiades protests, his son offers to prove its rightness. Strepsiades replies:

Miserable fellow! Why, 'tis I who had you taught how to refuse what is right, and now you would persuade me it is right a son should beat his father. (p. 370)

Using his newfound logic, Phidippides proves his rightness to his father's satisfaction. Phidippides gloats, "How pleasant it is to know these clever new inventions and to be able to defy the established laws!" Then Phidippides demonstrates the extreme consequences of his new learning and his contempt for convention. He says, "I shall beat my mother just as I have you."

At this threat, the full horror of Strepsiades' wickedness is revealed to him. Leo Strauss interprets the seemingly inconsistent violent reaction of the father to his son's assertion as meaning "if a son can lawfully beat his mother, why should it be unlawful for him to commit incest with his mother."[10] Aristophanes has sharply spiced the comedy in the satire by subtly suggesting the taboo of taboos, and by confronting the buffoon with the ultimate in cuckoldry.

Strepsiades, beside himself, blames the Clouds, but they reply, "you alone are the cause, because you have pursued the path of evil." They add:

We always act thus, when we see a man conceive a passion for what is evil; we strike him with some terrible disgrace, so that he may learn to fear the gods.[11]

Strepsiades asks Phidippides to join him in punishing Socrates, but the son tells him "keep your stupid nonsense" and departs. Strepsiades then asks the gods' aid and burns down Socrates' house while mocking his nebulous wisdom. When Socrates asks him what he is doing, he shouts back the first words of Socrates to him, "I traverse the air and contemplate the sun" (p. 377).

There are two targets of the satire in *Clouds*. Though the historic person and teachings of Socrates is the most concrete butt of it, the lengthiest and most biting parody is of the Athenian citizenry, caricatured in Strepsiades. He cannot manage his fortune or family; his values are superficial and self-serving; his obedience to law and religious piety are matters of personal convenience. His impiety takes second place to his constant effort to learn to violate the laws with impunity. For instance, his son demonstrates his successful graduation by displaying his legal chicanery. If he were not such a buffoon, Strepsiades would be seen as the villain of social decay.

Phidippides was but a playboy, due to family indulgence. He only becomes a potential moral monster at the insistence of his father, who is incapable of carrying out his own scheme. And, note, he is the instrument of the gods for punishing Strepsiades and Socrates. Phidippides' instinctive

10. Strauss, pp. 43.
11. Aristophanes, pp. 374-75.

understanding of the clouded wisdom of Socrates and his sophistical school is demonstrated in a paradoxical utterance of disgust at his father's new logic. He says, "These then are the fine things you have just learnt at the school of these sons of the Earth!" (p. 344).

Socrates' school of heaven-gazers is called "sons of the Earth," a colloquial phrase meaning enemies of the gods, in allusion to the mythical giants who had attempted to scale heaven. One wonders if the paradox is not more than sarcasm, if it does not express the paradoxical wisdom that the earthbound mortals who seek heavenly wisdom do not thereby worship the gods, but seek to destroy them.

The Just Discourse, like Strepsiades, is no more representative of true justice than is the Unjust Discourse, corresponding to Socrates. Aristophanes does not take the side of any of the play's protagonists, and his satirizing of the gods is even more ambiguous. Without a doubt he employs comic blasphemy, but to what purpose?

The Clouds are placed in rivalry to Zeus, and Socrates uses a comic version of a natural phenomenon to explain their beneficence to man. At the same time, Socrates argues convincingly the earthly impotence of Zeus. The Clouds are also shown to be two-faced, encouraging and entrapping Strepsiades (and to some extent Socrates) before pronouncing the justice of his punishment.

Interestingly, the Clouds, as goddesses, do not punish Strepsiades' wickedness. They merely foretell his downfall according to the logic of events and his actions. When Strepsiades blames them, the Clouds answer, "No, you alone are the cause, because you have pursued the path of evil" (p. 374).

Overtly, Socrates and Strepsiades are being punished for impiety, which leads to filial defiance and, ultimately, incest—the destruction of family and society. But there is another possibility lurking beneath the comic surface and the seeming vindication of the conventional verities.

Aristophanes may be ridiculing the conventional worship as much as he ridicules Socrates' unconventional heavenly

worship. Conventional piety is the worship of earthly irrelevance for the purpose of seeking favors that can not be
fulfilled and seeking excuses for self-generated disasters.

It must be noted that the Clouds are perfect comic representations of gods. The Clouds are imitators par excellence. They change shape constantly and assume various figures. They are ephemeral, "nebulous"; one can see in
them what one wants to. Thus, they can deceive and convince by appearing to be what one wants them to be. As
Strauss remarks, "this is the reason why they are the sole
god for Socrates as a man who teaches rhetoric."[12] Finally,
Aristophanes speaks to the audience, not as a protagonist in
the play, but as a Cloud and yet the author of the play. Is it
that in this satire he imitates the audience and the city, and
only through comic distortion and selectivity does he speak?

Before trying to deduce the positive from Aristophanes'
comic negativism, we should consider his satirizing of Socrates, for it falls into the same pattern. The centuries-old
criticism of Aristophanes for his supposedly unjust parody of
Socrates overlooks the open comedy of the satire—the audience knew and discounted its exaggeration. But the criticism in its blind obeisance to the Socratic-Platonic
philosophical tradition and its shotgun marriage with Christ-
ianity overlooks the valid issue between politics and
philosophy—a continuing one, finding ever-new comic expression ("pointy-headed intellectuals," "ivory-tower scholars," "memorize the encyclopedia, but can't remember to
zip up their pants," etc.).

Despite the undeniable contributions of Socrates in moral
and philosophic knowledge, the issue must be broached. Is
Socrates (Aristophanic or Platonic) an enemy of the city, not
because of his personal conduct, but precisely because of
his philosophy and the effect of its propagation on the citizens of the polis?

The personal behavior of Socrates and his disciples is

---

12. Strauss, p. 21. The present study owes to Strauss the insight into the Clouds
as imitators, but their symbolic mockery of conventional religion is my interpretation.

made a subject of comedy, but so is much conventional behavior. The brunt of the Aristophanic satire is directed at
the heavenly conceits of the Socratic teaching. From his
appearance in the sky-suspended basket to the final mockery of him by Strepsiades, he is parodied for his study and
worship of heavenly things in reference to earthly matters.

The comedy ridicules Socrates' abnormalities. All depar-
tures from the accepted norm are easy targets for laughter,
but the ridicule points up their importance. The mundane
interferes with the pursuit of heavenly truths. Yet, the rejection of earthly appearances in search of heavenly es-
sences leads to an acceptance of the most apparent and
least substantial of heavenly phenomenon—the clouds. Man
in seeking heaven finds only a mirror of himself, and that
which is least real for man on earth.

Socrates' teaching in itself is not the cause of Strepsiades'
dishonesty, Phidippides' beating of Strepsiades, or of potential incest. Men divorced from political reality are interested in heavenly truths, not for their eternal beauty,
but for their material advantage and selfish interest. Socrates' error is one of omission. He fails to realize or is totally unconcerned that more earthbound mortals will use or
be affected by his teaching in such a way as to destroy the
laws and ultimately the family.

Socrates believes that knowledge of the eternal truths
will reform bad conduct and perfect human society. For
Socrates, there are eternal and universal truths that apply
as much to political men and their social relationships as to
all other things. Because earthly matters are contingent and
relative—mere appearance—they cannot constitute a basis
for unchanging truths. Only the heavens in their all-
inclusiveness and ever-presence can be the source of basic
truth. Earthly man and changing society must be patterned
after the immortal heavens and their final Truth.

Clouds is the superb Aristophanic parody of the "truth"
of the immortal heavens. The subversion of law and the destruction of family are the consequences of a search for
transcendent truths. Man must not imitate the heavens (for

they become but a clouded mockery of himself at his most self-serving), but the heavens must mirror, and thereby support, man's earthly necessities, his political and social realities.

Aristophanes is not an atheist; he is a pagan. And the Olympian gods were projections of Greek behavior and earthly ideals onto the heavens. They lent supernatural sanction and mythical understanding to ancient Greek society and practices. Aristophanes comprehends this, and he wishes a return to the conventional religion of the "men of the Marathon," not the conventional and self-serving piety of the new citizens. His message is: look neither to the gods nor to their denial. Understand and respect the gods in the light of the polis and its political necessities. It is man's social deeds and earthly realities that are the anchors of wisdom.

Aristophanes is not religious, except in his recognition of the social function of religion in support of the laws as the foundation of society. To use the heavens for mortal man's benefits is to subvert the law, which is to disavow parental authority—commit incest.

It is not incidental that Socrates through Plato is considered a pre-Christian, quasi-saint, almost entitled to heaven. Beneath the comic caricature, Socrates preaches a revolutionary spiritual morality, opposed to the worldly morality of ancient Greece, which was founded on tribal customs and the partnership of word and deed. Aristophanes recognizes the new morality as a destroyer of the polis—the closed society with its own gods and civic morality. Despite the Platonic Socrates' glorification of the closed society in the *Republic*, the elevation of heavenly and universal truths over civic morality presages Christian monotheism and the open-world society.

For Aristophanes, Socrates' heavenly morality also heralds the elevation of "the word" over deeds.

The Clouds are the imitation of rhetoric, and their apostle renounces political action as the way of truth ("I have to suspend my brain and mix the subtle essence of my mind with air"). Aristophanes, the truly political man, condemns by ridicule the philosophical realism of the Platonic Socrates. Divorced from earthly reality, it is the apotheosis of unreason. Revelation is the new rationality of anti-political man.[13]

The interpretation of *Lysistrata* by Aristophanes need not detain us for long. The most phallic of his comedies (Strauss: "the most indecent and the most moral"), its political satirizing is simple and direct. He ridicules (in 411 B.C.) the continuing Peloponnesian War among the Greeks, and he parodies an almost fanatically masculine society by making women a positive political force. And Lysistrata is the heroine, the embodiment of so-called masculine virtues—rationality and statesmanship.

There is another uproarious parody that lurks beneath the surface of the comedy. Many Greeks were openly homosexual and to this practice military practices and warlike ideals may have been contributing factors. Women were a private concern, confined to housekeeping and procreation, unfit for ideal love or valorous action. Yet, in *Lysistrata*, when a totally male-determined civil war has almost destroyed the economy and decimated the population, women stage a political coup d'état and end the war by depriving the men of feminine sexual favors, something akin to barring bordellos to the current "Boys in the Band."

There is a possible indication of Aristophanes' ridicule of homosexuality within the play. When the men of the warring city-states come together to negotiate a peace, they call upon Lysistrata to aid them. They address her, "Lo! the foremost men in Hellas[,] seduced by your fascinations, are agreed to entrust you with the task of ending their quarrels." Lysistrata replies, "Twill be an easy task—if only they refrain from mutual indulgence in masculine love; if they do, I shall know the fact at once."[14]

If Aristophanes is ridiculing Greek homosexual practices,

13. Hannah Arendt, *The Human Condition* (New York: Doubleday Anchor Books, 1959). I am indebted to Arendt for this understanding of ancient Greek civic morality, but the interpretation of Aristophanic satirizing of Socrates is mine.
14. Aristophanes, p. 285.

it may be another indirect means of attacking the war. Martial values and military practices are conducive to homosexuality. Homosexuality undermines the home and the protective boundaries of the polis by depriving the women of their most persuasive weapon for peaceful living and family concern—their sexual favors. The final bond of marriage is sexual appetite. Diminish or divert the sex drive because of militarism and patriotism has become an enemy of patriotism. Military love of country destroys love of country as home and family.

In *Lysistrata* the war has been going on for years between the Greek city-states, led by Athens against Sparta. The women, led by Lysistrata, organize a conspiracy to take over the politics of the city-states and end the war through withholding sex from their men*

The satirical *Lysistrata* is enhanced by the sexual conspiratorial technique and its difficulties of implementation. The women must deny their husbands and lovers any sexual fulfillment while deliberately exciting them sexually. Women from the various city-states, and predominantly Sparta, enter into the conspiracy, but there is considerable talk about whether they themselves can abstain from the intense pleasures of the flesh long enough to succeed. However, after many ribald situations and much comically obscene dialogue—something of a war between the sexes—the women secure the men's surrender in exchange for their surrender.

In between, they have taken over Athens, where the action centers, by having the old women capture the Acropolis and hold it against recapture by the old men. Through sex, they force negotiations between the warring city-states—a recognition of their common plight (and common humanity) and indirect acceptance of the principle that war should not be made between Greeks. The women

---

*To cite a contemporary joke about Governor George Wallace: When he ran his wife Lurleen for governor and secured her election as his successor to the Alabama governorship in order to perpetuate his state political control, it was remarked, "Bedfellows make strange politics." A comic reverse twist on an old political axiom, it is certainly illustrative of *Lysistrata*.

are representative of the home, and use its biological base to forge the links between homes and across political boundaries to establish the true homeland—Greece itself.

Though Aristophanes argued implicitly for the laws and the earthly city in *The Clouds*, it is all of Greece that is that city. Its common culture of home and family is the basis for the conspiracy against intercity war.

Aristophanes, in his practical political understanding, completely eclipses Plato and Aristotle in ridiculing the parochial suicide of the city-states and their attendant civil wars. Male politics is war-oriented and is destroying the very basis of the polis for which war is supposedly waged. Imperialism is derided as a destructive male-child game, which the women, in their biologically rooted superior wisdom, decide to bring to a halt; they haul the naughty children home by their ears (or more vulnerable appendages) for the more pressing concerns of life.

To some extent, not uncommon in political satirists, Aristophanes reveals an antipathy to politics. He reverses Aristotle's political philosophy, which proceeds from family to polis as the rational culmination of the good life. The family remains the nuclear unit of the polis, but also retains the realistic rationality to restrain the destructive hubris of the polis.

We have seen that attacks on social and political authority are a stock element of popular comedy. In *Lysistrata*, Aristophanes adds to the broth with a complicated sexual unmasking, which proceeds to level military prowess and imperialistic pretensions by an overt sexual parody and a possible covert ridicule of homosexuality.

In the *Republic*, Plato allows elite women to become warriors and guardians, equally with the men. Their equality, however, is accompanied by a denial of their familial roles. The women are not admitted to equality with men as women; they must become "manly." On the contrary, Aristophanes in his satire extols the common sense of women as due to their very womanhood.

Women are rooted in the basic realities of existence, and

their realism in politics can check man's overweening pride, which leads to militarism and imperialism. Moreover, the women are not portrayed as unrealistic pacifists. They admit the need for defense against barbarians, that is, alien values. They deny the justice of war between a common people artificially divided by parochial political boundaries.

In effect, Aristophanes denies that the polis is defined by the Platonic and Aristotelian limitations of the number of people and by narrow geographical considerations. A political community is defined by the oneness of a people with a common way of life.

One cannot take the satirical techniques as fully indicative of Aristophanes' political beliefs. The women's "political" action is a parody intended to ridicule male politics and militarism. A gynecocracy is not Aristophanes' political ideal, but his extreme parody and bawdy ridicule do assert negatively the familial roots and function of politics, and the destructive consequences of the imperialistic politics of the Greek city-states. Through the very indecency of his comedy, he has been able to subversively proclaim the most profound morality and scathing social criticism of all his plays.

The sage as satirist cannot be a systematic or comprehensive philosopher. His positive doctrine is veiled in comedy, presented negatively through satire and ridicule. It is liable to be dismissed as pure nihilism or cynicism, and to be misunderstood because of its indirection and the necessities of comic technique.

If the comic techniques of satire and the other necessities of political humor are kept in mind, an educated guess can be made as to what the satirist is against. A more speculative deduction can be made as to his positive political thought. There is general agreement that Aristophanes is against the extreme democracy of Athens. But there is no agreement that he favors an agricultural type of democracy in which the aristocrats are also limited. This will be the conclusion of the present study.

There is general agreement that Aristophanes viciously

ridicules the self-serving citizenry and cruelly caricatures supposedly Socratic sophistries. *Clouds* is a concealed political polemic against civic selfishness and the new rhetoric. But there would be little agreement that Aristophanes is a proponent of the ancient civic morality and its *vita activa* (Arendt) against a new spiritual morality, denying earthly reality and idealizing the *vita contemplativa*.

There is general agreement that Aristophanes is totally opposed to Athenian imperialism and the Peloponnesian War. But there would be little agreement that he holds the family and the almost-biological wisdom of women to constitute the bedrock of political reality and the limits of political action. And there would be no concurrence whatsoever that *Lysistrata* is a veiled satirical attack on homosexuality as a militarily fostered vice that aids in severing the cord between the basic familial realities and the masculine political pride of imperialism.

Yet, the comic perspective makes reasonable, for one instance, the latter speculative conjecture. Ancient Greeks condoned, and even glorified, homosexuality, and it was associated with military practices. Greek women were severely confined to privacy and were considered inferior, even for love. The satire makes the men insistently virile, and the women positively lecherous, impassioned for husbands, lovers, or substitute sex devices. The comic reversal or parody could be stated thus: if this ideal parody of the corrupt reality were an actuality, the war could be ended. The negative of the negative, then, is that, as long as the corrupted reality prevails, the war and the destruction of family and polis will proceed.

In conclusion, the sage as satirist uses a full panoply of comic devices to attack his social and political targets. By inducing a humorous response in his audience, he suspends within them their initial defensive reaction to his scathing criticism, or, sublimating his critical aggressions comically, he avoids, through their humorous expression, reactions of violence that would tend to destroy the social fabric. Aristophanes can mercilessly criticize, under a veil of comical satire, almost hallowed Greek institutions: pederasty, patriotism, military values, and civic parochialism.

In the comic concealment, direct and unambiguous alternative ways, or positive doctrines of social reform, are not presented. Nevertheless, the satirizing sage dramatizes his criticism through use of a logic opposed to the conventional one. Humorously seducing his audience into his own chain of logic, he hopefully leads them back to a reexamination of the basic premises or values from which their social thinking proceeds. Suddenly, with a burst of laughter, they are confronted with a more "rational" premise for viewing the satirized situation—one that can overcome the disparity between the now comically absurd or ridiculous and the dimly perceived more "rational" or "natural" way.

The sage has a comic vision, however concealed, of what for him should be the right way, the right reason, or the right society. It would seem that a good part of the success of his satire or humor will be dependent upon the rapport of his audience with his sense of "rightness." Strauss notes that *Lysistrata*, the most moral of all Aristophanes' plays, was his most popular. Certainly the populace had to have some apprehension of both the prevailing corruption and right reform of it.

Reform is the right word, for Aristophanic satire is fundamentally conservative. Change is intrinsic to social satire, for the satire comically criticizes its target. But the comic form of social criticism has an innate conservatism in it, particularly Aristophanic satire.

Briefly, the political conservatism of social satire can be seen in its effects upon author and audience, and in its inspiration and its outlook. First, the author is the initial aggressor against a political personage or social institution. By his comic genius he has translated his anger or resentment into a satirical attack in which his target is made the butt of humor for an audience. The target becomes a victim and the aggressor's anger is expended peacefully and, possibly, constructively. He has revealed his victim's vices or failings for public correction, and he may have educated some of the public to his standards.

Second, the audience has participated vicariously in the satirist's sublimated aggression. They too have been purged of the need for more direct action in expression of their aggressions. And the satirist's use of sexual allusions, comic blasphemy, and ridicule of authority allows the audience in its imaginative participation and laughter to express forbidden emotions and thoughts in a socially permissible and cathartic manner. The social and political system gains added stability at the same time that it views itself critically. The people become prepared for reform and are relieved of the need for rebellion.

Third, there always lurks in the dim background of satire a vision or standard of rightness. Ridicule, parody, irony proceed from a sensed wrongness of social reality to some apprehension of the rightness of what could be. But comedy is not moral censure, otherwise it would become diatribe or preachment. The satire humorously prods or tickles its audience into an awareness of absurdity or abnormality. They have become more rational, but they aren't aware of their education, and their subsequent political action is their own. Satire is negative on its first level, and the positive remedy for the satirized must be inferred.

Last, political comedy and satire have something of both a cynical and tolerant outlook on man and his failings. The comic perspective has lenses fitted for viewing human weaknesses, and the lenses make it difficult not to detect one's own shortcomings. The necessary fanaticism of the rebel or prophet is antipathetic to the comic view. Aristophanes' gods get cuckolded, his comic hero passes gas, and his heroine is horny; they are only human.

Aristophanes' satire, like politics, is a compromise. It scorns the reality, calls up some ideality, and then settles for a laugh at human foibles and a hint that things could be better. But not too much better; we are all only human!

3

Socrates, Sage Satyr

Wherein the wise man becomes clown

In diametrical opposition to the politics of Aristophanes' satire stands Socrates, both in his Aristophanic caricature and his Platonic sainthood. This study holds that there is a comic consistency between the two, especially in Socrates' antipodal relationship to Aristophanes.

And there is startling affinity also. Aristophanes is the satirical genius, the greatest of comic political writers. Socrates is in a precise sense a philosophic clown—a divine fool. He is for Alcibiades, his disciple and adulator, a living satyr and the wisest of men. He is named by Aristotle in the *Nichomachean Ethics* as an ironist (self-depreciator), includes the satirical techniques of understatement, pretending ignorance, mock modesty, and sometimes overtones of slyness.[1]

I intend to examine Socrates as a comic character and wise man whose wisdom comes from his satyrical nature. I

1. Aristotle, *Nicomachean Ethics* (Indianapolis, Ind., and New York: Bobbs-Merrill Co., Inc., 1962), IV, 7, 1127a, 24, 1127b-26, pp. 105-6.

shall use the Platonic Socrates of the *Symposium* for the characterization of Socrates as he philosophizes. The *Symposium* is Plato's comic masterpiece; not directly political, it still reveals Socrates' essential beliefs and intimately describes the living Socrates.

Then, Plato's enduring classic, the foundation-stone of sober political philosophy, the *Republic*, will be considered here from a comic perspective. As Socrates will be viewed as a divine fool, so will the *Republic* be presented as a form of divine comedy. I do not intend to challenge the traditional understanding of scholarship on the *Republic*. I merely contend that a comic view of the *Republic* is justified in dramatic criticism and may yield valuable insights into it. Conversely, a failure to account for this dramatic structure of the *Republic* will lead to a default in understanding the work in its entirety.

Lane Cooper in *An Aristotelian Theory of Comedy* points to the ancient recognition of the similarity of Plato's dialogues to dramatic comedy. They are in the form of mimetic compositions, and mimesis was recognized as a chief source of comedy, even by Plato. Cooper finds the *Republic* to be of the mixed type of comedy, containing both narrative and imitative elements, and he regards the *Symposium* as a whole to be comedy.[2]

The dialogues of Plato, with their oftentimes ridiculous verbal exchanges, have distracted generations of students who, with pedantic seriousness, have sought to plumb their philosophic depths. Yet, Cooper says, "the sharp mental inquisitions naturally form a part of the literary technique in the Platonic dialogue; Plato systematically introduces them for comic effect" (p. 276). I believe that it is of importance to answer the question "What is that comic effect?"

Before I attempt to answer this question, I would point out that there is an overall comic aspect to the Platonic dialogues, noted by Cooper that may enter into the final estimation of comic effect. Plato, within the dialogues, particularly in the *Republic* and the *Philebus*, gives a theory of

2. Lane Cooper, pp. 100-111.

comedy and, as a consequence of his reasoning on it, he would prohibit comedy in his "ideal" polis. But here is the almost-comical reverse twist; under his theory, the *Symposium*, of course, would be barred, and, laughably, the *Republic* itself falls under his moral proscription.

The comic conception of Socrates that I shall adopt is that of the divine fool. It is suggested by Aristophanes' caricature of Socrates in the *Clouds*, but is confirmed by Alcibiades' soliloquy on Socrates in the *Symposium*. Interestingly, in that speech Plato has Alcibiades quote Aristophanes' description of Socrates in the *Clouds*.

The conception of the divine fool, divine clown, or holy fool has a long history—witness the much later Don Quixote of Cervantes. However, this study's conception is that of the man who acts from some personal vision of the "divine" or ideally good society as a standard for earthly polities. The divine fool's actions, teachings, or prophecies are abnormal in that they are opposed to, or conflict with, the customs and conventions of his society and culture. In consequence, his logic and thoughts proceed from different premises and values, and his conclusions and judgments are opposed to the conventional wisdom.

If he expresses this opposition in a humorous manner, and society accepts him and his views humorously, he may be perceived as a fool or a clown. Note that the divine fool's vision provides him with a built-in base for satirizing society. Moreover, his alternative and unconventional logic, when it intersects with the conventional logic, reduplicates the comic thought-process of the child (Jules Feiffer's technique) or the creative thinker (Koestler, *The Act of Creation*).[3]

That the divine fool chooses to present his wisdom humorously may be a tactical, temperamental, or philosophical decision. In the case of Socrates, it will be contended that the latter is the deciding factor. Socrates, however temperamentally suited to the role of divine fool,

3. Cf. chap. 1.

seems in several passages to consciously express a view of life as a form of comedy best approached "comically."

Thus, Aristophanes' portrayal of Socrates as a fool to the Athenian populace is correct, though humorously exaggerated. But Socrates knows himself to be a "fool." His loving disciple, Alcibiades, so describes him. And his "foolishness" is essential to his teaching and concomitant with his ironic view of man in society—the human comedy.

The interpretation of Socrates as a divine fool, and of the *Republic* as a divine comedy, proceeds from Plato. In short, if Socrates and the *Republic* are comical, then, necessarily, is Plato. Moreover, if there is some credibility in the interpretation, Plato is a much more mundane and humane philosopher than he is Karl Popper's totalitarian.*

The specific term *divine comedy* is derived from Dante's *Divine Comedy*, but it easily could be maintained that the genus is epitomized in the *Republic*. The disparity between the divine and the real is the constant theme of the *Republic*, and the comical or humorous is one consequence of that disparity. In translation, the terms *laughable, absurd, ridiculous*, and *foolish* form a repetitious litany in the *Republic*, matched only by the constant calling upon the "divine" as the final arbiter.

Feibleman, in *In Praise of Comedy*, describes beautifully the spirit of the divine comedy as "the largest field that comedy can take for criticism and remain comedy, *i.e.*, not lose all of its criticism through diffusion and become pure joy." He states that:

the criticism of divine comedy is directed at nothing less than the whole field of the finite predicament: the glorious effort and partial failure of that which is limited as it strives to comprehend (and thus partially to transcend) its limitations. The breadth that comedy can achieve and remain comedy is, then, wider than might at first have been supposed. For limitations are nowhere as narrow as they are

*Karl Popper in *The Open Society and Its Enemies* interprets the *Republic* as the model of a dogmatically closed society in the modern sense of a totalitarian society.

often conceived to be. Beyond any limited order there is always a less limited order, and so on in infinite progression. God in this sense could almost be defined as the least limited or most unlimited order. Comedy thus has an infinite range, and the divine comedy is still criticizing something. Nietzsche had some such conception as this in mind when he said, in *Also Sprach Zarathustra*, "I could never believe in a God who did not know how to laugh." To accept actuality just as it is, even for a God, would mean not to be a ruler of the logical order.[4]

Plato's Socrates is God's prophet who knows how to laugh. He lives the divine order and insists upon its earthly relevance, but he is the ultimate man of irony—the divine must be our calling, the human is our failing. First we must picture Socrates as one of his most loving admirers did— Alcibiades in the *Symposium*, the most uproarious and yet deeply beautiful of Plato's dialogues.

In the *Symposium*, friends, including Socrates and Aristophanes (and, later in the evening, Alcibiades) have come together at a dinner party to celebrate the public victory of one of them, Agathon, for his tragedy. After dinner, the group decide to entertain themselves by giving speeches on the subject of love. The speeches are some of the most lyrical and penetrating on love in all of the world's literature, but the comedy of their dramatic presentation is the focus of this essay.

The conversation at the drinking party (*in vino veritas*—a loosening of inhibition in order to "soberly" discuss the most intimate of human concerns) is witty and competitive, but the subsequent speeches present graphically the philosophical opposition of Aristophanes and Socrates as it applies to a particular issue. Though we are not at this point directly concerned with Aristophanes, we are concerned with the *Symposium* and the *Republic* as dramatic comedies. Moreover, Aristophanes has had his comic Soc-

---

4. James K. Feibleman, *In Praise of Comedy* (New York: Horizon Press, 1939, 1970), pp. 212-13.

rates considered previously; let us now view Plato's comic
Aristophanes.

Aristophanes' eulogy of love is preceded by his sneezing
to relieve himself of hiccups, and his jesting about it.
Another speaker introduces his presentation by remarking,
"Don't try to raise a laugh before you've even started."
Then "Aristophanes laughs," and replies:

But don't be too hard on me. Not that I mind what I'm
going to say is funny—all the better if it is; besides a comic
poet is supposed to be amusing. I'm only afraid of being utterly absurd.[5]

Aristophanes on love is amusing, but as far from absurd
as is the realistically rational. In short, love is beautiful but
comical. He says that once there were three races of men.
One was hermaphroditic, man-woman; another was man-
man; and the third was woman-woman. He describes them
as follows:

each of these beings was globular in shape, with rounded
back and sides, four arms and four legs, and two faces, both
the same, on a cylindrical neck, and one head, with one
face one side and one the other, and four ears, and two lots
of privates, and all the other parts to match. They walked
erect, as we do ourselves, backward or forward, whichever
they pleased, but when they broke into a run they simply
stuck their legs straight out and went whirling round and
round like a clown turning cartwheels. And since they had
eight legs, if you count their arms as well, you can imagine
that they went bowling along at a pretty good speed. (pp.
542-43 [189e6-90a8])

Aristophanes continues that these beings tried to rival the
gods, and Zeus, to weaken them, split them in half. He recounts of Zeus that

5. Plato, "Symposium," trans. Michael Joyce, in *The Collected Dialogues*
(Princeton, N.J.: Princeton University Press, 1963), p. 542 (189 a-b 6).

he cut them all in half just as you or I might chop up sorb apples for pickling, or slice an egg with a hair. And as each half was ready he told Apollo to turn its face, with the half-neck that was left, toward the side that was cut away—thinking that the sight of such a gash might frighten it into keeping quiet—and then to heal the whole thing up. So Apollo turned their faces back to front, and, pulling in the skin all the way round, he stretched it over what we now call the belly—like those bags you pull together with a string—and tied up the one remaining opening so as to form what we call the navel. As for the creases that were left, he smoothed most of them away, finishing off the chest with the sort of tool a cobbler uses to smooth down the leather on the last, but he left a few puckers round about the belly and the navel, to remind us of what we suffered long ago. (p. 543 [190d7-91a4])

But Aristophanes says that the bisection "left each half with a desperate yearning for the other, and they ran together and flung their arms around each other's necks, and asked for nothing better than to be rolled into one." Their yearning was so great that it affected their survival and they began to die out. Zeus, in sympathy for them, "devised another scheme":

He moved their privates around to the front, for of course they had originally been on the outside—which was now the back—and they had begotten and conceived not upon each other, but, like the grasshoppers, upon the earth. So now, as I say, he moved their members round to the front and made them propagate among themselves, the male begetting upon the female—the idea being that if, in all these clippings and claspings, a man should chance upon a woman, conception would take place and the race would be continued, while if man should conjugate with man, he might at least obtain such satisfaction as would allow him to turn his attention and his energies to the everyday affairs of life. So you see, gentlemen, how far back we can trace our innate love for one another, and how this love is always trying to redintegrate our former nature, to make two into one, and to bridge the gulf between one human being and another. (p. 544 [191b7-d4])

Aristophanes goes on in comic prose to describe the raptures of lovers seeking to reunite in their natural oneness, of their desire "to be merged, that is[,] into an utter oneness with the beloved." And he concludes, "for love must never be withstood—as we do, if we incur the displeasure of the gods. But if we cling to him [love] in friendship and reconciliation, we shall be among the happy few to whom it is given in these latter days to meet their other halves." Yet, characteristically, Aristophanes qualifies his speech with "if this be a counsel of perfection, then we must do what, in our present circumstances is next best, and bestow our love upon the natures most congenial to our own" (pp. 545-46 [193b3-c8]).

Aristophanes' view of love is earthy and a matter of flesh and fornication (interestingly, with some resemblance to evolutionary theory of bisexuality). Nevertheless, his comic sense of the ridiculous somehow becomes sublime. Men, rooted in the earth and fixed in their flesh, can through love of one another restore the unity of their fellowship, which belongs to their original nature.

Plato's Aristophanes is true to the Aristophanes of the political comedies. His comic sense looks upon the living world and laughs at its foibles from the vantage point of its immanent potential. His comic vision is of this world, and though it criticizes human failings, it attests to Aristophanes' love of life in all its absurdity.

On the contrary, the comic nature of Socrates finds expression in the world of men, but takes aim from beyond it. Aristophanes wants to be "funny" and he presents his understanding of love as comedy; Socrates' teaching is never comical. As we will see, he approaches his subject humorously, he himself remains amusing, and he treats his "students" ironically, but his teaching is of the utmost gravity and piety.

In the *Symposium* Socrates begins his discourse by questioning the poet Agathon on the latter's eulogy of love. He diffidently asks Agathon to clear up several points on which he is in confusion. Swiftly, he shows the poet that love is not a thing in itself, but an impulse beyond the self possessed of it. He says, "the object of his love and of his desire is whatever he isn't, or whatever he hasn't got—that is to say, whatever he is lacking in" (p. 553 [200e3-210c8]).

Agathon agrees, and Socrates, as usual, points out to him that he has contradicted his previous assertion that "love is beautiful." For Socrates launches his own discourse by revealing that love proceeds from lack of beauty, and thus, good, toward its fulfillment in the lover. Socrates has established his premise for a view of love as an impulse toward transcendence in man.

Socrates explains the nature of love as a spirit with another device of Platonic dramatic comedy, the humorous fable or myth. He says that his teacher Diotima, the wise woman, told him the following:

On the day of Aphrodite's birth the gods were making merry, and among them was Resource, the son of Craft. And when they had supped, Need came begging at the door because there was good cheer inside. Now, it happened that Resource, having drunk deeply of the heavenly nectar—for this was before the days of wine—wandered out into the garden of Zeus and sank into a heavy sleep, and Need, thinking that to get a child by Resource would mitigate her penury, lay down beside him and in time was brought to bed of Love.

So Love became the follower and servant of Aphrodite because he was begotten on the same day that she was born, and further, he was born to love the beautiful since Aphrodite is beautiful herself.

Then again, as the son of Resource and Need, it has been his fate to be always needy; nor is he delicate and lovely as most of us believe, but harsh and arid, barefoot and homeless, sleeping on the naked earth, in doorways, or in the very streets beneath the stars of heaven, and always partak-

ing of his mother's poverty. But, secondly, he brings his
father's resourcefulness to his designs upon the beautiful
and the good, for he is gallant, impetuous, and energetic, a
mighty hunter, and a master of device and artifice—at once
desirous and full of wisdom, a lifelong seeker after truth, an
adept in sorcery, enchantment, and seduction.

He is neither mortal nor immortal, for in the space of a
day he will be now, when all goes well with him, alive and
blooming, and now dying, to be born again by virtue of his
father's nature, while what he gains will always ebb away as
fast. So Love is never altogether in or out of need, and
stands, moreover, midway between ignorance and wisdom.
(p. 555-56 [203b-4])

Socrates continues his story of being instructed in love by
Diotima, and he puts forth that love is a longing to make
the good one's own for the sake of happiness. Diotima, he
says, qualified this proposition with the sexual metaphor of
procreative urge in love. Love, then, becomes "a longing
not for the beautiful itself, but for the conception and generation that the beautiful effects." And it follows that love
as procreation "is the one deathless and eternal element in
our mortality." Thus, love as the longing for the good leads
to "love as a longing for immortality" (pp. 558-59 [206c-
7a2]).

As Socrates shows procreation to be toward the immortal,
he goes on to transpose procreation from things of the flesh
to those of the spirit. He says that Diotima instructed him
that

those whose procreancy is of the body turn to woman as the
object of their love, and raise a family, in the blessed hope
that by doing so they will keep their memory green,
"through time and through eternity." But those whose
procreancy is of the spirit rather than of the flesh—and they
are not unknown, Socrates—conceive and bear the things of
the spirit. And what are they? you ask. Wisdom and all her
sister virtues; it is the office of every poet to beget them,
and of every artist whom we may call creative. (p. 560
[208e2-9a6])

Wisdom is then associated with the art of governing, "which goes by the names of justice and moderation." And Diotima tells Socrates that the Spartan Lycurgus and the Athenian Solon left behind "offspring" and fathered children far beyond any mortal issue. Diotima continues that this art is but one of "the more elementary mysteries of Love," and she thereupon unfolds the higher mysteries to Socrates (pp. 560-61 [209a7-e5]):

She says of the candidate for Love: Starting from individual beauties, the quest for universal beauty must find him ever mounting the heavenly ladder, stepping from rung to rung—that is, from one to two, and from two to *every* lovely body, from bodily beauty to the beauty of institutions, from institutions to learning, and from learning in general to the special lore that pertains to nothing but the beautiful itself—until at last he comes to know what beauty is. (pp. 562-63 [211c2-8])

Socrates concludes his story of the teaching of Diotima by saying that, ever since, it has been his mission "to bring others to the same creed, and to convince them that, if we are to make this gift our own, Love will help our mortal nature more than all the world." The spiritual message is ended, and Socrates returns his audience to earth with a witticism, saying "so you may call this my eulogy of Love, Phaedrus (a guest), if you choose; if not, well, call it what you like" (p. 563 [212b2-c2]).

And Plato returns his comic masterpiece to the mundane with the noisy entrance into the party of a very drunken Alcibiades. There then follows the comic drama of jesting and mock-romantic flirtation, a challenge by Alcibiades to the party to get drunk with him, and a return challenge to Alcibiades to give his discourse on love.

He settles for a eulogy of Socrates, and he pledges to tell the solemn truth (in drunkenness) "just as it comes into my head." Alcibiades starts:

Well, gentlemen, I propose to begin my eulogy of Socrates with a simile. I expect he'll think I'm making fun of him, but, as it happens, I'm using this particular simile not because it's funny, but because it's true. What he reminds me of more than anything is one of those little sileni that you see on the statuaries' stalls; you know the ones I mean—they're modeled with pipes or flutes in their hands, and when you open them down the middle there are little figures of the gods inside. And then again, he reminds me of Marsyas the satyr.

Now I don't think even you, Socrates, will have the face to deny that you look like them, but the resemblance goes deeper than that, as I'm going to show. You're quite as impudent as a satyr, aren't you? If you plead not guilty I can call witnesses to prove it. And aren't you a piper as well? I should think you were—and a far more wonderful piper than Marsyas, who had only to put his flute to his lips to bewitch mankind. (p. 566 [215a5-c1])

Alcibiades relates that the divine tunes that are played "show which of us are fit subjects for divine imitation." However, he adds, the tunes of Socrates have the same effect without any instrument; they are Socrates' "few simple words, not even poetry." Only Socrates can make Alcibiades feel ashamed for his prodigal living, and the latter says, "well, that's what this satyr does for me, and plenty like me, with his pipings."

Alcibiades clinches the portrayal of the sage satyr with these words:

Then again, he loves to appear utterly uninformed and ignorant—isn't that like Silenus? Of course it is. Don't you see that it's just his outer casing, like those little figures I was telling you about? But believe me, friends and fellow drunks, you've only got to open him up and you'll find him so full of temperance and sobriety that you'll hardly believe your eyes. Because, you know, he doesn't really care a row of pins about good looks—on the contrary, you can't think how much he looks down on them—or money, or any of the honors that most people care about. He doesn't care a curse for anything of that kind, or for any of us either—yes, I'm telling you—and he spends his whole life playing his little game of irony, and laughing up his sleeve at all the world. (pp. 567-68 [216b-c6, 216d3-e6])

The sage satyr is a divine fool whose comic approach to life camouflages and cushions his heavenly morality. And Plato has Alcibiades himself, in comical drunkenness, continue to extol the saintliness of Socrates. He says that it is better to be bitten by a poisonous snake than by Socrates' philosophy, which fills its victims with a "sacred rage."

Making allowance for the cultural homosexuality of the ancient Greeks, Alcibiades then describes his attempted seduction of Socrates in one of the most comical passages possible. But Socrates remains undisturbed and untouched by the encounter, and Alcibiades says that Socrates ends by laughing and jeering at Alcibiades' youthful beauty (pp. 569-70 [218c-19d]).

Alcibiades goes on to tell of Socrates in war. Again there emerges the laughable incongruity of his heroic and soldierly bearing and his comical behavior. In fact, Alcibiades quotes Aristophanes' caricature of Socrates' walk in the *Clouds*. After he tells the others that they will "never find anyone like Socrates, or any ideas like his ideas, in our own times or in the past" unless he is compared with sileni or satyrs, Alcibiades concludes:

Which reminds me of a point I missed at the beginning; I should have explained how his arguments, too, were exactly like those sileni that open down the middle. Anyone listening to Socrates for the first time would find his arguments simply laughable; he wraps them up in just the kind of expressions you'd expect of such an insufferable satyr. He talks about pack asses and blacksmiths and shoemakers and tanners, and he always seems to be saying the same old thing in just the same old way, so that anyone who wasn't used to his style and wasn't very quick on the uptake would naturally take it for the most utter nonsense. But if you open up his arguments, and really get into the skin of them, you'll find that they're the only arguments in the world that have any sense at all, and that nobody else's are so godlike, so rich in images of virtue, or so peculiarly, so entirely pertinent to those inquiries that help the seeker on his way to the goal of true nobility. (p. 572 [221d-22a6])

And Plato concludes the dialogue on a humorous note by having the narrator of the party tell how almost everyone goes to sleep or goes home. The narrator awakens near daybreak and observes Socrates still arguing and drinking with Agathon and Aristophanes. Finally, Socrates gets the other two "to admit that the same man might be capable of writing both comedy and tragedy—that the tragic poet might be a comedian as well" (p. 574 [223d3-5]).

With that, the others fall asleep and Socrates stalks off to the baths, and the *Symposium* closes with "he spent the rest of the day as usual, and then, toward evening, made his way home to rest" (p. 574 [223d10-12]).

The note on which Plato ends the dialogue could be taken as symbolic of the ambiguity of his philosophical drama and its hero, Socrates, the divine fool. Plato writes both tragedy and comedy, and in one dramatic form, and Socrates is, in one sense, a tragic poet who is also a comedian.

The tragic sense is conveyed in the *Symposium* (and in the *Republic*) by the vision of the good in contrast to the actuality of human failings, or by the knowledge of man's infinite possibilities confronted with the constant corruption of his flesh. But Plato and his Socrates are saved from the fullness of tragedy by an equally strong sense of the ridiculous in the human predicament. Man in his ignorance and confusion is like a child, who must be coddled and coaxed while he is haltingly taught.

The dramatic device of the dialogue and its comedy can be understood as the indulgent teaching of wayward children. The story of the drinking party quickens our interest and holds our attention. Historic personalities and their idiosyncracies are presented for the reader's consideration. Then comic fables are introduced in the narrative as a humorous seduction into deeper thought.

In the Aristophanic fable of human origins, the idea of love as the oneness of man is contained in the comic thought itself. However, the Socratic fable of the birth of love is but comic bait in his dialectical ascending to the highest notion of love, the pure idea of beauty. Humor is not present again until Socrates has completed his eulogy. Then he says to call it his eulogy of love or, "well, call it what you like." From utmost seriousness to feigned indifference, Socrates swiftly becomes ironic in the face of the chance effects of his contribution.

The dramatic, comical role of Alcibiades is more difficult to explain. After Socrates' ascent to the spiritual heights of the love of pure beauty, why the seemingly sudden descent to the drunken Alcibiades, his ridiculous recounting of the attempted seduction of Socrates, and above all, his comical personification of Socrates?

First, Plato, as one of the world's greatest prose dramatists, relieves the tension of deep reflection on the question of the love of beauty by introducing a conflict or startling contrast. The attention of the audience is revived, and the injection of copious humor facilitates the continued consideration of love and beauty, but by other means. The consideration returns to the study of beauty at the elementary level of particular personalities, and the Platonic teaching continues by means of example—the example of the inner beauty of Socrates versus the anarchic soul of Alcibiades.

The *agon* or conflict between Alciabiades and Socrates is not a competition for a material prize. It is rather a clash between two souls—one anarchic, the other rightly ordered—for the boundless prize of earthly happiness and eternal bliss. Diotima had told Socrates that if "man's life is ever worth living, it is when he has attained this vision of the very soul of beauty." She had added that, once the vision was attained, one would never again be seduced by the gross material pleasures (in the pursuit of which Alcibiades is the renowned champion). Diotima concluded that the man who has attained the virtue of the truly beautiful "shall be called the friend of god, and if it is ever given to a man to put on immortality, it shall be given to him" (p. 563 [211d-12b]).

In conflict with this ideal stands the disordered soul of Alcibiades, the playboy hero of Athens—handsome, wealthy, noble, and militarily courageous. As a sensualist and sybarite, he is the popular epitome of the happy man. In many ways, Socrates' description in the *Republic* of the youth with philosophical potential who is stunted by the corrupted polis resembles Alcibiades. Socrates says:

And even supposing, said I, that owing to a fortunate disposition and his affinity for the words of admonition one such youth apprehends something and is moved and drawn toward philosophy, what do we suppose will be the conduct of those who think that they are losing his service and fellowship? Is there any word or deed that they will stick at to keep him from being persuaded and to incapacitate anyone who attempts it, both by private intrigue and public prosecution in the court?[6]

Socrates asks if there is any chance of such a one's continuing to philosophize. He accepts the answer, "none at all." Thus the conflict of souls is not for victory over each other. Alcibiades' loss is symbolized by his failure to seduce Socrates, and Socrates' loss is portrayed both by Alcibiades' present state and in the later *Republic* by Socrates' acknowledgment that the disordered polity cannot rightly orient the potential of able but ambivalent youth. Rather, the conflict is for the dialogue's victory over the audience. Plato, as it were, dramatically displays the ordered and the anarchic souls and their effects on their exemplars, Socrates and Alcibiades.

Moreover, the contest is not even. The anarchic Alcibiades subordinates himself to Socrates ("Socrates is the only man in the world that can make me feel ashamed"). As the graphic portrayal of Alcibiades reveals by contrast the

6. Plato, *Republic*, p. 801 (564 d 12-75 a 7).

superiority of Socrates, the eulogy of Socrates by Alcibiades acknowledges it.

For Plato, Alcibiades has a stunted potential and an anarchic soul, but, like all men, he can know the good, and to know it is to acknowledge its superiority. However, without providence or chance, in the disordered polity the soul will lack the training and learning to achieve its potential and attain its share in the good.

Enter divine comedy. Even association with the perfectly good man, Socrates, cannot counter the effects of the disordered polity. Socrates' knowledge of his own limitations in the face of human fallibility, his failure to convert his close friend and fervent admirer, leads him to irony. Socrates speaks to Alcibiades with "ironical simplicity," and has "the infernal arrogance to laugh" at Alcibiades' youthful beauty and "jeer at the one thing" that he was really proud of.[7]

Socrates' retreat into humor from his vision of beauty is matched from the outside by Plato's retreat from the "divine" dialogue between Socrates and Diotima into the drunken discourse of Alcibiades. Both retreats are the equivalent of the philosophical descent back into the cave in the *Republic*—the comic concession to the human condition.

Oddly, the descent from the pure vision of beauty and truth into the cave of the human condition, which requires comic dissimulation, resembles the psychology of humor as analyzed by Freud. The pure knowledge of the truth of existence, expressed in its unalloyed fullness, would engender a violent reaction to it as a kind of aggression upon man's hallowed customs. The man of truth, faced with violence and the death of truth, represses the full expression of it to man. The truth, buried in the subconscious but demanding expression, forms mental associations and comes forth in comic form. In its comic camouflage it allays counteraggression, makes allies of the audience, permits the attack of truth on human fallibility, and somehow conveys something of the message of the divine fool.

7. Plato, *Symposium*, p. 570 (218 d 7, 219 c 3).

Platonic comedy is the compromise of truth with human fallibility, and Socrates is a divine fool because his "foolishness" ensures the transmission of a bit of his "divinity" to worldly man. Of course, his foolishness is also the commonly perceived disparity between his abnormal thoughts and behavior and the conventional wisdom. Yet, it occasions laughter instead of hostility among his audience.

There is a final comic technique in Socrates and his philosophical Frankenstein, Plato. But the technique is not incidental; it is, and must be, consistent with the mystic philosophy of Plato and the resultant divine comedy. It is precisely described by Alcibiades, classically portrayed by Socrates in his Platonic depictions, and dramatically employed by Plato in the dialogues. And it is a direct simile of the psychology of humor.

Alcibiades compares the arguments of Socrates with the satyrlike sileni that "open down the middle." The outside is laughable because of the common and utterly nonsensical expressions of a satyr. But the inner meanings "are so godlike, so rich in the images of virtue, or so peculiarly, so entirely pertinent to those inquiries" directed to man's true nobility in the world that, if they were not comically concealed, as Alcibiades puts it, "there are times when I'd honestly be glad to hear that he was dead, and yet I know that if he did die I'd be more upset than ever—so I ask you, what is a man to do?" (pp. 572, 567 [222a3-5, 216c1-3]).

In the *Symposium* we have seen Socrates employ the full panoply of comedy, sexual metaphor, irony, and the constantly camouflaged aggression of divine truth. Alcibiades describes its comical technique and its disarming and infectious effect. Socrates then demonstrates it with the story of Diotima, a story within a story, and then another story, a comic fable of the birth of Love.

There is yet another outer shell to the sileni, "you know the ones I mean—they're modeled with pipes or flutes in their hands, and when you open them down the middle there are little figures of the gods inside" (p. 566 [215b1-5]). Where the *Symposium* introduces the divine fool or the sage satyr, the *Republic* presents the divine comedy, the earthly city in which the divine fool must carry out his divine mission, knowing full well its necessity and futility.

4

Republic, Divine Comedy

Wherein philosophy becomes comical

Comically, the *Republic* is conceived in contradiction, only possible in impossibility, and, if the Republic could be privately achieved, it would be publicly destructive. That the *Symposium* is a kind of dramatic comedy has long been understood, though it is seldom considered so in political philosophy; that the *Republic* is also dramatic comedy, in fact, the most sublime in form, a divine comedy, is almost never mentioned, let alone systematically considered.

Yet, the comic genre of the *Republic* is indisputable.[1] By Plato's own analysis, the *Republic* is an example of the mimetic art,[2] and its techniques and inner structure make it comedy, not tragedy. Thus, again we are led to ask what meanings and insights can be gained from a comic perspective on the *Republic* that are not generally yielded by the traditional analyses. Above all, why does Plato cast in the

1. Cooper, pp. 100-101, 107, 113, 276.
2. Plato, *Republic*, pp. 820-32 (595b-607d).

98

form of a dramatic comedy what is almost the founding philosophical treatise on the most serious and elevated of human concerns.

Answers in detail to questions of comic meaning will be developed in the following analysis, but a tentative answer to the why of a dramatic comedy can be hazarded. It is precisely because Plato is trying to transmit some grasp of the most serious and elevated of matters that he resorts to dramatic comedy, albeit divine comedy. For him, the chasm in men's understanding between the mundane world of conventional opinions and the eternal universe of essential truths is so great that it can only be bridged by myths and metaphors. Then men can only be induced to cross the bridge—to tolerate the approach to truth—through playful humor (p. 768 [536e]).

If anything is clear in the text and in its "myth of the cave" in respect to the highest truths and the ultimate good, it is that almost all men are children. Moreover, they are dangerous children. Socrates says of the philosopher who, having seen the idea of the good, descends back into the cave of human society and attempts to relate his wisdom, "and if it were possible to lay hands on and to kill the man who tried to release them and lead them up, would they not kill him?" (p. 749 [517a7]). The divine comedy is both persuasive and a protective adaptation by Plato to a hostile society, and the role of the divine fool is partly the same for Socrates.

Of course, Plato's (and Socrates') own view of mankind has a comic dimension. He views man's earthly failings from his vision of heavenly perfection and finds them sorely but humorously trying. He doesn't become fanatically religious or reformist, nor does he withdraw into sullen silence. He laughs, puns, parodies, satirizes, while at the same time he communicates with utmost seriousness his vision of the good. Perhaps the most that can be said is that Plato, with all of his pre-Christian austerity, still partakes of the Dionysian spirit of the Greeks. It alone saves him from the religious fanaticism of heavens-on-earth.

The first matter to be considered in approaching the *Republic* as divine comedy is its dramatic form and the use of dialogue.[3] The dramatic form includes several levels, much like the inner and outer meanings of the sileni in the *Symposium*. The outer drama is the meeting of Socrates and his friends at the house of Cephalus during a religious festival at Piraeus. They begin to discuss the meaning of justice, and Socrates goes on to develop its meaning through dialectical conversation with the others. In the course of the conversation, the personalities of the discussants and their modes of questioning and responding to Socrates enter into the audience's understanding of the dialogue.

For understanding the drama as a divine comedy, it is important to note that the discussion about justice by Socrates takes place when the party of Socrates absents itself from the religious celebration of the goddess Bendis, a Thracian deity. Religious conformity must be temporarily suspended if one is to seek the divine sources of justice. On the other hand, the civic religion has already been compromised by its invasion by alien deities.

The first person to state his view of justice is Cephalus, the owner of the house in which the dialogue takes place. He is a wealthy old man and the father of several young men who take part in the dialogue. Socrates asks him, as a representative of age and civic virtue, what he can say of his life and feelings now that he is so aged. Cephalus testifies to his own contentment and speaks of the one anxiety of those approaching death—that they may have been unjust. He says that the chief advantage of his wealth is that he has been able to tell the truth and to render to each man what he, Cephalus, owes him.

Socrates quickly demonstrates the contradiction in this definition of justice and, therefore, its weakness. Cephalus admits to it, but excuses himself to attend the sacrifices.[6]

---

3. Eric Vogelin, *Plato* (Baton Rouge, La.: Louisiana State University Press, 1966). This study is deeply indebted to Vogelin for his detailed exposition of the dramatic form and techniques of the *Republic*. Vogelin's interpretation is heavily theological, but that is in accord with the idea of divine comedy. However, the comic perspective is solely my own interpretation.

He turns over the argument to Polemarchus, his son and heir, who insists on the validity of his father's decision.

The representative of the ruling order gives the simplistic and accepted definition of justice. He is unconcerned with its weakness or with pursuing its full meaning, and returns with a laugh to the sacred rites (social conformity).[4] As he passes on to his son the question of justice, Socrates jests, "Is not Polemarchus the heir of everything that is yours?" The younger generation is heir to the failings of justice in their elders, and Polemarchus is heir to all the material wealth and the spiritual poverty of Athens.

Socrates easily disposes of Polemarchus's refined definition that justice is to render each man his due, but in doing so he displays the comic technique of his argumentive logic. First, he gets Polemarchus to agree to a slightly altered premise—what is one's due is what befits one, and the person who can render to another what most befits him is the craftsman with the skill related to the befitting. Having gained agreement, Socrates by a string of associations draws Polemarchus into absurd conclusions. Socrates states, "So justice, according to you and Homer and Simonides, seems to be a kind of stealing, with the qualification that it is for the benefit of friends and the harm of enemies. Isn't that what you meant?"

Polemarchus, aghast, protests that he no longer knows what he meant, but he still believes that "justice benefits friends and harms enemies" (pp. 580-84 [331e-34c]).

Socrates goes on from Polemarchus's admission of ignorance to further demonstrate how his new definition leads to absurd conclusions. He then leads Polemarchus to a new understanding of justice that is not contradictory. Socrates says:

If, then, anyone affirms that it is just to render to each his due and he means by this that injury and harm is what is due to his enemies from the just man and benefits to his friends, he was no truly wise man who said it. For what he

4. Plato, *Republic*, p. 580 (I, 331b2-e).

meant was not true. For it has been made clear to us that in no case is it just to harm anyone. (p. 585 [335e])

Socrates has led Polemarchus in a seemingly logical manner to the acceptance of a resolutionary principle of morality. He has done so by dialectically forcing unacceptable conclusions from initial premises while at the same time posing acceptable associations with the premises as alternative paths of reasoning. When a repugnant or contradictory conclusion is rejected by his respondent, Socrates employs the alternative reasoning to lead him from the flawed opinion to the true wisdom.

Yet, the dialogue is not one of dry-as-dust logic. Plato encases Socrates' logic in almost comic utterances and punctuates it with absurd contradictions as Socrates demonstrates to his interlocutor the fallacies in the latter's initial belief or opinion. Thus, in the preceding dialogue with Polemarchus, Socrates at one point has Polemarchus agree about just men that "it is then just for them to benefit the bad and injure the good." And, again, "by justice then do the just men unjust, or in sum do the good by virtue make men bad?"

Each time Polemarchus is brought to the ridiculous conclusion, he must reverse his thought; then Socrates can correct its error and lead him to the true wisdom. As was quoted earlier from the *Symposium*, Alcibiades says that "anyone listening to Socrates for the first time would find his arguments simply laughable; he wraps them up in just the kind of expressions you'd expect of such an insufferable satyr."[5]

The arguments remain humorous, and Socrates employs the best comic technique in using the art of contradiction to draw from his interlocuters the most deeply moral conclusions. This is something of a contradiction itself, for he is dealing frivolously with the most weighty of matters. There is also a kind of comedy present in Plato's personification of

5. *Symposium*, p. 572 (221 e).

the participants in the dialogue. Of course, always present is Socrates as the divine fool with his "satyrical" character. We have seen Cephalus, the aged establishmentarian, and now his son, Polemarchus, more deeply concerned and possibly disturbed, as befits an heir to the superficial and self-satisfied justice of the regime. His arguments are shallow but good-natured, and he is easily confused. Socrates convinces him easily of his errors, almost too easily, for we are left with the feeling that where there is little depth or resistance, there can be little commitment and less understanding of the momentous nature of Socrates' moral assertion.

The next character to be personified by Plato in the *Republic* is Thrasymachus, the Sophist. In every way he comically personifies what Plato considers to be the character of the new rhetorician. If Aristophanes caricatures Socrates mercilessly, certainly Plato does the same to the Sophist. Yet, the dramatic encounter of Thrasymachus with Socrates is not vicious; it is ridiculously funny. Unless one is alive to its comedy, it is an annoying distraction, but when read aloud, it is high humor. In Socrates' recounting of the argument, it is also a kind of gentle mockery of his opponent and of himself, whereby their styles and personal attributes complement their beliefs. Socrates begins the encounter:

Now Thrasymachus, even while we were conversing, had been trying several times to break in and lay hold of the discussion but he was restrained by those who sat by him who wished to hear the argument out. But when we came to a pause after I had said this, he couldn't any longer hold his peace. But gathering himself up like a wild beast he hurled himself upon us as if he would tear us to pieces. And Polemarchus and I were frightened and fluttered apart.

He bawled out into our midst, What balderdash is this that you have been talking, and why do you Simple Simons truckle and give way to one another? But if you really wish, Socrates, to know what the just is, don't merely ask questions or plume yourself upon controverting any answer that anyone gives—since your acumen has perceived that it is easier to ask questions than to answer them—but do you yourself answer and tell what you say the just is. And don't you be telling me that it is that which ought to be, or the beneficial or the profitable or the gainful or the advantageous, but express clearly and precisely whatever you say. For I won't take from you any such drivel as that![6]

Socrates says that Thrasymachus's aggressive attack dismays him and fills him with fear, and he answers Thrasymachus timidly and pleads for mercy. At this, the latter "gave a great guffaw and laughed sardonically," and he exclaims, "Ye gods! Here we have the well-known irony of Socrates, and I knew it and predicted when it came to replying you would refuse and dissemble and do anything rather answer any question that anyone asked you" (p. 587 [337a-b]).

Despite Thrasymachus's rudeness and demand for money for instructing the group on justice, Socrates continues to act humble and insist on Thrasymachus's own wisdom concerning justice. Though Thrasymachus has proclaimed in advance the Socratic technique of argument by interrogation, his pride in his wisdom is too great for him: "Thrasymachus was eager to speak in order that he might do himself credit since he believed that he had a most excellent answer to our question." He must speak because he has the mortal pride that one's opinion is true knowledge. The human clown delivers himself up for ritual sacrifice to the divine fool. Opinion, the human masquerading of private prejudice as knowledge, is to be confronted with wisdom, the essential truths of the cosmos.

After Thrasymachus had delivered his opinion, "justice is nothing else than the advantage of the stronger," Socrates immediately begins questioning him despite his resistance. For Thrasymachus again brands Socrates, even as he gives in to his questioning. He says, "you are a buffoon, Socrates, and take my statement in the most detrimental sense" (p. 588 [338d3]).

6. *Republic*, p. 586 (331 b-d 4).

As is to be expected, Socrates quickly has Thrasymachus embroiled in ridiculous contradiction. The latter must then revise his statement, and he falls into the trap of a favorite Platonic-Socratic analogy—the likening of a ruler to a craftsman. As Thrasymachus replies to Socrates' questions about the skill of the craftsman and its aims, he continues to bombastically insult Socrates. He says, "you won't get the better of me by stealth and, failing stealth, you are not of the force to beat me in debate," and "bring on against this your cavils and your shyster's tricks if you are able," and adds "paltry fellow though you may be" (p. 591 [341b-c3]).

All the while, Socrates drives Thrasymachus by his questioning, based on the latter's original analogy, to another contradiction of his idea of justice:

Then, said I, Thrasymachus, neither does anyone in any office of rule in so far as he is a ruler consider and enjoin his own advantage but that of the one whom he rules and for whom he exercises his craft, and he keeps his eyes fixed on that and on what is advantageous and suitable to that in all that he says and does. (pp. 592-93 [342e5-43])

But Thrasymachus refuses to assent to Socrates' superior logic. He is being beaten at his own game or words and can only react with comic boorishness. He asks, "tell me, Socrates, have you got a nurse?" Socrates protests and inquires his meaning. Thrasymachus replies:

Because, he said, she lets her little snotty run about driveling and doesn't wipe your face clean, though you need it badly, if she can't get you to know the difference between the shepherd and the sheep. (p. 593 [343a3-8])

Thrasymachus means, of course, that the shepherds take care of the sheep for their advantage and that of their masters. He goes on to insist on the real advantage of the unjust man over the just man, and he states that this can best be seen in the epitome of injustice, namely tyranny. He concludes, "injustice on a sufficiently large scale is a stronger, freer, and more masterful thing than justice, and, as I said in the beginning, it is the advantage of the stronger that is the just, while the unjust is what profits a man's self and is for his advantage" (p. 594 [344c-d]).

Socrates continues to press the analogy of the craftsman on Thrasymachus, but he abruptly drops that line of argument and says, "a far weightier matter seems to me Thrasymachus' present statement, his assertion that the life of the unjust man is better than that of the just" (p. 597 [347e3-7]). Again, Socrates gets Thrasymachus to accede to a premise from which he can proceed to pin him to a contradiction; in the course of examining the latter, he again uses the analogy of the craftsman. Yet, the vaunted rhetorician, the skilled craftsman in debate, accepts ths Socratic premise and analogy.

However, Thrasymachus is not unaware of being trapped. He says, "Either then allow me to speak at such length as I desire, or, if you prefer to ask questions, go on questioning and I, as we do for old wives telling their tales, will say, 'Very good,' and will nod assent and dissent" (p. 601 [350e1-4]).

Oddly, though Thrasymachus protests, he does it politely, even respectfully. Moreover, Socrates does not let him speak at will, but goes on questioning him. In fact, he compliments Thrasymachus for his conduct: "Admirable, Thrasymachus, I said. You not only nod assent and dissent, but give excellent answers." Docilely, Thrasymachus replies, "I am trying to please you" (p. 601 [351c3-5]).

Nevertheless, Thrasymachus has not been won over. His replies, for the remainder of his active part in the dialogue, remain courteously mocking: "So be it, he replied, not to differ from you." "By all means." "Have it that it keeps it, he said." "Revel in your discourse, he said, without fear, for I shall not oppose you, so as not to offend your partisans here."

And Socrates is not offended or disappointed at what has become mock ceremony for his rival. As he recounts, "Fill up the measure of my feast, then, and complete it for me, I said, by continuing to answer as you have been doing" (pp. 601-2 [351d7-52b6]).

Near the end of the Thrasymachus-Socratic dialogue, Socrates asks the question, "the just soul and the just man then will live well and the unjust ill?" Thrasymachus replies, "so it appears . . . by your reasoning." When Socrates concludes, "never, then, most worshipful Thrasymachus, can injustice be more profitable than justice," Thrasymachus sarcastically mocks, "let this complete your entertainment, Socrates, at the festival of Bendis."

Socrates expresses his appreciation to Thrasymachus, but admits his dissatisfaction with the outcome. He has not found out what justice is, and so "the present outcome of the discussion is that I know nothing."

What has been the purpose of the comic encounter? Though civilly tamed, Thrasymachus is unregenerate. He does not agree with Socrates' reasoning, and he seems to consider himself to have been forced by the superior skill of Socrates' false logic into providing entertainment for the group.

Socrates knows that he has not won over Thrasymachus. In fact, he has blithely ignored the latter's request to speak uninterruptedly. In short, he used Thrasymachus to complete his thought and develop interest in his audience. Still, he too remains dissatisfied.

Can it be that, in this introduction to the *Republic* proper, Plato merely sets the stage for the drama of justice? Thrasymachus has been beaten at his own game. He is tamed, not by recognition of the truth, but by Socrates' superior rhetoric. Socrates is a better sophist than the sophist. And to what avail? Possibly entertainment alone. Thus, words and logic used purely for argument, to best or persuade another, are empty. They have become play without the power to penetrate to truth or reveal it to others.

Socrates' sophistical defeat of Thrasymachus has not even satisfied the other participants. Glaucon at the beginning of Book II says, "for Thrasymachus seems to have given up to you too soon, as if he were a serpent that you have charmed, but I am not yet satisfied with the proof that has been offered about justice and injustice." Exactly; the entertainment offered has been that of the satyr-snake charmer playing the flute of his words (*Symposium*, 215 d) to tame the rude serpent.

To break through the level of opinion-versus-opinion to the truth of things, Socrates must go beyond argument. He must proceed by myth and allegory to arouse in his "partisans" (Thrasymachus, 352,b3) their emotional kinship with or impulse toward the truth. He poetically retraces for them the ascent of the philosopher from out of the cave to the light of the truth.

Without a prior spiritual receptivity, Thrasymachus cannot be convinced (converted?) to the truth of justice by any wordplay. Words must become other than counters in a game of wits; as dim representatives of the reality of things, they must become "markings" of the path upward toward the truth. Socrates will be the guide, but each man must make the journey and find the truth for himself.

Two more points may be made in respect to this wrestling match of opinion, its rejection as unsatisfactory, and the abrupt reversal toward the upward pursuit of the truth. The reversal constitutes in itself a contradiction—truth is not to be discovered in the opinions concerning it. And another contradiction of far greater magnitude for the divine comedy lurks between Socrates' refutation of Thrasymachus's opinion of earthly justice and Socrates' later denunciation of that same earthly justice as hopelessly corrupt. Socrates has strongly, though gently, refuted Thrasymachus's opinion and arguments on the injustice of earthly justice. He himself later will espouse similar views. Though Socrates condemns this injustice in the name of a higher justice, and Thrasymachus seems to condone it, Socrates has been able to draw the latter into contradictions only through the presence in him of "good-willing" confusion about the nature of justice. He too is receptive and remains with the Socratic group on its journey toward truth.

Second, even in its inception, the contradiction between the essentially private (or intensely personal) nature of the quest for justice and truth and the overtly public character of justice (in the *Republic*) is apparent. The supremely gentle Socrates is totally unyielding to Thrasymachus's entreaty to state his views of justice uninterruptedly. Socrates would rather take over the dialogue and push it in a stilted manner to a wooden conclusion, unsatisfactory to all.

For him, even the truth of public matters is not a matter of discussion, a product of the dialectic of public argument. Thrasymachus, however, "good-willing" and honest in his view of public justice, does not possess a partial truth of the matter at hand to be supplemented by Socrates' partial truth. The truth is whole, and Socrates through his vision is possessed by it. He cannot compromise it for the sake of agreement. He can only soften its impact through humor. Socrates is a "fool" in presenting the truth, but the truth is divine and the fool is an iron man in adhering to it.

From this point on, the way to the truth is not a collective effort but an emotional reaching out to the poetic representations of the divine fool. He has the authority of the final truth. His vision, if possible politically, would destroy politics. To the extent to which it is possible personally, it would deprive politics of man.

Nevertheless, though the genuine dialogue of a real clash of opinions has been abandoned, its form continues. Two brothers, Glaucon and Adimantus, insist that Socrates continue his inquiry into the nature of justice. To facilitate the inquiry, Glaucon poses the social or conventional opinion of justice, a social-contract theory of the origins of justice in which justice is held to be "a compromise between the best, which is to do wrong with impunity, and the worst, which is to be wronged and be impotent to get one's revenge" (p. 606 [359a]).

Glaucon is satirizing the conventional opinion of justice, saying that both the just and unjust man are swayed by their self-interest. Justice is not at all inborn goodness or a rational perception of an objective good. To illustrate,

Glaucon relates the myth of the ring of Gyges, the story of a ring that made its bearer invisible. Gyges then committed injustice with impunity in order to gain his desires. Glaucon continues that if both the just and the unjust men had such rings, their behavior would be indistinguishable, for no one would

persevere in justice and endure to refrain his hands from the possessions of others and not touch them, though he might with impunity take what he wished even from the marketplace, and enter into houses and lie with whom he pleased, and slay and loose from bonds whomsoever he would, and in all other things conduct himself among mankind as the equal of a god. (pp. 607-8 [359d-60c])

Here Plato resorts to a kind of psychological satire that he uses a number of times in the *Republic*. The relating of man's yielding to the temptations of power if he could become invisible is a comic fantasy or daydream. It is easily recognizable to most of us, either as one of our own daydreams or as the perennial story of the invisible man. We laugh in recognition, while we may go on to ponder its import for human justice.

Glaucon continues his posing of the real question of justice for Socrates by reversing the situation of the invisible man and speaking of the just man whose justice is invisible to all and results in no material or social rewards. At the same time, the unjust man is consummately skilled at injustice, fully reaping its rewards and enjoying the reputation for justice.

Finally, Adimantus completes the conventional views and understanding of justice by relating how society educates its children to justice and what it teaches about the gods in relation to justice (pp. 608-14 [360e-68]). Though the brothers are asking Socrates to refute the implications of the social understandings and teachings of justice, at the same time they are truthfully relating the actual opinions and practices of society on justice. It is a biting and bitter satire of society only partly relieved by the humor in the disparity between our ideals and our practices. The satire flays the social authorities and permits some release of aggression against them, but it is too telling for much comedy.

Glaucon and the group then call on Socrates to pursue to the end the inquiry about the nature of justice. He replies that it will be easier to observe justice when it is writ large in the city, and from there look for its likeness in the individual. They all agree, and Socrates proceeds to imaginatively construct a city.

The city that Socrates constructs is a simple one in which men come together and contribute their various skills toward the supply of the common necessaries. The life that would be led is austere but wholesome; Socrates concludes, "and so, living in peace and health, they will probably die in old age and hand on a like life to their offspring" (p. 619 [372a-d]).

Glaucon is disgusted and cries out, "if you were founding a city of pigs, Socrates, what other fodder than this would you provide?" Glaucon must have comfort and luxury. If justice is only to be found in a simple, healthy city, then it is only fit for pigs. Surprisingly, Socrates yields:

Good, said I. I understand. It is not merely the origin of a city, it seems, that we are considering but the origin of a luxurious city. Perhaps that isn't such a bad suggestion, either. For by observation of such a city it may be we could discern the origin of justice and injustice in states. The true state I believe to be the one we have described—the healthy state, as it were. But if it is your pleasure that we contemplate also a fevered state, there is nothing to hinder. For there are some, it appears, who will not be contented with this sort of fare or with this way of life, but couches will have to be added thereto and tables and other furniture, yes, and relishes and myrrh and incense and girls and cakes—all sorts of all of them. And the requirements we first mentioned, houses and garments and shoes, will no longer be confined to necessities, but we must set painting to work and embroidery, and procure gold and ivory and similar adornments, must we not?
Yes, he said. (p. 619 [372d3-73b])

One can almost hear the eager, greedy Yes of Glaucon, and, without too much imagination, one may hear also the gentle, resigned tones of the divine fool as he continues to elaborate on the wealth and comforts of the luxurious city. He includes the consequences of luxury, inquiring, "Doctors, too, are something whose services we will be much more likely to require if we live thus than as before?" Glaucon easily acquiesces.

Moreover, additional territory will be required by the city and its neighbors also, "if they too abandon themselves to the unlimited acquisition of wealth, disregarding the limits set by our necessary wants." Again Glaucon assents, and Socrates says that war will necessarily follow expansion. He points out:

And we are not yet to speak, said I, of any evil or good effect of war, but only to affirm that we have further discovered the origin of war, namely, from those things from which the greatest disasters, public and private, come to states when they come. (p. 620 [373d-74])

The once-argumentative Glaucon merely affirms "certainly." At this point, Socrates calls forth an army, which, of course, must be skilled in its art. We are at the inception of the guardian class, the center stone in that supposedly possible ideal commonwealth whose pattern is laid up in heaven, the Republic.

Yet, pause a moment; Socrates has already sketched his best possible city, Glaucon's "city of pigs." He does not stand corrected by Glaucon, nor does he then sketch an equally good alternative. I have quoted him as he changes course toward Glaucon's luxurious city. He stresses that "the true state I believe to be the one we have described—the heavenly state, as it were. But if it is your pleasure that we contemplate also a fevered state, there is nothing to hinder."

Cephalus, representative of the successful, older generation was unconcerned with the question of justice. Glaucon, spokesman for the younger generation represented in Socrates' circle, is deeply troubled by the problem. But he is the child of his parents, educated to affluence and habituated to luxury. For him, justice is not a primary purpose in the creation of the city, but a secondary problem following upon the primary purpose of the city—luxurious living. In short, justice is a cure for the ills of affluence, but those ills are in no way allowed by Glaucon and his peers to shake their unquestioning assumption of civic materialism. No wonder that Socrates later in the dialogue bars all children above ten years of age from the Republic. Despite their good intentions toward justice, Socrates' friends are corrupted adults in respect to the truly healthy state.

The divine comedy of the *Republic* is comically founded on a joke of the divine fool. His joke is his response to the human comedy of his audience, who cannot distinguish justice from selfishness, whose greed is so great that they ignore Socrates' ridiculing of the injustices of the fevered, luxurious city.

And have not thousands upon thousands of students of the *Republic* been so fooled by Plato's comedy on human avarice? How could men even consider living in a city of pigs, and doesn't justice necessarily arise as a problem of the inevitable drive of men toward materialistic civilization?

The divine fool's wisdom is too strong for human weaknesses. Plato must send comedy to the rescue of the clown and the cosmos. First, the comedy plays a cathartic function for Socrates (and, ultimately, Plato). Socrates is possessed by his vision of the good and compelled by his sense of divine mission to deliver it; yet, the message cannot be delivered in its purity. The irony of Socrates is an escape from the anguish of the divine messenger.

Second, the *Republic* as divine comedy is the transmutation of the untransmissible divine message into a humanly acceptable counterfeit of it. The *Republic* is literally a joke played by Plato, and his Socrates, on base mankind. As jokes often do, the *Republic* proceeds from a standard of the good, contains a truth, and conceals a message. But in itself, it is a compromising of the eternal truth of the good with the mundane reality of man.

The *Republic* may condemn politics and its practice would destroy politics, but, in itself, it is a profoundly political response to the reality of things—a compromise of the good with the given. Its humor is the language of politics, and its ambiguous and ambivalent divine fool, Socrates, is the politician of perfection, seeking the votes of materialistic man.

In the following consideration of the function of comedy in the *Republic*, this view will be supported in more detail. However, one more point may be noted in asserting that the Socratic turning from the city of pigs to the luxurious city is the pivot upon which the divine comedy turns.*

If the city of pigs would have been the habitat for just men, the luxurious city is fit for doglike men. Socrates, having established the need for an army in the expansionist state, further asserts that the army must be composed of skilled soldiers, termed guardians. He says, "it becomes our task, then, it seems, if we are able, to select which and what kind of natures are suited for the guardianship of a state" (p. 621 [374e4]).

The guardianship of the luxurious state demands a nature somewhat paradoxical for justice. Socrates asks, "do you think . . . that there is any difference between the nature of a well-born hound for this watchdog's work and that of a well-born lad?" (p. 621 [375]). He points out to Glaucon how a dog's attributes are consistent with those which will be required of the guardian class. In short, the guardians are the soldiers of a garrison state and, certainly, a good soldier does resemble a good watchdog.

But in case Glaucon may have missed the humor in the

---

*Contrary to Eric Vogelin's thesis in his *Plato*, the comic perspective would hold that this Socratic creation of the Republic does not represent a spiritual turning around to the truth of the good, but a turning back to mundane reality and the necessity of compromise. The Republic remains a symbolic representation of the road to the truth, but it is the road downward to the approximation of the truth for earthly man. There is in the proximate justice of the compromise Republic the possibility for a few philosophically gifted youths to use it as the road upward, but they are the very few, and their truth is not social.

paradox of a dog's nature and the guardians of justice, Socrates proceeds to make the contradiction even more outrageously ridiculous. First he says "you surely have observed in well-bred hounds that their natural disposition is to be most gentle to their familiars and those whom they recognize, but the contrary to those whom they do not know." Upon his agreement with this, Socrates adds, "and does it not seem to you that our guardian-to-be will also need, in addition to being high-spirited, the further quality of having the love of wisdom in his nature?" (p. 622 [375e]).

The brute capacity for the recognition of familiars has been transformed into a love of wisdom. And when Socrates is asked how the watchdog shows "a true love of wisdom," he carries the ridiculous even further:

> In respect, said I, that he distinguishes a friendly from a hostile aspect by nothing save his apprehension of the one and his failure to recognize the other. How, I ask you, can the love of learning be denied to a creature whose criterion of the friendly and the alien is intelligence and ignorance?
> It certainly cannot, he said.
> But you will admit, said I, that the love of learning and the love of wisdom are the same?
> The same, he said.
> Then may we not confidently lay it down, in the case of man too, that if he is to be in some sort gentle to friends and familiars he must be by nature a lover of wisdom and of learning? (pp. 622-23 [376b4-c])

Socrates has stretched the ridiculous into the totally absurd by a series of incongruous associations, and the guardian of the state like a watchdog "must be by nature a lover of wisdom and learning." Surely Plato, the founding philosopher, can distinguish between animal recognition and human rationality, between learning as conditioning to the familiar and learning as the development of wisdom away from the familiar to the general.

Have not Plato and his Socrates added an even more absurd contradiction than the original contradiction of the true, healthy "city of pigs" to the fevered, luxurious state? At the beginning of the discourse on the required nature of the guardian, Socrates had referred to the seeming contradiction in the qualities required, saying, "but yet if one lacks either of these qualities, a good guardian he can never be. But these requirements resemble impossibilities, and so the result is that a good guardian is impossible" (p. 622 [375d]).

However, as we have seen, Socrates goes on to demonstrate the possibility—in effect, the possibility of a philosophical dog. Now, Plato cannot be taken too literally; he is a dramatist as well as a philosopher, and the demands of the one will affect the other. What, then, is the philosophical significance, if any, in these comical contradictions?

Men who are committed to the gross materiality of the luxurious city over the spiritual goal of the truth of the good—justice, are no better than dogs. Bringing justice to them will resemble the imposition of justice upon a kennel. The likelihood of achieving the fullness of justice in any one of their souls is equivalent to the breeding of a philosophical dog.

The vision of philosophical truth in the *Republic* remains, but the Republic itself is a cure for the dog natures of men, and its kennel-like structure is an adaptation of justice to those natures. At the same time, it facilitates the escape from dogdom to manhood for a few of them. It will be noted that not the least of the Socratic jokes on Glaucon and his luxury-bent friends is the conditioning of the dog-like guardians of the Republic to poverty by associating it with the seeming material rewards of civic honor and power and a "material" afterlife of bliss. They willingly accept the poverty, after having made the luxurious city the *sine qua non* of justice.

The conditioning of the kennel begins with Socrates setting the basis for the education of children in the Republic. Because he deals with children, the education can most closely resemble animal conditioning. Yet, the model of

education presented is essentially the dramatic method of
Plato for the instruction of all men. Socrates says that the
education of the children is two-fold—"gymnastics for the
body, and for the soul, music." Music must come first, for
it molds the soul in the manner desired. Under music is included the tales for children of which there are "two
species, the one true and the other false." Education uses
both species, but first, the false. Socrates explains:

Don't you understand, I said, that we begin by telling
children fables, and the fable is, taken as a whole, false, but
there is truth in it also? And we make use of fable with
children before gymnastics. (p. 623 [376e-77b])

But, again, in almost comical discourse, Socrates has
added meaning to meaning, and concealed meaning within
both. Just previously he had said that the discussants must
continue the consideration of the topic if they are to pursue
the inquiry into justice. And, speaking of the future guardians, he says, "come, then, just as if we were telling
stories or fables and had ample leisure, let us educate these
men in our discourse" (p. 623 [376d-e]).

To educate men to justice, one must tell stories or fables.
To mold children's souls toward justice, one begins with the
telling of fables that are, on the whole, false, but contain
truth. Fables are necessary for telling truth to children, but
men without justice are like children toward the truth.
Moreover, the indulged, and thus corrupted, men of the
dialogue who crave luxury are spoiled children toward justice, and they are being told the tale of the Republic by
Socrates. And, we, the children of the human condition and
the audience of Plato, are being told the tale of the
Republic—a divine comedy!

The three chief myths of the *Republic* must now be considered in this vein. Their use resembles Alcibiades' simile
for Socrates of the sileni and Marsyas the satyr—meaning
within meaning, and finally "there are little figures of the
gods inside (*Symposium*, 215 b, 222)." Therein, Alcibiades

says that he uses the simile not because it is funny, but because it is true. Yet, it is still funny! Tales within tales and myths as intellectual puzzles present in humorous guise otherwise unacceptable or incomprehensible truths.

The myth of the cave will be considered first, because it falls outside the structure proper of the Republic and addresses itself to the general problem of truth and society. In doing so, it also provides an analogy to the function of political comedy and gives an explanation of its use as myth.

It will be remembered that the myth of the cave is an allegory of how men think (opine) in society and the relation of that thought to the truth of things. Essentially, that thought is never about reality itself—the eternal and universal truths and the final good of things. Rather, men think about the dim reflections of reality, portrayed in the myth as shadows on the wall of a cave. In the cave, the men are chained into positions at the bottommost level in such a manner that they can only look upon the wall while conversing with one another. Their conversations are social opinions about truth as reflected in the shadows.

The shadows on the wall are caused by a fire burning behind a wall to the rear and on a level above the prisoners. The shadows reflect images cast by "men carrying past the wall (and between the fire) implements of all kinds that rise above the wall, and human images and shapes of animals as well, wrought in stone and wood and every material, some of these bearers presumably speaking and others silent" (p. 747 [514-15]).

One of the prisoners is freed and forced to view the manner in which the shadows are cast and the light of the fire which causes them. Moreover, he is dragged by force past the second level of the cave out into the light of the sun itself. First, he is greatly pained and can see but little. Socrates relates:

Then there would be need of habituation, I take it, to enable him to see the things higher up. And at first he would most easily discern the shadows and, after that, the likenesses or reflections in water of men and other things, and later, the things themselves, and from these he would go on to contemplate the appearances in the heavens and heaven itself, more easily by night, looking at the light of the stars and the moon, than by day the sun and the sun's light. (p. 748 [516a5-b2])

Finally, the ex-prisoner sees the true nature of things and comprehends the movements of the universe. Socrates asks whether this man would wish to return to the cave among his former fellows, and whether he could ever be content to compete with them for material honors in best reasoning on the shadows of the cave's wall? He quotes Homer that perhaps such a man would "greatly prefer while living on earth to be serf of another, a landless man, and endure anything rather than opine with them and live that life?" When he is answered with agreement, Socrates further poses:

Now if he should be required to contend with these perpetual prisoners in "evaluating" these shadows while his vision was still dim and before his eyes were accustomed to the dark—and this time required for habituation would not be very short—would he not provoke laughter, and would it not be said of him that he had returned from his journey aloft with his eyes ruined and that it was not worth while even to attempt the ascent? And if it were possible to lay hands on and to kill the man who tried to release them and lead them up, would they not kill him? (p. 749 [517])

Socrates' respondents answer Certainly, and Socrates, after speaking of the idea of the good and the necessity of its vision for all public and private wisdom, speaks of the reluctance of men who have "attained to this height" to "occupy themselves with the affairs of men." He says:

And again, do you think it at all strange, said I, if a man returning from divine contemplations to the petty miseries of men cuts a sorry figure and appears most ridiculous, if, while still blinking through the gloom, and before he has become sufficiently accustomed to the environing darkness, he is compelled in courtrooms or elsewhere to contend about the shadows of justice or the images that cast the shadows and to wrangle in debate about the notions of these things in the minds of those who have never seen justice itself? (p. 750 [517d5-e2])

There have been many interpretations of the meaning of the myth of the cave, and probably a number of them are true in one way or another. The comic interpretation does not claim to truth, only to the parallel between the myth and one explanation of the function of comedy, and to the likelihood that, in turn, the parallel may explain the *Republic* as divine comedy and Socrates as a divine fool.

The philosophic man who has been forced upward out of the cave and has, through pain, seen the light of the ultimate truth may have to descend into the cave again (Socrates' divine mission). If he does, he will be subject to laughter, and, if he tries to release the prisoners from their opinions toward the truth, they may kill him. In effect, Socrates perceives himself to be regarded as a laughable fool, and it is because of his vision of the truth that is so unlike conventional opinion. Yet, he is compelled by his mission to be the champion or aggressor for the truth in a society viciously hostile to it. Earlier in the discourse, Socrates has spoken of the possibility of there being a true philosopher in a corrupt polity, and refers to his own situation:

My own case, the divine sign, is hardly worth mentioning—for I suppose it has happened to few or none before me. And those who have been in this little company and have tasted the sweetness and blessedness of this possession and who have also come to understand the madness of the multitude sufficiently and have seen that there is nothing, if I may say so, sound or right in any present politics, and that there is no ally with whose aid the champion of justice could escape destruction, but that he would be as a man who has fallen among wild beasts, unwilling to share their misdeeds and unable to hold out singly against the savagery of all, and that he would thus, before he could in any way benefit his friends or the state, come to an untimely end without doing any good to himself or others—for all these reasons I say the philosopher remains quiet, minds his own affair, and, as it were, standing aside under shelter of a wall in a storm and blast of dust and sleet and seeing others filled full of lawlessness, is content if in any way he may keep himself free from iniquity and unholy deeds through this life and take his departure with fair hope, serene and well content when the end comes. (p. 732 [496c3-e2])

But Socrates, "the champion of justice," cannot remain quiet and mind his own affairs, and, thereby, escape destruction. What is he to do, the anguished soul who must descend into the depths of the cave, speak the truth, suffer laughter, and court destruction?

Socrates would seem to give away the secret of the divine fool and the divine comedy when he speaks of the technique of educating the young in his Republic. First, he is unwontedly severe in several observations; then he relents, saying that he forgot "we were jesting and I spoke with too great intensity." He continues that the indispensable preparation for the dialectic must be given to the young in their education, but "not in the form of compulsory instruction:"

Because, said I, a free soul ought not to pursue any study slavishly, for while bodily labors pursued under constraint do not harm the body, nothing that is learned under compulsion stays with the mind.

And Socrates adds:

Do not then, my friend, keep children to their studies by compulsion but by play. That will also enable you to discern the natural capacities of each. (p. 768 [536c-37])

Undoubtedly, the best evidence for Socrates' solution to the dilemma of the philosopher in the depths of the cave is the *Republic* itself, and in Socrates' almost constant use of humor throughout the dialogue. The above quotations, with their educational context, make the comic technique explicit. Socrates admits to jesting, and apologizes for speaking with too great intensity. He says that compulsion is worthless in matters of the mind, and that play is the method for keeping children to their studies.

The constant wordplay, the jest, the fable, the myth, the dramatic comedy is the play of the philosopher with men who are children toward justice. It is also the palatable disguise of the truth whereby it may militate against the opinions of the multitude and yet escape their hostility by encouraging their laughter. As for Plato and Socrates, comedy permits them to vent their aggressions against falsehood and by humor to displace their anguished frustration at the unbridgeable chasm between their vision of the good and their presence in the cave of the actual.

In short, in the comic interpretation of the myth, the cave represents the point of encounter between two paths of reasoning. The comic path has descended downward from an unconventional standard or idea of truth into the laughable distortions and shadows of the cave. The other path of reasoning is conventional and proceeds from the cave itself, reflecting only the cave's reality or accommodations to the given. The point of contact between the two paths will necessarily conflict, for, on the one hand, the accustomed accommodation is threatened, and, on the other, the basic understanding of the truth, essential to the integrity of its bearer, is being violated.

The conflict can become violent, and often does. But the incongruity of the two paths presents the key elements of comedy—contradiction, impossibility, satire, paradox, and the like. The shock of conflict can be deflected into humor, threat allayed by playfulness, and tension relieved by laughter. The comic guise finally wore too thin for the historic Socrates, but for the timeless Socrates of the *Republic*, and

or the *Republic* itself, comedy remains the medium for divine truth amid earthly falsehood.

The second myth is a no less comical tale for conveying a
divine truth into the cave. Socrates terms it "a sort of
Phoenician tale," "an opportune falsehood," "a noble lie to
persuade if possible the rulers [of the Republic] themselves,
but failing that the rest of the city." Thus, the tale seems to
be founded on contradiction in its very description.
Moreover, Socrates begins the tale by referring to the great
unlikelihood of persuading the citizens to believe the ethical myth necessary to full justice for their city. He says:

And yet I hardly know how to find the audacity or the
words to speak and undertake to persuade first the rulers
themselves and the soldiers and then the rest of the city
that in good sooth all our training and educating of them
were things that they imagined and that happened to them
as it were in a dream, but that in reality at that time they
were down within the earth being molded and fostered
themselves while their weapons and the rest of their
equipment were being fashioned. And when they were
quite finished the earth as being their mother delivered
them, and now as if their land were their mother and their
nurse they ought to take thought for her and defend her
against any attack and regard the other citizens as their
brothers and children of the selfsame earth.

Socrates continues the story:

While all of you in the city are brothers, we will say in our
tale, yet God in fashioning those of you who are fitted to
hold rule mingled gold in their generation, for which reason
they are the most precious—but in the helpers silver, and
iron and brass in the farmers and other craftsmen. And as
you are all akin, though for the most part you will breed
after your kinds, it may sometimes happen that a golden
father would beget a silver son and that a golden offspring
would come from a silver sire and that the rest would in
like manner be born of one another. So that the first and
chief injunction that the god lays upon the rulers is that of

nothing else are they to be such careful guardians and so intently observant as of the intermixture of these metals in the souls of their offspring, and if sons are born to them with an infusion of brass or iron they shall by no means give way to pity in their treatment of them, but shall assign to each the status due to his nature and thrust them out among the artisans or the farmers. And again, if from these there are born sons with unexpected gold or silver in their composition they shall honor such and bid them go up higher, some to the office of guardian, some to the assistantship, alleging that there is an oracle that the state shall then be overthrown when the man of iron or brass is its guardian. Do you see any way of getting them to believe this tale? (p. 659 [414d-15d])

Socrates is answered No for the founding generation, but Possibly for succeeding generations in the Republic. He replies that "even that would have a good effect in making them more inclined to care for the state and one another" (p. 660 [415d-d4]). Socrates' reply glosses over the confirmation of the impossibility of establishing the myth—if the founding citizens will not believe in the equal brotherhood of all citizens, then how can the Republic become a just city, and why would they then inculcate the myth in their children?

Yet, the myth has served to impart the basic ethic of the divine comedy, the brotherhood of man. Its contradictory nature and aura of impossibility reveal the saving comic grace of the Platonic Socrates' truth in confrontation with the fallibility of man. Eric Vogelin translates "noble lie" of the Phoenician tale as "big lie," but for him the contradiction is enhanced by it. He states that with "the contents of the 'lie,' the satirical intention of the Tale becomes clear." Vogelin asks, "what is that 'Big Lie'? It is the simple truth that all men are brothers."[7]

The Republic cannot succeed as the just city unless men will subordinate their differences in skill and ability (through which they have come together in the city and

7. Vogelin, p. 105.

contribute toward its welfare) to their primary equality in common origin and social kinship. Even here, the divine comedy points to the contradiction within the human condition—the city is founded on difference, but must be grounded in equality to attain justice.

Vogelin holds that the satirical intention of the myth is directed towards Athens. He says that "the introduction of the supreme truth as an unbelievable Big Lie is one of the bitterest pages in a work that heaps so much bitter scorn on Athens" (p. 106). The interpretation of divine comedy fully accepts the Phoenician tale as a bitter satire, but not of Athens alone, rather of all the earthly cities of man.

In support of the divine satire on the cities of man, Socrates continues his myth of metals to justify the communal poverty of the guardians. He says, "gold and silver, we will tell them, they have of the divine quality from the gods always in their souls, and they have no need of the metal of men nor does holiness suffer them to mingle and contaminate that heavenly possession with the acquisition of mortal gold, since many impious deeds have been done about the coin of the multitude, while that which dwells within them is unsullied."[8]

Socrates goes on to say that the acquisition of private possessions transforms the guardians "from the helpers of their fellow citizens to their enemies and masters," that is, destroys the equal justice of brotherhood. Now, the model for the Republic is laid up in heaven, so all actual cities fall short of it, and nowhere more so than in the class divisiveness of their citizenry.

Later in the discussion, Socrates says that the guardians must keep the extremes of wealth and poverty for all classes out of the city, "since the one brings luxury, idleness, and innovation, and the other illiberality and the evil of bad workmanship in addition to innovation." He is asked how such a city, lacking wealth, will be able to defend itself against a wealthy state. Socrates replies with a humorous

8. *Republic*, p. 661 (416 e 5-17 a 3).

riddle, "it would be rather difficult to fight one such, but easier to fight two" (p. 663 [422a-b]).

He explains by stating that only the Republic will be able properly "to use the name city." All the other cities "are each one of them many cities, not a city, as it goes in the game. There are two at the least at enmity with one another, the city of the rich and the city of the poor, and in each of these there are many" (p. 664 [422e3-23a2]).

Thus, in the divine comedy Athens is but another of the divided cities of man, and the satire is of the cities within the city—the class warfare between the occupants over private property and power. The satire bears out the once-refuted Thrasymachus on the facts of earthly rule, but it ridicules even more scathingly any notion of its justice.

The final myth that I shall consider is also a sustaining myth for the ethic of justice in the Republic. It is not so much a satire, though elements of satire are present, as a humorous capstone to the divine comedy. Socrates has described the living happiness of the just man, thereby vindicating his original argument against Thrasymachus. Yet he says that these rewards are as nothing compared to those which await after death. He proposes to tell of them through the tale of the Pamphylian warrior, Er.

Er was slain in battle, but at the moment of his funeral he came back to life. He said that he had been in the world beyond and told the story of it. When he had died, he traveled with many others to a place of judgment where there were openings into the earth and others, above them, into the heavens. Here the people were judged, and the good went upwards, and the bad ones downward into the earth. Here, also, were openings upward and downward which served as exits from heaven and earth.

Er is told by the judges that he is to be a messenger to the outer world, and that he should observe everything so that he can tell of it. He watches as from the exits poured "clean and pure" heavenly souls and squalid and dusty earthly souls. They all proceed to an encampment where they renew acquaintances and relate their thousand-year sojourns above or below the earth where, respectively, the good have lived in bliss, and the bad have suffered ten-fold for their wrongs.

After eight days, the returning souls are taken to a place of departure for new life on earth. Socrates continues the tale of Er:

Now when they arrived they were straightway bidden to go before Lachesis, and then a certain prophet first marshaled them in orderly intervals, and thereupon took from the lap of Lachesis lots and patterns of lives and went up to a lofty platform and spoke, "This is the word of Lachesis, the maiden daughter of Necessity, 'Souls that live for a day, now is the beginning of another cycle of mortal generation where birth is the beacon of death. No divinity shall cast lots for you, but you shall choose your own deity. Let him to whom falls the first lot first select a life to which he shall cleave of necessity. But virtue has no master over her, and each shall have more or less of her as he honors her or does her despite. The blame is his who chooses, God is blameless.' " (p. 841 [617d2-e6])

After each has taken up his lot, the souls are allowed to choose from patterns of lives before them on the ground, and the lives are of all kinds of men and animals and of every variety. However, "there was no determination of the quality of a soul, because the choice of a different life inevitably determined a different character" (p. 842 [618b3]).

Socrates says that this is the supreme hazard for man, and that he must live a life on earth that will enable him to choose life anew correctly. Thus, a man must seek to live justly and to know justice, so that he "may know how always to choose in such things the life that is seated in the mean and shun the excess in either direction, both in this world so far as may be and in all the life to come, for this is the greatest happiness for man" (p. 842 [619a4]).

So far, the myth of Er would seem to be a rather straightforward religious myth, though in the Platonic dialogue it is beautifully symbolical and almost a poetry of justice. However, when the choosing of new lives by the returning souls begins, comedy enters. The tale of Er continues thus:

The drawer of the first lot at once sprang to seize the greatest tyranny, and that in his folly and greed he chose it without sufficient examination, and failed to observe that it involved the fate of eating his own children, and other horrors, and that when he inspected it at leisure he beat his breast and bewailed his choice, not abiding by the forewarning of the prophet. For he did not blame himself for his woes, but fortune and the gods and anything except himself. He was one of those who had come down from heaven, a man who had lived in a well-ordered polity in his former existence, participating in virtue by habit and not by philosophy, and one may perhaps say that a majority of those who were thus caught were of the company that had come from heaven, inasmuch as they were unexercised in suffering. But the most of those who came up from the earth, since they had themselves suffered and seen the sufferings of others, did not make their choice precipitately. For which reason also there was an interchange of good and evil for most of the souls, as well as because of the chances of the lot. (p. 843 [619b8-d7])

Er relates that the choosing "was a strange, pitiful, and ridiculous spectacle, as the choice was determined for the most part by the habits of their former lives." The myth then tells how heroes and characters of ancient Greek classics made choices of new lives that are comically related to, or comic reversals of, their past lives. For instance, Odysseus had drawn the last lot and makes the last choice. Because of the many toils of his former life, he searched unceasingly for "the life of an ordinary citizen who minded his own business." When he found it, he declared his contentment complete (p. 843-44 [619e7-20d2]).

After each of the souls has made his choice, all of them pass beneath the Throne of Necessity into the Plain of Oblivion, where they drink of the River of Forgetfulness, where some without good sense drink more than their measure. Then they are reborn.

Socrates concludes the myth, "and so, Glaucon, the tale was saved, as the saying is, and was not lost. And it will save us if we believe it" (p. 844 [621b10-c]). And so Socrates closes the myth with an expression close to a contemporary witty cliché, "you'd better believe it." Within a few more sentences, he closes the *Republic*, declaring the belief in the immortality of the soul and its rewards in the hereafter to be conducive of commitment to the upward way and the pursuit of righteousness—a rough equivalent of Voltaire's "if there were no God, it would be necessary to invent him."

The myth of Er is not comical in itself, but little Platonic drama is. Its intent is divinely serious—to propose a religious myth that will motivate or sustain just behavior and wise justice on earth. Yet, as with the other Platonic myths, its very use has an element of divine comedy in it which, in turn, leads to the use of comic techniques.

The divine comedy, again, consists in the disparity between the final truth of the good, and the flawed actuality of the human condition. For Socrates it is abundantly clear that justice is its own happiness; a healthy soul is happiness in being, and justice is the health of the soul. Health does not have to prove its superiority to sickness, nor have reward beyond itself.

But Socrates deals with men of matter who consider the just city a pigsty, and the kennel-city of philosophical dogs the foundation of earthly justice. No wonder the psychological conditioning proper to animals and children must be extended to a heaven-hell, reward-punishment myth. The joke is another sarcasm about base man.

Now the myth itself and its playful symbolism are jokes within the divine comedy. Whether Plato believes in the personal immortality of the soul is another matter. Certainly the *Republic* seems to hold out the possibility of the ultimate salvation of the soul through true knowledge of the good. However, the myth of Er, like the Phoenician tale before it, presents this highest truth as an explicit false-hood, a comical commentary on the mortal condition.

An ironic pessimism pervades the content of the myth it-self, concerning the political perfecting of earthly man or his salvation in general. The returning soul who seizes the greatest tyranny is from heaven, but he had been good in his previous existence only because of the habituation of a well-ordered polity. Thus, in his next afterlife he will suffer ten times a thousand punishments for having innocently chosen tyranny. So would be the fate of most of the sub-jects of the most nearly perfect Republic, even assuming its earthly possibility. Perfection, indeed!

An Odysseus would seem to fare no better, for he chooses the life of an ordinary citizen—a man of habit? Others, too, present the "strange, pitiful, and ridiculous spectacle" of choosing new lives that are comical reversals of their past existences, because "the choice was deter-mined for the most part by the habits of their former lives." Finally, some are condemned in their next cycle of life-afterlife because they drink too much at the River of Forgetfulness, due to their lack of good sense. Presumably these poor souls will not have the memory traces of their immortal souls to guide them aright in their new lives.

Yet, the *Republic* is not an early Calvinist tragedy, for the tale "will save us if we believe it." Socrates closes the dialogue, "and thus both here and in that journey of a thousand years, whereof I have told you, we shall fare well" (p. 844 [621c-d3]).

The *Republic* ends, then, with a joyous affirmation, a vir-tual blessing. Men can through wisdom and individual choice break with the eternal flux and attain the light of the good. The myth of Er is instructional, the playful education of childlike men. It ridicules the haphazard nature of habituated goodness, and it suggests dreadful punishments, but only figuratively. The possible horror of eternal damna-tion is overcome by the gentle amusement of the myth. Materialistic man has been given a materialistic myth of the hereafter. Justice does pay off—after all.

The *Symposium* closed on the argument of Socrates that the same poet could write "both comedy and tragedy—that the tragic poet might be a comedian as well." The *Republic* closes with the tragicomic myth of Er, and it ends the divine comedy as a tragicomedy. The tragedy is in man's failure to see and act on the truth of the good and the consequent earthly corruption of soul and commonwealth. The comedy lies, first, in Socrates' compassion toward man's failings. He clowns; he does not crusade.

Plato may retreat to humor as the sublimated aggression of his sense of the good. He may use humor to ward off hostility while he speaks truth to error. Nevertheless, Plato and his Socrates look upon earthly men as corrigible children, amusing and destructive, but not inevitably damned.

Then it can be said that the psychological merges with the tactical. The second use of comedy in the *Republic* is educational. The divine wisdom of the Platonic Socrates speaks to man dramatically in myth, symbolism, wordplay, satire. It distracts them from their ego defenses and amuses them while it indirectly imparts truths otherwise too strong for human weaknesses.

Herein may lie the partial explanation for the deepest paradox of the *Republic* as a narrative drama—its full and continuous use of comedy as a dramatic form and its full and repeated condemnation of comedy. In prescribing the education of the children and youth in the Republic, Socrates severely criticizes the tragic and comic poets, and especially Homer. The gist of his indictment is that the poets imitate the unworthy, and they offer the gods up to ridicule.

Moreover, poetry is a kind of mimicry and requires a man capable of doing or being more than one thing (a twofold or manifold man), but in the Republic everyone will do his one function well. Included within the criticism of mimetic poetry by Socrates is "narration through imitation," or the Platonic dialogues themselves, and they would also be barred. What poetry would be left in the Republic would resemble the art of socialist realism of the Soviet Union. After Socrates has ordained the exile of tragic or comic geniuses, he concludes:

we ourselves, for our souls' good, should continue to employ the more austere and less delightful poet and taleteller, who would imitate the diction of the good man and would tell his tale in the patterns which we prescribed in the beginning, when we set out to educate our soldiers. (p. 643 [398a9-b4])

In case we have not understood the denunciation, Socrates repeats it at considerable length toward the end of the dialogue (597e6-608b). Again, he condemns all poetic imitation, and this time explicitly on the grounds that it appeals to feelings or emotions instead of reason. He says:

For it waters and fosters these feelings when what we ought to do is to dry them up, and it establishes them as our rulers when they ought to be ruled, to the end that we may be better and happier men instead of worse and more miserable. (p. 832 [606d4-8])

Socrates criticizes tragedy, "for after feeding fat the emotion of pity (for others) there, it is not easy to restrain it in our own suffering." He then extends the same principle to comedy, in no uncertain terms:

Does not the same principle apply to the laughable, namely, that if in comic representations, or for that matter in private talk, you take intense pleasure in buffooneries that you would blush to practice yourself, and do not detest them as base, you are doing the same thing as in the case of the pathetic? For here again what your reason, for fear of the reputation of buffoonery, restrained in yourself when it fain would play the clown, you release in turn, and so, fostering its youthful impudence, let yourself go so far that often ere you are aware you become yourself a comedian in private. (p. 831 [606b7-c10])

Does not Socrates, the clown of divine necessity, risk the likelihood of becoming "a comedian in private"? If so, the myth of Er foretells the next fate for his soul. Thersites, the offensive clown of Homer's *Iliad*, is described in his choice of a new soul: "Far off in the rear [Er] saw the soul of the buffoon Thersites clothing itself in the body of an ape" (p. 843 [620c3-4]). If we were to follow the lead of Alcibiades, Socrates could be described a thousand years hence "as clothing himself in the body of a satyr."

There are two exceptions to this unequivocal condemnation of comedy, aside from the permission of a kind of "socialist realism" comedy in the purged Republic. First, and the remark is almost offhand, Socrates cautions that the unworthy should not be imitated "unless it be for jest" (p. 641 [396e]). He would seem to be distinguishing between a good and a bad humor. First, a good kind of pure humor of wordplay, which does not imitate, degrade, or ridicule other people or things, would be ethically permissible. But all other humor is bad; that which is satirical, aggressive, phallic, or otherwise negative would be proscribed.

Needless to say, this distinction would proscribe most of the comedy that performs a political function. Phallic comedy, which levels social superiors and the rulers toward a common equality, would be barred. Comedy as sublimated aggression against authority would be barred. The cathartic function of comedy thereby would be almost nullified. For one is unlikely to receive relief from the tensions of political order and other "civilized discontents" through comic support of the establishment or good-humored mimicry of the most worthy men.

The second exception to the proscription of comedy is more speculative. Socrates has begun his indictment of the poets and Homer, and he has criticized laughter and a passage from Homer that would provoke it. He adds:

But further we must surely prize truth most highly. For if we were right in what we were just saying and falsehood

is in very deed useless to gods, but to men useful as a remedy or form of medicine, it is obvious that such a thing
must be assigned to physicians, and laymen should have
nothing to do with it. (p. 634 [389b2-6])

In short, comedy, including the myths and tales of the
Republic and the *Republic* itself, is a kind of falsehood that
is "useful as a remedy or form of medicine." Socrates has
spoken of the fictional tales as necessary in the education of
children, and he has spoken of keeping children to their
studies not by compulsion but by play. Comedy is an educational medicine for the disease of the luxurious city; it is
an educational remedy for the impaired vision of the men
in the cave.

However, for Plato and his Socrates, comedy is a negative thing, a necessary expedient for man's shortcomings. It
can be used to expose man's folly and to educate him to the
good, and Socrates states that

he talks idly who deems anything else ridiculous but evil,
and who tries to raise a laugh by looking to any other pattern of absurdity than that of folly and wrong or sets up any
other standard of the beautiful as a mark for his seriousness
than the good. (p. 691 [452d6-9])

Conversely, if the good were to be achieved, comedy as a
concession to mortal defects and differences would be obso-
lete. The political need of comedy would have been superseded along with the supersession of politics itself. The Republic under the governance of the truth needs no humorous reminder of its imperfections, nor do its citizens need
an emotional release from the "unnatural" repressions of
society.

The contradiction of use and criticism of comedy in the
Republic returns us to the original statement of it as divine
comedy. "Comically, the *Republic* is conceived in contradiction, only possible in impossibility, and if privately
achieved, publicly destructive." The constant theme of divine comedy is contradiction—the contradiction between

the divine truth of the good and the earthly failings toward justice.

As the myth of the cave has been interpreted in comic perspective, once the philosopher has been possessed by the vision of the good, all that is within the cave of earthly society and its conventional opinions of the truth will fall short of, or be contradicted by that vision. If the philosopher chooses not to be a fanatic for his truth and yet must seek to express it meaningfully, the comedy of contradiction is a projection of the contradictory nature of the divine comedy itself. All that remains is the genius of the author. With Plato and his divine fool, Socrates, there is that providential match.

But providence is an unlikely helpmeet in the most famous of the contradictory passages of the *Republic*, that is, the question of the actualization of the Republic through the merging of the philosophers and kings. Socrates recognizes the great paradox when he reluctantly undertakes the question. He says, "you will be very ready to be lenient, recognizing that I had good reason after all for shrinking and fearing to enter upon the discussion of so paradoxical a nature" (p. 711 [472a5-8]).

He adds, "our purpose was not to demonstrate the possibility of the realization of these ideals" (p. 711 [472c9-10]). But Socrates then announces that he is on the verge "of what we likened to the greatest wave of paradox. But say it I will, even if, to keep the figure, it is likely to wash us away on billows of laughter and scorn." With this, Socrates states the paradox of paradoxes:

Unless, said I, either philosophers become kings in our states or those whom we now call our kings and rulers take to the pursuit of philosophy seriously and adequately, and there is a conjunction of these two things, political power and philosophical intelligence, while the motley horde of the natures who at present pursue either apart from the other are compulsorily excluded, there can be no cessation of troubles, dear Glaucon, for our states, nor, I fancy, for the human race either. Nor, until this happens, will this constitution which we have been expounding in theory ever be put into practice within the limits of possibility and see the light of the sun. But this is the thing that has made me so long shrink from speaking out, because I saw that it would be a very paradoxical saying. For it is not easy to see that there is no other way of happiness either for private or public life. (pp. 712-13 [473c6-e7])

The likelihood of philosopher-kings approximates that of the earlier philosophical dogs. Socrates rests the case on chance and providence ("divine sign") (p. 732 [496d-97]), a kind of cosmic comedy. But, truly, Socrates gives few chances. He goes on to speak of why no philosopher who had seen the light of the good would descend back into the cave willingly. Only the philosopher whose city had nurtured him toward the truth would be so obliged (p. 752 [520a6-d5]). Thus, it takes a Republic to ensure the philosopher-king, but no philosopher-king, no Republic. And the perfectly ruled city would be the one in which the man least willing to rule, ruled.

Yet, Socrates gives us a final chance of the Republic—an *easy* one! He relates this:

All inhabitants above the age of ten, I said, they will send out into the fields, and they will take over the children, remove them from the manners and habits of their parents, and bring them up in their own customs and laws which will be such as we have described. This is the speediest and easiest way in which such a city and constitution as we have portrayed could be established and prosper and bring most benefit to the people among whom it arises. (p. 772 [541a-b])

The amenable Glaucon replies, "much the easiest, . . . and I think you have well explained the manner of its realization if it should ever be realized." Here then is the joke of jokes mounted on the greatest of paradoxes. "The speediest and easiest way" to realize the Republic is for philosophers upon assuming rule to exile all adults and take over their children.

If the radical contradictions of the *Republic* can be resolved, then, it is not a divine comedy. It proclaims the possibility of perfection, and man's failure to even approach the pattern of heaven could hardly be laughable. But Plato and his Socrates believe in the reality of the good, and laughter and the play of comedy is seldom absent in the *Republic*. There is but one conclusion consistent with the genius and seriousness of Plato. The Republic is possible only in impossibility.

Impossibility is necessary to the comic genius of Plato. The actualization of the good would eliminate the necessity of negative political comedy. For Plato proclaims the inferiority of comedy as he authors the greatest work of comic philosophy. However, the end of comedy is contingent on the end of earthly man. The impossibility of the Republic yields the human necessity of comedy, and the *Republic* is its testimony.

Though the Republic as the commonwealth of man is impossible, the Republic as the commonwealth of the soul is present in the person and promise of Socrates. Using dream analogies, Socrates has described the various political constitutions as paralleling various psychological conditions of man, depending on the predominance of reason within them. He demonstrates tyrannical man to be the most miserable of men, for his soul is the most discordant. Socrates rounds out his psychology of souls with a description of the wise or just man's soul:

He will rather, I said, keep his eyes fixed on the constitution in his soul, and taking care and watching lest he disturb anything there whether by excess or deficiency of wealth, will so steer his course and add to or detract from his wealth on this principle, so far as may be.
Precisely so, he [Glaucon] said.
And in the matter of honors and office too this will be his guiding principle. He will gladly take part in and enjoy those which he thinks will make him a better man, but in public and private life he will shun those that may overthrow the established habit of his soul.
That seems probable, he said. (p. 819 [591e-b])

The wise man will shun the politics of all cities other than the heavenly patterned Republic, because the politics of earthly cities may overthrow the rational rule of the soul. In effect, the politics of the right relationships between men in society has been overthrown for the private politics of personal salvation.

The revolutionary consequences of the philosophical assumptions and procedure of the *Republic* are now apparent. To discover justice in the soul, it was to be observed in a just city created for that purpose. The requirements of justice in the soul (a man-eternal good relationship) were projected onto the city (a man-man earthly relationship). When the imagined city of the just soul was found to be incapable of translation into an earthly city of men's justice, the earthly city was found to be wanting. Therefore, the city is denounced as destructive of the soul, and the right soul must abandon the earthly justice of the city. Yet, the soul of man in its mortal existence continues to occupy the earthly city, and the problems of proximate justice remain. The divine comedy comes full circle.

The good and wise man must forsake politics for the sake of his soul, unless providence bids him otherwise, or unless the city becomes as its pattern in heaven. If the former, he will not become political, but, acting upon his vision of the truth, he will be compelled to absolutism or, at the least, the Socratic role of the divine fool. If the latter, the Republic made manifest, the good man will be either guardian or ruler, and acting in full captivity to truth, he will govern in full freedom from the opinions and controls of others. Either way, politics is at an end. Politics is the earthly corruption of divine truth.

The *Republic* is the most profoundly anti-political philosophy ever written. Its political comedy is the humor of invective, scorn, condemnation, ridicule, and satire against the human condition and man's political accommodations to it. Conversely, the *Republic* is the supreme political comedy, for it is the ultimate aggression against earthly rule disguised as Socratic irony and dramatic comedy.

The ironic Socrates is humorous, gentle, and dramatically lovable—witness his encounter with Thrasymachus. Yet, Socrates is the most unyielding, dogmatic, and duplicitous of men. The dramatic genius of Plato portrays accurately a normal reaction to Socrates' teachings in Thrasymachus's rage at him and then passive frustration.

For Socrates, there is no truth in the opinion of Thrasymachus, nor, for that matter, in the opinions of the other discussants. He may later confirm the facts of their views, but he totally denies that their views of justice, as formed by those facts, have any truth value. The truth of justice is not, for Socrates, an accommodation of the highest good to the contingent given. The truth is the good, and it stands forever against the worldly givens. The truth is not prudential or political.

For Plato and his Socrates, the only compromise of the divine truth to man's world is comedy. Comedy expresses the political wisdom of Socrates and remains the saving grace in this greatest of philosophical diatribes against politics. Comedy is the concession that Plato makes to man's differences and the world's shortcomings. It is ultimately his admission of the unbridgeable chasm between the divine good and earthly error.

Yet, the comic sense, which leads Plato to adopt comedy for the instruction of mortal weaklings and to disguise the aggressions of truth against hostile opinion, does not lead him into a prudential justice. Comedy is his only politics. Thus, in this most anti-political of political philosophers, the ultimate political function of comedy is revealed; comedy serves as the politics of perfectionism.

5

Lincoln, Satyr Statesman

Wherein satyr serves state

Thus educated men troubled themselves to reduce to simple points the shifting lights and glooms of the Lincoln personality. They would deny the wriggling in one human frame of Hamlet and Falstaff.
—Carl Sandburg, *Abraham Lincoln: The War Years*

If it can be said that Aristophanes was the comic genius on politics, and the Platonic Socrates was the comic genius against politics, then, Abraham Lincoln is the comic genius in politics. Yet, though each of the three differ radically in respect to politics, their common comic perspective toward politics imposes arresting similarities.

Aristophanes' earthiness and sense of vulgar humor toward politics is matched by Lincoln's folk humor and use of the vernacular. In fact, for me the first thought of Lincoln as epitomizing the comic character in democratic politics came when analyzing Aristophanes' characterization of Agoracritus. However, the Agoracritus is a matter of political invective; Lincoln seldom used this comic mode. He is the master storyteller. One of his own stories illustrates the differing usage in this comic approach:

A high official came to him [Lincoln] in a towering rage, but went away perfectly satisfied. "I suppose you had to make large concessions?" the President was asked. "Oh, no," was the answer. "I did not concede anything. You have heard how the Illinois farmer disposed of the log that was too wet to burn, too big to haul away, and too knotty to split? He plowed around it. Well, that is the way I got rid of Governor Blank. I plowed around him. But it took three mortal hours; and I was afraid every minute that he would find me out!"[1]

But Lincoln resembles Agoracritus in a much deeper way. He is the political man of lowliest origins and almost no formal education who speaks the language of the people to communicate with them and lead them. His historic success lies in restoring the unity of political society while advancing it toward its highest truth of equality in freedom. His comic sense and its political functions are indispensable to this historic task.

Lincoln's comic genius is that of the greatest of democratic politicians. It cannot be a vicious genius, because he is the thoroughly political man. He acts within politics to persuade, to reconcile, to allay strife. On the other hand, Aristophanes' genius is a critical one, acting from outside politics.

Lincoln and the Platonic Socrates are polar opposites on politics, and Lincoln's political opinion of Socrates might well have approximated that of Aristophanes in *Clouds*. Then again, Lincoln, as did Aristophanes in the *Symposium*, might well have conversed far into the night with Socrates, exchanging comic anecdote for humorous myth. Carl Sandburg's poetic description of Lincoln, "the wriggling in one human frame of Hamlet and Falstaff," could

1. Helen Nicolay, *Personal Traits of Abraham Lincoln* (New York: The Century Co., 1912), p. 253.

equally have been said of Socrates. Lincoln's tragic sense of missed possibilities, human fallibility, and divine mystery proceeds from different roots, but lends an ambiguity to his thoughts not unlike that of Socrates.

Oddly, the two men are so satyrlike, ironical in their personalities, and martyred in their callings, that it is not difficult to fantasize a transmigration of souls, and in the comic vein of the myth of Er. Recall the description of Socrates by Alcibiades in *Symposium* and compare it with a recurring theme in Lincoln's stories about his own ugliness:

Lincoln was, naturally enough, much surprised one day, when a man of rather forbidding countenance drew a revolver and thrust the weapon almost into his face. In such circumstances "Abe" at once concluded that any debate or argument was a waste of time and words.

"What seems to be the matter?" inquired Lincoln with all the calmness and self-possession he could muster.

"Well," replied the stranger, who did not appear at all excited, "some years ago I swore an oath that if I ever came across an uglier man than myself, I'd shoot him on the spot."

A feeling of relief evidently took possession of Lincoln at this rejoinder, as the expression upon his countenance lost all suggestion of anxiety.

"Shoot me," he said to the stranger; for if I am an uglier man than you I don't want to live."[2]

I shall go on to analyze the sources and political nature of Lincoln's humor, but it is not totally irrelevant to point to the seeming coincidences of Socrates, the ugly stone mason, and Lincoln, the ugly railsplitter; the Peloponnesian civil war and the American civil war; and even the logic of the Socratic dialogue, employing myths, and the logic of Lincolnian story and anecdote, employing frontier vernacularisms. Finally, despite the political antithesis of Socrates' heavenly vision to Lincoln's earthy common sense,

2. Alexander A. McClure, *Abe Lincoln's Yarns and Stories* (Chicago: The Educational Co., 1901), p. 65

Lincoln displays an aloofness and partisan political dispassion that fully rivals Socrates' visionary impartiality.

In sum, as Socrates was depicted as a sage-satyr, Lincoln is the satyr-statesman, for whom a gentle form of satire is essential to life and politics. The political comedy of Abraham Lincoln is a comedy of politics, and Abraham Lincoln, the humorist, is the supreme politician; each is but the reverse side of the other.

The Marginal Man and Frontier Humor

However risky, certain psychological inferences must be made concerning the roots of Abraham Lincoln's humor. The least speculative means of doing so is to consider the man in relation to the objectively known facts of his individuality and in conjunction with his formative environment. Most important in understanding the comic Lincoln are his lowly familial origins and the formative influence of the American frontier.

Lincoln's ancestry and early years are briefly summarized in a brilliant ironical sketch of his life by himself. In a letter written in 1859 to his friend and political promoter, J. W. Fell, he wrote:

Herewith is a little sketch, as you requested. There is not much of it for the reason, I suppose, that there is not much of me. If anything be made out of it, I wish it to be modest, and not to go beyond the material. If it were thought necessary to incorporate anything from any of my speeches, I suppose there would be no objections. Of course, it must not appear to have been written by myself.

Yours very truly,
Abraham Lincoln

I was born February 12, 1809, in Hardin County, Kentucky. My parents were both born in Virginia, of undistinguished families—second families, perhaps I should say. My mother, who died in my tenth year was of a family of the Hanks, some of who now reside in Adams, and others in

Macon County in Illinois. My paternal grandfather, Abraham Lincoln, emigrated from Rockingham County, Virginia to Kentucky about 1781 or 1782, where a year or two later he was killed by the Indians not in battle, but by stealth, when he was laboring to open a farm in the forest. His ancestors, who were Quakers, went to Virginia from Berks County, Pennsylvania. An effort to identify them with a New England family of the same name ended in nothing more definite than a similarity of Christian names in both families, such as Enoch, Levi, Mordecai, Solomon, Abraham and the like.

My father, at the death of his father, was but six years of age, and he grew up literally without education. He removed from Kentucky to what is now Spencer County, Indiana, in my eighth year. We reached our new home about the time the State came into the Union. It was a wild region, with many bears and other wild animals still in the woods. There I grew up. There were some schools, so called, but no qualification was ever required of a teacher beyond "readin', writin', and cipherin' " to the rule of three. If a straggler supposed to understand Latin happened to sojourn in the neighborhood, he was looked upon as a wizard. There was absolutely nothing to excite ambition for education. Of course, when I came of age, I did not know much. Still, somehow, I could read, write, and cipher to the rule of three, but that was all. I have not been to school since. The little advance I now have upon this store of education, I have picked up from time to time under the pressure of necessity.[3]

Lincoln finished this rare advertisement for a blossoming presidential candidate in two more terse paragraphs, ending with a simple description of his physical characteristics. His irony, however, is double-edged. The "second families" of Lincoln's parents implicitly ridicules "the First Families of Virginia" and their social pretensions. Along with the "effort to identify" with a New England family, both statements are solid examples of comic democratic leveling directed

3. Abraham Lincoln, *The Collected Works of Abraham Lincoln* (New Brunswick, N.J.: Rutgers University Press, 1953), 3:511-12.

against attempts at social superiority. Lincoln also levels fun at the limited education of the frontier, but his sketch is eminently factual about his own limited background.

It is this background that made Lincoln a marginal man, even in the frontier settlements of Illinois and, particularly, as he moved upwards in politics and law. A marginal man can be understood as one who exists on the fringes of society's culture, in it but not fully of it. Generally, he possesses some social attributes, and lacks other ones of the dominant culture, which hinders his full acceptance into society. Most often, these characteristics are religious, ethnic, or racial ones that are rejected by society, but they can be those of a subculture of poverty or of an isolated group. In the latter case, the norms and behavior of the dominant culture fail to fully penetrate the subculture, and it develops its own life-style, suited to its more immediate needs.

Perhaps the most famous recent example of the humor of the marginal man is that derived from the Jewish subculture. Jewish humor and the Jewish type of humor are the most pervasive elements of comedy in the United States. Jews create comedy about themselves and gentiles in part because of a latent hostility between their culture and the socially dominant one. Thereby they sublimate potentially dangerous aggressive impulses and can assert their superiority and uniqueness boldly but harmlessly. To a lesser extent, black humor and the older Irish humor display similar traits.

All subcultures endow their marginal men with a special comic advantage. They are possessed of a vantage point with alternate ways of thought from which to observe critically society's conventions and ways of behavior. In some men these observations will be channeled into a kind of critical comedy. Most important, all marginal men are enabled to see social conventions as merely one way of human behavior among others while being sustained in their own pattern by their subculture.

For the Jews, as for Lincoln in his special case,[4] there is another critical factor. Because of the ancient and literate Jewish culture, Jews have a sense of intellectual superiority. They not only regard the dominant culture differently, they also regard it intellectually. Their comedy is cathartic and presents critical alternatives to convention, but it also possesses an informing intelligence. The humor of Abraham Lincoln, who had less than a year of formal school but went on into law and politics and became President of the United States, is both culturally marginal and intellectually informed. Lincoln is a master logician of comedy.

Lincoln's marginality is compounded of two factors, family poverty and frontier existence. One of Lincoln's critics states in a negative manner the influence of poverty on his humor. Colonel Dom Piatt did not believe that Lincoln's humor could be attributed to his gentleness or relief from the heavy cares of office. He said:

What man of keen, delicate sensibility could find relief from cares of any sort in jests so coarse that they could not be put to record? . . . This habit ran through his life from the day he was a day-laborer. While a railsplitter in his early manhood he was noted for his jokes and stories. Had he then the necessity for relief?[5]

Carl Sandburg goes on to write, "Lincoln's tough hide or lack of fine sensibilities in Piatt's view was traced tersely by Wendell Phillip's expression that Lincoln was 'the white trash of the South spawned on Illinois' " (3: 335). The "aristocratic" estimates of Lincoln by Phillips and Piatt supply a needed balance to the simplistic and sentimentalist views of his humor. Yet, they are but partial truth, for they miss completely the creative, intellectual, and democratically political functions of his humor.

4. Lincoln is related to the Jews in a joke about him that he particularly enjoyed. The North had to issue greenbacks in the Civil War, and the joke posed the question, why is a greenback like a Jew? The answer was that it is an issue out of Father Abraham in search of a redeemer.
5. Carl Sandburg, *Abraham Lincoln: The War Years* (New York: Harcourt, Brace and Co., 1936), 3:334-35.

Without becoming mired in the subjective swamp of pseudo-psychology, some mention should be made of the Hamlet in Lincoln. His melancholy is well known, and most biographers relate his occasional bouts with depression. This trait may be related to his marginality and is certainly part of his comedy. Carl Sandburg quotes and comments on the observations of Lincoln's close friend, Isaac N. Arnold:

"What has made this joyous merry man so sad? What great sorrow lies at his heart?" The mingling of these extremes in Lincoln affected his loyal friend. "Mirthfulness and melancholy, hilarity and sadness, were strangely combined in him. His mirth was sometimes exuberant. It sparkled in jest, story, and anecdote, while at the next moment his peculiarly sad, pathetic, melancholy eyes would seem to wander far away, and one realized that he was a man 'familiar with sorrow and acquainted with grief.' " (3: 308-9)

Arnold's and Sandburg's pairing of Lincoln's sorrow and humor is a reminder of the kinship of tragedy and comedy. Whatever purely personal traits contributed to Lincoln's melancholy, the early loss of his mother, the harsh existence of his youth, the crudity and cruelty of the frontier settlements, an unstable wife, the Civil War, the death of several children, they provide sufficient objective reasons for his melancholy. Of course, they must be taken in conjunction with his deep intelligence, and his dispassion and compassion for others that were to be so evidenced in the war years.

A gentle man of deep intelligence and driving ambition who would far surpass his lowly origins and cultural limitations would be likely to be aware of the constant tragedy of human existence on the frontier and among the poor. The settlers were his people and he was formed by them. He would know their humanness, their unfulfilled potentials but heroic achievements. As he rose in society, he would look back in sorrow and forward to his new peers with critical detachment. Their fashions and foibles, the civilized glosses on their refined cruelties and cultured selfishness, would be fully apparent to him.

The story is told of Hugh McCulloch, the Secretary of Treasury in Lincoln's second term, escorting a delegation of New York bankers to Lincoln. He whispered to Lincoln:

These gentlemen from New York have come on to see the Secretary of Treasury about our new loan. As bankers they are obliged to hold our national securities. I can vouch for their patriotism and loyalty, for, as the good Book says, "Where the treasure is there will the heart be also."

Lincoln replied, "There is another text, Mr. McCulloch, I remember, that might equally apply: 'Where the carcass is, there will the eagles be gathered together.' "[6]

Lincoln's tragi-comic sense of man would be founded on an experience of meanness and mortality, coupled with his own realization of possibilities; a desire to achieve and be accepted in the highest reaches of society, coupled with an alien detachment toward its habitués and their conventions. A man of two worlds, at home in neither, Lincoln would know the weaknesses of both in the disparity between them. As he despaired in the reality of things, he might well yearn for the unity of mankind and seek comic relief. Sandburg relates this anecdote:

A beaming and officious visitor slid into the office one day as Lincoln sat writing and chirruped, "Oh, why should the spirit of mortal be proud?" The President turned a noncommittal face, "My dear sir, I see no reason whatever," and went on writing.[7]

Inextricable from the marginality arising from Lincoln's lowly origins is his frontier existence. The frontier in American history constituted in itself a subculture, and a historically unique one in which for a man of Lincoln's intelligence and sensitivity there could develop a comic sense

6. Anthony Gross, ed., *Lincoln's Own Stories* (New York and London: Harper & Bros., 1912), p. 120.
7. Sandburg, 2:288.

of the disparity between the harsh realities of existence and the refinements and conventions of civilization. The conditions of living on the frontier were primitive and, in some ways, a throwback to prehistoric times, but the settlers came from, and remained aware of, a complex advanced civilization. Many of the pioneers possessed the literacy and consciousness of educated people. In a man of Abraham Lincoln's intellect, this clash of two worlds would enable him to see into the artificiality of society's conventions along with their necessity or expendability.

In short, one gift Lincoln would bring to a nation at civil war would be a grasp of the necessities of survival and of the proper order of things beneath their civilized gloss. His expression of reality versus convention would often be in comic form. Sandburg gives an account of an interview between the President and Solomon Chase, his Secretary of Treasury, and financier Amasa Walker. It concerned a proposed greenback issue, which Chase feared was unconstitutional yet seemed necessary for financing the war. Sandburg quotes Dom Piatt's report:

Mr. Chase made a long and elaborate constitutional argument against the proposed measure. "Chase," said Mr. Lincoln, after the Secretary had concluded, "down in Illinois I was held to be a pretty good lawyer, and I believe I could answer every point you have made, but I don't feel called upon to do it. This thing reminds me of a story I read in a newspaper the other day. It was of an Italian captain, who ran his vessel on a rock and knocked a hole in her bottom. He set his men to pumping and he went to prayers before a figure of the Virgin in the bow of the ship. The leak gained on them. It looked at last as if the vessel would go down with all on board. The captain, at length, in a fit of rage at not having his prayers answered, seized the figure of the Virgin and threw it overboard. Suddenly the leak stopped, the water was pumped out, and the vessel got safely into port. When docked for repairs, the statue of the Virgin Mary was found stuck head-foremost in the hole."

"I don't see, Mr. President, the precise application of your story," said Mr. Chase.

"Why, Chase, I don't intend precisely to throw the Virgin Mary overboard, and by that I mean the Constitution, but I will stick it in the hole if I can. These rebels are violating the Constitution to destroy the Union. I will violate the Constitution, if necessary, to save the Union, and I suspect, Chase, that our Constitution is going to have a rough time of it before we get done with this row. Now, what I want to know is whether, Constitution aside, this project of issuing interest-bearing notes is a good one?" (3: 397)

The frontier not only endowed Lincoln with a basic grasp of reality, it also taught him a colorful language, a vernacular of the people, and a comic mode of communication. Sandburg quotes the *Saturday Review* of London:

One of the advantages the Americans now have in national joking is the possession of a President who is not only the First Magistrate, but the Chief Joker, of the land . . . . The basis of nearly all American wit was irreverence, speaking lightly of serious events, treating alligators, lightning, big rivers, trackless mountains, as mere material for jest. This was natural enough, in the English view, for the lank, lean-faced pioneers had faced all these things, had given out their dry-daring jokes with smileless lips amid swamp fever, starvation, and death itself." (3: 301)

The English critic captures a major element of frontier humor, turning tribulations and terrors into comedy, as Lincoln would do throughout the war. Obviously, the comic function is cathartic; it provides relief from man's fears, and it also constitutes a defiance of seeming destiny, and supplies courage for continuing effort. However, the writer overlooks a major characteristic of frontier humor—its anecdotal and storytelling modes.

Alexander McClure, a friend of the President and an editor of his humor writes, "the Western people thus thrown together with but limited sources of culture and enjoyment, logically cultivated the story-teller, and Lincoln proved to be the most accomplished in that line of all members of the Illinois bar."[8]

Helen Nicolay writes:

As a boy he loved a story for the pure fun in it; and, since he was human, liked to tell one, because in those pioneer times of few amusements and almost no books, the exercise of the faculty carried with it popularity, even more than it does today. Aesop's Fables, one of the few books that fell into his hands, was a mine of wealth to such a lad, and a formative influence as well.

Grown to manhood, he faced juries by day, or appeared after nightfall before scanty groups of settlers, gathered solemn and expectant in dimly lighted log cabins to hear his views on State politics or National tariff or internal improvement. In such conditions the power of a story to rivet attention or illuminate the dismal surroundings was not to be thrown away.[9]

It would seem that on the frontier, man, lacking many of the graces of civilization, was thrown back on his more basic resources. In redeveloping the art of storytelling, the settlers were returning to the past of fables and folk tales, sagas and myths. In fact, keeping in mind the frontier stories, one may wonder whether modern students of the more ancient modes of storytelling may take them too seriously at times.

The story falls back on a most fundamental social characteristic of human beings, their speaking to one another. Its comic element is to keep interest and to entertain, but the comic form with its cathartic function also serves to record experience, to point up a moral, to educate, and to develop thought itself.

Chauncey Depew, United States Senator from New York, related that Lincoln told him, "They say that I tell a great many stories; I reckon I do, but I have found in the course of a long experience that common people, take them as

8. McClure, p. xiv.
9. Nicolay, p. 13.

they run, are more easily informed through the medium of a broad illustration than in any other way. . . ."[10] His close friend Ward Lamon explained that Lincoln "used stories as a laugh cure for a drooping friend or for his own melancholy, yet also to clinch an argument, to lay bare a fallacy, to disarm an antagonist, but most often the stories were 'labor saving contrivances.' "[11]

Lincoln developed the art of comic story-telling into a consummate political skill, and in analyzing its comedy we will see that he was fully conscious of his uses of it. However, one basic element of his comic stories should first be noted. Their language is that of the farm and frontier, and Lincoln spoke it naturally and in his usual discourse. But he could also speak and write in the most beautiful, clear, and direct prose ever known to American politics. Helen Nicolay comments that "Lincoln knew no foreign tongue, yet he spoke two languages—the vernacular, and a strong, majestic prose akin to poetry."[12]

His stories and their vernacular language brought vicious criticism on him, but a great part of their political appeal is in their common tone. In response to the almost violent opposition of United States Senator Benjamin Wade, Henry Davis, and Wendell Phillips to his reelection, Lincoln said that he was not much interested in their activities and told a story:

I feel on this subject as an old Illinois farmer once expressed himself while eating cheese. He was interrupted in the midst of his repast by the entrance of his son who exclaimed, "Hold on, Dad! There's skippers in that cheese you're eating!"

"Never mind, Tom," said he, as he kept on eating his cheese, "if they can stand it I can."[13]

In this somewhat vulgar, seemingly simple, comic story, there is contained a profound truth of democratic

10. McClure, p. xviii.
11. Sandburg, 3:305.
12. Nicolay, p. 359.
13. McClure, pp. 96-97.

politics—a sense of the necessity of tolerance between rivals in politics. No comedy is neutrally amusing, and the comedy of a conscious and consistent political humorist like Lincoln reflects a particular morality, as we shall see.

Another rustic tale with a biting moral to it was told by Lincoln to the Southern peace commissioners during the famous Hampton Roads negotiations seeking an end to the Civil War. The journalist Henry J. Raymond asked the President if he had told the rebels a story. He said that he had, and related that, in discussing the emancipation of the slave, Mr. Hunter, a Confederate representative, said that the ending of slavery would ruin the Southern economy. Hunter concluded, "no work would be done, nothing would be cultivated, and both blacks and whites would starve!" Lincoln countered with this:

Mr. Hunter, you ought to know a great deal better about this argument than I, for you have always lived under the slave system. I can only say in reply to your statement of the case, that it reminds me of a man out in Illinois, by the name of Case, who undertook, a few years ago, to raise a very large herd of hogs. It was a great trouble to feed them, and how to get around this was a puzzle to him. At length he hit on the plan of planting an immense field of potatoes and, when they were full grown, he turned the whole herd into the field, and let them have full swing, thus saving the labor of feeding the hogs, but also that of digging the potatoes. Charmed with his sagacity, he stood one day leaning against the fence, counting the hogs, when a neighbor came along.
"Well, well," said he, "Mr. Case, this is all very fine. Your hogs are doing very well just now, but you know out here in Illinois the frost comes early, and the ground freezes for a foot deep. Then, what are you going to do?"
This was a view of the matter which Mr. Case had not taken into account. Butchering time for hogs was way on in December or January! He scratched his head and at length stammered: "Well, it may come pretty hard on their snouts, but I don't see but that it will be root, hog, or die.' "
(p. 84)

"Root, hog, or die" not only expresses Lincoln's work ethic, but it reflects a humor-tempered fatalism toward the inevitable that will be seen to be an integral part of his political morality. The story illustrates, in addition to its moral, a method of political argument and use of the common language. Sandburg quotes the *Chicago Tribune* reporter, Horace White, a close and continuous observer of Lincoln from the time of the Douglas debates through the Civil War as writing with "feeling and color of how Lincoln's sense of humor was fatefully intermeshed with the man's everyday behavior and democratic habits." White wrote:

I never heard him express contempt for any man's honest errors, although he would sometimes make a droll remark or express a funny story about them. Deference to other people's attitudes was habitual with him. There was no calculation, no politics in it. It was part and parcel of his sense of equal rights.[14]

The comic stories and their common language emerge as integral to Lincoln's acceptance of, and accommodation to, democratic politics and its equal rights. Sandburg reports his constant use of colloquial expression, common to farm and frontier. Lincoln referred to "a mighty onhandy man," "grub," "it has petered out," "it won't jibe," and "a heavy hog to hold" (3: 335-36).

The Government Printer Defrees complained to the President about printing one of his messages in which he used the term "sugar-coated." He felt that it was undignified and told Lincoln so. The President replied, "Defrees, that word expresses exactly my idea, and I am not going to change it. The time will never come in this country when people won't know exactly what 'sugar-coated' means."[15]

Lincoln's language and stories came to him naturally out of his marginal status and frontier development, but he used them consciously for a clarity and directness in political communication that have never been equaled. Above

14. Sandburg, 3:335-36.
15. McClure, p. 204.

all, it is "political" communication through allaying aggression and creating good feeling while doing what must be done.

Sandburg writes that the impression his humor conveyed "reached as far and as deep as any made by the President's addresses or letters in winning affection for him, in blunting the edges of war hatred."[16]

The Comic Lincoln's Genius of Language and Logic

It must be apparent by now that Lincoln's stories and their language were consciously used and had a systematic consistency to them. Of course, much of his humor was employed for the sheer fun of it, and he sought to amuse and entertain to please others. Certainly, its origins are in this rudimentary pleasure and sociability. Even then, the humor reveals a personality trait invaluable to politics, and a psychological balance against the ever-present power drive of politics.

But Abraham Lincoln went on to develop a way of thought, expression, and argumentation that in its fullness may be unique in the history of politics. The *Boston Transcript* called his first inaugural speech "the plain homespun language of a man of the people, who was accustomed to talk with 'the folks' . . . the language of a man of vital common sense, whose words exactly fitted his facts and thoughts." Helen Nicolay comments further:

Lincoln, with his straightforward sentences made up of short forceful words, was not playing the game according to accepted rules. Ex-President Tyler complained that he did not even play it according to rules of grammar.[17]

Lincoln told one story in response to the demands that he remove Grant from the army command. Grant was being viciously criticized for many characteristics incidental

16. Sandburg, p. 316.
17. Helen Nicolay, pp. 359-60.

to his military ability. Lincoln's story graphically illustrates his use of stories and his understanding of the function of speech in politics. He said:

Out in my State of Illinois there was a man nominated for sheriff of the county. He was a good man for the office, brave, determined, and honest, but not much of an orator. In fact, he couldn't talk at all; he couldn't make a speech to save his life.

His friends knew he was a man who would save the peace of the county and perform the duties devolving on him all right, but the people of the county didn't know it. They wanted him to come out boldly on the platform at political meetings and state his convictions and principles; they had been used to speeches from candidates, and were somewhat suspicious of a man who was afraid to open his mouth.

At last the candidate consented to make a speech, and his friends were delighted. The candidate was on hand, and, when he was called upon, advanced to the front and faced the crowd. There was a glitter in his eye that wasn't pleasing, and the way he walked out to the front of the stand showed that he knew just what he wanted to say.

"Feller citizens," was his beginning, the words spoken quietly, "I'm not a speakin' man; I ain't no orator, and I never stood up before a lot of people in my life before; I'm not goin' to make no speech, 'xcept to say that I can lick any man in the crowd."[18]

Grant could do his job; all else was secondary. However, the story itself is used by Lincoln to get across the essential point in the most forceful and understandable manner. In turn, the political speech has as its almost sole function communicating, briefly and clearly, a basic message to the people. But, to the extent that the humorous story is its medium, the political speech also seeks to accomplish its purpose in the most amusing and conciliatory manner. Lincoln's political anecdotes are seldom politically evasive; they combine a logic of communication and a gentleness toward political differences.

18. McClure, p. 436.

Of course, Lincoln's tolerance and appreciation of political differences often led him to tell a story to avoid a direct refusal or escape an embarrassing situation. The logic of his stories is in part intended to serve a flexible accommodation to the differences of politics. The common words of his stories also serve a double purpose. They are the language of the people and communicate most effectively with them, but their homespun quality imparts to the stories the flavor of humor and eases the acceptance of their moral. Emerson wrote:

I believe it to be true that when any orator at the bar or in the Senate rises in his thought, he descends in his language.—that is, when he rises to any height of thought or of passion he comes down to a language level with the ear of all his audience. It is the merit of John Brown and Abraham Lincoln—one at Charlestown, one at Gettysburg—in the two best specimens of eloquence we have had in this country.[19]

Just as with his language, Lincoln's stories originated among the common people out of their everyday experiences. Through exaggeration, distortion, caricature, and satire, people took actual incidents of daily living and turned them into comical accounts of their activities that pointed up some lesson-principle. Sometimes Lincoln did the fashioning of the stories himself; most of the time, he said that he was a mere retailer of others' stories. But he did far more than merely recount others' stories. He adapted them to his own political and legal needs, and it is highly likely that this self-educated genius developed his thought through the medium of comic stories.

The comic stories of the farm and frontier that Lincoln typically utilized were not exercises in absurdity, nor did they display a satirical criticism of accepted truths. There were stories of those kinds, and Lincoln occasionally used them. However, the usual Lincoln's story employed a kind of analogical logic. Ward Lamon has already been quoted

19. Ralph Waldo Emerson, *Works* (Boston and New York: Houghton, Mifflin Co., 1875), 8:125.

on Lincoln's use of stories "to clinch an argument, to lay bare a fallacy, to disarm an antagonist." Helen Nicolay agrees, and ties the facility to the facing of juries and speaking "before scanty groups of settlers." She writes, "in such conditions the power of a story to rivet attention and illuminate dismal surroundings was not to be thrown away."[20]

Lincoln's understanding of his storytelling is manifest in a reply that he gave to a person who made an insistent demand for one of his stories. He replied:

I believe I have the popular reputation of being a storyteller, but I do not deserve the name in its general sense, for it is not the story itself, but its purpose or effect that interests me. I often avoid a long and useless discussion by others, or a laborious explanation on my own part, by a short story that illustrates my point of view. So, too, the sharpness of a refusal or the edge of a rebuke may be blunted by an appropriate story so as to save wounded feelings and yet serve the purpose. No, I am not simply a story-teller, but story-telling as an emollient saves me much friction and distress.[21]

Colonel McClure recounts a time the President was in a minority on a diplomatic issue within his Cabinet, and "didn't want to argue the points raised, preferring to settle the matter in a hurry, and an apt story was his only salvation." Lincoln said, "I don't propose to argue this matter, because arguments have no effect upon men whose opinions are fixed and minds are made up. But this little story of mine will make some things which now are in the dark show up more clearly."

Lincoln went on to tell of a time in his youth when he had worked as a peddler on the frontier. And McClure quotes Lincoln:

"Just before we left Indiana and crossed into Illinois," continued Mr. Lincoln solemnly, speaking in a grave tone

20. Helen Nicolay, p. 13.
21. Gross, p. 210.

of voice, "we came across a small farmhouse full of nothing but children. These ranged in years from seventeen years to seventeen months, and all were in tears. The mother of the family was red-headed and red-faced, and the whip she held in her right hand led to the inference that she had been chastising her brood. The father of the family, a meek-looking, mild-mannered, tow-headed chap, was standing in the front door-way awaiting—to all appearances—his turn to feel the thong.

"I thought there wasn't much use in asking the head of that house if she wanted any 'notions.' She was too busy. It was evident an insurrection had been in progress, but it was pretty well quelled when I got there. The mother had about suppressed it with an iron hand, but she was not running any risks. She kept a keen and wary eye upon all the children, not forgetting an occasional glance at the 'old man' in the doorway.

"She saw me as I came up, and from her look I thought she was of the opinion that I intended to interfere. Advancing to the doorway, and roughly pushing her husband aside, she demanded my business.

" 'Nothing, madame,' I answered as gently as possible; 'I merely dropped in as I came along to see how things were going.'

" 'Well, you needn't wait,' was the reply in an irritated way; 'there's trouble here, an' lots of it, too, but I kin manage my own affairs without the help of outsiders. This is jest a family row, but I'll teach these brats their places ef I hev to 'lick the hide off ev'ry one of them. I don't do much talkin', but I run this house, an' I don't want no one sneakin' round tryin' to find out how I do it, either.'

"That's the case here with us," the President said in conclusion. "We must let the other nations know that we proposed to settle our family row in our own way, and 'teach these brats their places (the seceding States) if we have to 'lick the hide off' of each and every one of them. And, like the old woman, we don't want any 'sneakin' 'round' by other countries who would like to find out how we are to do it, either.[22]

22. McClure, pp. 430-31.

Nevertheless, the comic stories of Lincoln are a form of argument, and their purpose is to persuade others of a conclusion advanced by the teller. But the comic medium not only provides a humorous illustration of the point at hand; in the face of opposition to it, the humor depersonalizes the issue and facilitates by good feeling what may be a necessary acceptance of the conclusion.

The comic story has rarely been recognized as a form of reasoning and argumentation. We saw earlier that comic thought can constitute a kind of alternative logic, as in the childlike humor of Ffeiffer's cartoons or in the humor of the marginal men of a society. In the argumentative use of the comic story by Lincoln, we are confronted with a form of analogical reasoning. It would seem to have two sources for Abraham Lincoln—the practical reasoning of men arguing over actual problems of daily life, and the trained reasoning of men at law arguing the legal issues before a court.[23]

The analogical reasoning of folk tales used as a means of instruction and argumentation is dependent upon the verbal history of a group. It compiles a record of solutions to social problems through trial and error, and in the mode of stories recalls the essentials of each event. When a social issue arises, or a person must be instructed in the manner of resolving some problem, recourse is had to the story or tale that tells of a similar problem in the past and how with having deeply influenced him in boyhood is, as mentioned earlier, Aesop's Fables.[25] He absorbed its logic and developed a comic mode of argument from it, and many of his stories clearly reveal their Aesopian structure.

A strongly abolitionist delegation came to him demanding emancipation of the slaves prior to when he thought it would be practical and capable of enforcement. He asked them:

23. Cf. Edward H. Levi, *An Introduction to Legal Reasoning* (Chicago: University of Chicago Press, a Phoenix Book, 1948, 1970); Stephen Toulmin, *The Uses of Argument* (New York and London: Cambridge University Press, 1958, 1969).
24. Nicolay, pp. 37-38.
25. Carl Sandburg, *Abraham Lincoln: The Prairie Years* (New York: Harcourt, Brace & Co., 1926), 1:73-76.

"How many legs will a sheep have if you call the tail a leg?" They answered, "five." "You are mistaken," said Lincoln, "for calling a tail a leg don't make it so"; and that exhibited the fallacy of their position more than twenty syllogisms.[26]

Lincoln's intellectual genius had elevated a primal way of social reasoning into a powerful instrument of political and practical logic. Moreover, his choice of careers reinforced and refined the analogical reasoning of his storytelling. Legal reasoning, particularly that of common law, is analogical reasoning, proceeding from a case at hand to past and similar ones with guiding precedents. In turn, the precedents rest upon basic legal principles of right and wrong, set by society. Finally, in the less sophisticated courtrooms of the frontier settlements, Lincoln's storytelling to establish a point or point up a precedent was a major legal skill.

Judge David Davis said of Lincoln as a lawyer:

In all the elements that constitute the great lawyer he had few equals. . . . He seized the strong points of a cause, and presented them with clearness and great compactness. His mind was logical and direct, and he did not indulge in extraneous discussion. Generalities and platitudes had no charm for him. An unfailing vein of humor never deserted him; and he was able to claim the attention of court and jury when the cause was the most uninteresting, by the appropriateness of his anecdotes.[27]

Lincoln, in asking in 1856 for a new pass from R. P. Morgan, the Superintendent of the Alton Railroad, displayed his own awareness of the relationship of humorous anecdote to the law:

Dear Sir:
Says Tom to John: "Here's your old rotten wheelbarrow. I've broke it, using on it. I wish you would mend it, case I will want to borrow it this arter-noon."

26. Gross, p. 116.
27. Nicolay, p. 93.

Acting on this as a precedent, I say, "Here's your old chalked hat. I wish you would take it and send me a new one; case I shall want to use it the first of March."

Yours, truly,

A. Lincoln[28]

An excellent example of Lincoln's legal skill in story-telling is related by Judge Beckwith of Danville, Illinois:

A man, by vile words, first provoked and then made a bodily attack upon another. The latter, in defending himself, gave the other much the worst of the encounter. The aggressor, to get even, had the one who thrashed him tried in our Circuit Court on a charge of an assault and battery. Mr. Lincoln defended, and told the jury that his client was in the fix of a man who, in going along the highway with a pitchfork on his shoulder, was attacked by a fierce dog that ran out at him from a farmer's dooryard. In parrying off the brute with the fork, its prongs stuck into the brute and killed him.

" 'What made you kill my dog?' said the farmer.

" 'What made him try to bite me?'

" 'But why did you not go at him with the other end of the pitchfork?'

" 'Why did he not come after me with his other end?'

"At this Mr. Lincoln whirled about in his long arms an imaginary dog, and pushed its tail end toward the jury. This was the defensive plea of 'son assault demesne'— loosely, that 'the other fellow brought on the fight,'— quickly told, and in a way the dullest mind would grasp and retain."[29]

This comic analogical reasoning that Lincoln developed out of story-telling and his legal practice carried over into his most serious political declarations. In a famous letter to A. G. Hodges in 1864, in which he expressed his position as anti-slavery, he stated in part:

It was in the oath I took that I would, to the best of my ability, preserve, protect, and defend the Constitution of

28. Lincoln, *Collected Works*, 2:330.
29. McClure, p. 93.

the United States. I could not take the office without taking the oath. Nor was it my view that I might take an oath to get power, and break the oath in using the power. I understood, too, that in ordinary civil administration this oath even forbade me to practically indulge my primary abstract judgment on the moral question of slavery. I had publicly declared this many times, and in many ways. And I aver that, to this day, I have done no official act in mere deference to my abstract judgment and feeling on slavery. I did understand however, that my oath to preserve the Constitution to the best of my ability imposed on me the duty of preserving, by every indispensable means, that government—that nation, of which that Constitution was the organic law. Was it possible to lose the nation and yet preserve the Constitution? By general law, life and limb must be protected, yet often a limb must be amputated to save a life; but a life is never given to wisely save a limb. I felt that measures otherwise unconstitutional might become lawful by becoming indispensable to the preservation of the Constitution through the preservation of the nation.[30]

Perhaps imputing the structure of comic analogical reasoning to the majestic sobriety of Lincoln's declaration is unwarranted. Yet, there is an unmistakable similarity between the two. Lincoln likens the Constitution and nation to a limb and life and draws forth an Aesopian axiom. He begins with a simple premise resting on the logic of contradiction, and then employs a comic twist of wording ("take an oath to get power, and break the oath in using the power") to drive home his point. And he disavows all right to abstract judgment—here is an issue; there is its earthy analogy; so be it.

A much more concise statement by Lincoln on the same theme reveals even more clearly its kinship to the comic analogue. In 1860, when Lincoln was asked by a supporter to reiterate publicly his intention not to interfere with slavery in Southern states, he declined. He said that he had already done so many times, and his statements were in print and open to all. He concluded:

30. Lincoln, *Collected Works*, 7:281.

Those who will not read or heed what I have already publicly said would not read or heed a repetition of it. "If they
hear not Moses and the prophets, neither will they be persuaded though one rose from the dead." (4: 130)

The touch of humor to a powerful statement on the limits
of change in public opinion is in the phrasing, the biblical
quotation, and the extremism of the example. Moreover,
Lincoln, the master logician, states succinctly that, given an
unchanged prejudice or premise, any change in the objective circumstances matters little.

The key features of Lincoln's storytelling as a logic of
analogical thought and argumentation can now be summed
up. They are its democracy, practicality, conservatism, and
humor. The democratic nature of storytelling lies in its
humble and primal social origins. The story is composed
from everyday experiences of the people, related in their
mode and tongue, pointed to their problems, and geared to
their comprehension.

The logic of storytelling is eminently practical. It proceeds from a concrete issue or problem, seeks its essence,
and relates it to the tale of a similar problem that has been
previously encountered, and from which an appropriate
means for its resolution has been derived. The tale may be
fictitious, but it is composed of the familiar and the concrete actuality. Last, the goal of the story is to effect a result in action or thought to achieve an immediate end—
winning a political or legal argument, accepting a necessary
decision, guiding a course of action.

To the contrary of the usual satire, Lincoln's storytelling
is not radically critical; rather, the logic of storytelling depends upon shared values and ensures a continuity of social
thought and action. It poses no abstract ideals against social
reality. It implies no change in the future that would reverse the past. Like the law, which may be an institution
evolved from analogic folk tales, storytelling has the morality and structure of society built into it. Despite his revolutionary presidency, Lincoln was a social conservative,

and his chief mode of thought and political expression reveal it.

Finally, and most disputably, the comic may well not be merely incidental to Lincoln's use of analogy in storytelling. First, the humor of the story may be part and parcel of its popular communicability—it rivets attention and facilitates acceptance. But, more deeply, the structure of comedy has a kinship with the analogical reasoning of storytelling. Both deal with the earthiness of living actuality. Both have all the uncertainty of contingent events and their fallible human actors.

Again, though comedy thrives on contrast, and analogy depends on similarity, each is but a reverse of the other. For comedy finds difference in similarity, and analogy, similarity in difference. To seek the one is to become conscious of the other. To know both is to experience the ambiguity of existence. The comic perspective becomes the comic catharsis to relieve the tensions of that ambiguity.

The Humorous Lover of Practical Wisdom

Any attempt to assess the philosophy of Lincoln must come to grips with the pervasiveness of the comical in his thought. Philosophy in its literal translation as the love of wisdom becomes for Lincoln a humorous love of practical wisdom.

His search for wisdom is a desire for knowledge of man on earth and in society—a search for understanding real men in all the confusion of their relationships with one another. Here he encounters that ambiguity of man in his existence, which can be dogmatically denied or overcome through imposing an intellectual or religious unity from above. But Lincoln is no dogmatist or grant theorist. He chooses to live with ambiguity. He laughs, and is content with proximate answers to ever-present problems.

To start with Lincoln's view of himself, in the 1859 Fell

letter, he said of his life, "there's not much of it" because "there's not much of me." He ironically makes light of his own achievements, but, more deeply, he may be expressing his view of every man's limitations. Lincoln took a positive delight in ridiculing man's pretensions, including his own. He recalled an old, hard-boiled Democrat stepping up to him just after the Illinois Republican State Convention had made him their presidential nominee:

"So you're Abraham Lincoln?"
"Yes, that is my name."
"They say you're a self-made man."
"Well, yes, in a way what there is of me is self-made."
"Well," said the old man with a long survey, "all I got to say is that it was a damned bad job."[31]

Lincoln had once stated, "There are few things wholly evil or wholly good; almost everything is an inseparable compound of the two."[32] And he illustrated this belief with a story calculated to cut down any self-righteousness:

Riding at one time in a stage with an old Kentuckian who was returning from Missouri, Lincoln excited the old gentleman's surprise by refusing to accept either tabacco or French brandy.
When they separated that afternoon—the Kentuckian to take another stage bound for Louisville—he shook hands warmly with Lincoln, and said, good-humoredly:
"See here, stranger, you're a clever but strange companion. I may never see you again, and I don't want to offend you, but I say this: My experience has taught me that the man who has no vices has damned few virtues."[33]

Even in the midst of America's greatest crisis, Lincoln allowed himself no false pride at his leadership. A citizen in a reception said to him, "I am glad to take the hand of the man, who, with the help of Almighty God will put down

31. Sandburg, *The War Years*, 3:335.
32. Sandburg, *The Prairie Years*, 2:66.
33. McClure, p. 66.

this rebellion." Lincoln quickly replied, "You are more than half right, sir."[34]

Lincoln's view of men in general was permeated by the same duality. Carl Sandburg, in a brilliant chapter examining Lincoln's laughter and the humor of the Civil War period, succinctly expresses this sense of comic duality:

Life was ridiculous, its forms and appearances deceptive and ludicrous, and any pomp and power would drop into collapse and shuffle with a limping dignity if looked at long enough—such stark gargoyles of thought were implied by the horselaugh philosophers praised by Lincoln. The fields of politics and war saw swindlers, pretenders, hypocrites, demagogues, charlatans, bootlickers, snivelers, shifters, incompetents. They and their works implied constantly that democracy, the experiment of popular government, could never be anything else than a series of approximations, imperfections incessantly present or arriving. Democracy would be achieved only through humanity, its operations conducted by and through the members of the human family. And what was humanity, or as Lincoln termed it, "the family of man"? A species of biped creatures on the surface of the earth with which these horselaugh philosophers were concerned. Behind the exterior or mirth, under the jokery, seemed so often to be the quizzical thrusting: "What is man? Why does he behave as he does? Is it absurd that I, who am a man, should cut up and play such capers as you see me in?" (3: 353)

Two stories of Lincoln express his view of man's ambiguity. Lincoln, when a member of the Illinois State Legislature, wished to silence a fellow member who questioned the constitutionality of every motion made. Lincoln gained the floor and said that the incessant constitutionalist reminded him of an old friend. He described a grizzled frontiersman with shaggy, overhanging eyebrows, and spectacles, much like the objecting legislator. Lincoln continued:

One morning, on looking out of his cabin door the old gent-

34. Sandburg, *The War Years*, 3:306.

leman thought he saw a squirrel frisking on a tree near the house. He took down his gun and fired at it, but the squirrel paid no attention. Again and again he fired, getting more mystified and more mortified at each failure. After a round dozen shots he threw down the gun, muttering that there was "something wrong with the rifle."

"Rifle's all right," declared his son who had been watching him, "Rifle's all right, but where's your squirrel?"

"Don't you see him?" thundered the old man, pointing out the exact spot.

"No, I don't," was the candid answer. Then, turning and staring into his father's face, the boy broke into a jubilant shout. "Now I see your squirrel! You've been firing at a louse on your eyebrow."[35]

It would be difficult to more graphically express the impairment of man's sense of reality by his prejudices. But those same prejudices may drive a man to good works in the comically mixed world of Abraham Lincoln. Thus, when he was told of political activities by his Secretary of Treasury, Salmon B. Chase, whose overweening ambition drove him to contest the 1864 Republican presidential nomination of Lincoln, Lincoln told a story:

My brother and I were once plowing corn, I driving the horse and he holding the plow. The horse was lazy, but on one occasion he rushed across the field so that I, with my long legs, could scarcely keep pace with him. On reaching the end of the furrow, I found an enormous chin fly fastened upon him and knocked him off. My brother asked me what I did that for. I told him I didn't want the horse bitten in that way.

"Why," said my brother, "that's all that made him go."

Now, if Mr. Chase has a Presidential chin fly biting him, I'm not going to knock him off, it it will only make his department go.[36]

Men act out of a strange mixture of motives, and good may issue from bad. In politics, ambition may serve the

35. Nicolay, pp. 20-21.
36. McClure, p. 71.

purposes of state, and Lincoln comically displays a knowledge of this motivating force that mirrors Madison's philosophical statement in *The Federalist* 51:

Ambition must be made to counteract ambition. The interest of the man must be connected with the constitutional rights of the place.

For Lincoln to be able to profit from another's ambitions, especially when directed against him, required a rare dispassion. The ability to view oneself objectively in relation to others and to the scheme of things is invaluable politically and must be commented on. However, its sources for Lincoln appear to lie in his religious unorthodoxy. Mrs. Lincoln said that he never joined a church, but he was a religious man by nature. She said, "it was a kind of poetry in his nature, and he never was a technical Christian" (p. 386).

Lincoln's religious sense as expressed in his humor is totally lacking in any sense of certainty about divine purpose. He constantly, but gently, ridiculed any kind of dogmatism. He replied to a minister who "hoped the Lord was on his side," that that did not bother him. His concern was that he and his country should be on the Lord's side.[37] Another time, when a minister claimed to bring him a divine command to act immediately in emancipating the slaves, he replied:

I hope it will not be irreverent for me to say that if it is probable that God would reveal his will to others on a point so connected with my duty, it might be supposed He would reveal it directly to me. (pp. 265-66)

Lincoln never embraced a belief in the Christ, and it is not surprising that he regarded the squabbles of Christian denominationalism with amusement. When a delegation of clergymen from three denominations asked him for a change in the system of appointing regimental chaplains,

37. Nicolay, p. 351.

Lincoln said that, without disrespect, he would tell them a story:

"Once, in Springfield, I was going off on a short journey, and reached the depot a little ahead of time. Leaning against the fence just outside the depot was a little darkey boy, whom I knew, named 'Dick,' busily digging with his toe in a mud-puddle. As I came up, I said, "Dick, what are you about?'

" 'Making a *church*," ' said he.

" 'A church?; said I; 'what do you mean?'

" 'Why, yes,' said Dick, pointing with his toe, 'don't you see? there is the shape of it; there's the "steps" and "front-door"—here the "pews," where the folks set—and there's the "pulpit." '

" 'Yes, I see,' said I, 'but why don't you make a "minister?"' '

" 'Laws,' answered 'Dick,' with a grin, 'I hain't got *mud* enough!' "

The ultimate truth for Lincoln is a mystery, and he laughs at all pretensions of divine knowledge. Yet, he appears to have a deep and serene faith in a just and purposeful universe. Lincoln's Second Inaugural Address is not humorous; it is a profoundly beautiful statement of the faith of a political man. Nevertheless, in its juxtaposition to the harsh strictures of the self-righteous and the religious dogmatists in politics, it becomes a kind of satire, possessed by the humor of a divine fool. In it, Lincoln concluded:
Neither party expected for the war, the magnitude, or the duration, which it has already attained. Neither anticipated that the *cause* of the conflict might cease with, or even before, the conflict itself should cease. Each looked for an easier triumph, and a result less fundamental and astounding. Both read the same Bible, and pray to the same God; and each invokes His aid against the other. It may seem strange that any men should dare to ask a just God's assistance in wringing their bread from the sweat of other men's faces; but let us judge not that we be not judged. The

38. Sandburg, *The War Years*, 3:326.

prayers of both could not be answered; that of neither has been answered fully. The Almighty has His own purposes. "Woe unto the world because of offenses! for it must needs be that offenses come; but woe to that man by whom the offense cometh!" If we shall suppose that American slavery is one of those offenses which, in the providence of God, must needs come, but which, having continued through His appointed time, He now wills to remove, and that He gives to both North and South this terrible war, as the woe due to those by whom the offense came, shall we discern therein any departure from those divine attributes which the believers in a Living God always ascribe to Him? Fondly do we hope—fervently do we pray—that this mighty scourge of war may speedily pass away. Yet, if God wills that it continue, until all the wealth piled by the bondman's two hundred and fifty years of unrequited toil shall be sunk, and until every drop of blood drawn with the lash, shall be paid by another drawn with the sword, as was said three thousand years ago, so still it must be said "the judgments of the Lord, are true and righteous altogether."

With malice toward none; with charity for all; with firmness in the right, as God gives us to see the right, let us strive on to finish the work we are in; to bind up the nation's wounds; to care for him who shall have borne the battle, and for his widow, and his orphan—to do all which may achieve and cherish a just, and a lasting peace, among ourselves, and with all nations.[39]

The principles of Lincoln's Second Inaugural Address and the practices that flow from them, establish Lincoln as the greatest of political moralists. And the moral quality for politics that illuminates the Address is one of almost superhuman dispassion, a comic acceptance of the world and a tolerance for its flawed humanity that enables Lincoln to act with loving mercy toward all men. The divine is a mystery, but not one for man's license, but rather for love with trust in the ultimate benevolence of nature.

Sandburg speaks of Lincoln's dispassion as "an aloof qual-

39. Abraham Lincoln, *Selected Speeches, Messages and Letters*, ed. T. Harry Williams (New York and Toronto: Rinehart & Co., Inc., 1957), pp. 281-83.

ity, not alien to humor or even fantasy." He continues with several stories that illustrate this aloofness and, at the same time, an almost inhuman mercifulness toward the enemy. When a Confederate blockade-runner was released from prison and thanked Lincoln, the President replied, "I am happy to know I am able to serve an enemy." Sandburg also relates this anecdote:

Once a petitioner, of doubtful loyalty, handed the President a letter signed by an influential Marylander. While the President read it, another man in line spoke up saying the signer of the letter had been dead several months. The petitioner turned pale, sank into a chair in a half-faint. Lincoln: "Never mind, sir, never mind. I would rather get a letter from a dead man than from a live man any day."[40]

The many stories of Lincoln's pardoning prisoners in the Civil War illustrate again and again his comic mercifulness. The gentlest example is in a letter to Stanton concerning the crime of fourteen-year-old Daniel Winger, who had been sentenced to be shot:

My dear Sir:
    Hadn't we better spank this drummer boy and send him back home to Leavenworth?

A. Lincoln[41]

And the afternoon preceding his assassination, Lincoln signed a pardon for a soldier sentenced to be shot for desertion, remarking, "Well, I think the boy can do us more good above ground than under ground."[42]

Lincoln's comic mercifulness is surely a counterpart to his religious skepticism. However, his thoughts and behavior were in the main rooted in a hardheaded factualism. He did not so much seek inspiration for action from faith, since he

---

40. Sandburg, *The War Years*, 3:332.
41. H. Jack Lang, *The Wit & Wisdom of Abraham Lincoln* (New York: Greenberg Publishers, 1941), p. 113.
42. McClure, p. 386.

acted from a lack of faith in any definite directives from the Almighty. When it came to right action, he sought the facts and right thinking about them. Thus, one of Lincoln's stories was related by him to the conduct of the newspapers. It told of

a traveler lost during a terrific thunder-storm, blundering and floundering along in thick darkness, except when vivid lightning flashes showed him trees falling around him, and the heavens apparently rent asunder. At last a flash and a crash more terrible than all the rest brought him to his knees. He was not a praying man. His petition was short, and to the point. "O Lord," he gasped, "if its all the same to you, please give us a little more light and a little less noise!"[43]

Sandburg recognizes Lincoln's comical philosophizing about reality when he writes:

In the White House Lincoln philosophized no less than in the earlier days, in the same manner as when, after hearing many theories and noisy wranglings in a big law case, he had walked out on the Rock Island bridge, coming on a boy with a fishing-pole whose legs dangled idly from the ties above the water. "I suppose you know all about this river," he ventured. The boy, brightly: "I guess I do. It was here when I was born, and its been here ever since." And Lincoln smiled. "I'm mighty glad I walked out here where there is not so much opinion and a little more fact."[44]

Perhaps Carl Sandburg has written more fully and acutely about Lincoln's humor than any other author. Interestingly, the chapter that he devotes to Lincoln's humor is entitled "Lincoln's Laughter—And His Religion." In this chapter Sandburg sees the comic in Lincoln and his favorite humorists as a part of the comedy of democracy, which merges for Lincoln into the religious mystery of man and his works. For Sandburg, Lincoln's nature combined a

43. Nicolay, pp. 22-23.
44. Sandburg, *The War Years*, 3:321.

wildly irrepressible comic attitude with a deep strain of melancholy. His melancholy would seem to be tied in with his religious views. Nevertheless, each aspect of his personality was but a part of the whole man, who was supremely a democratic politician.

Sandburg tells a story of Senator Fessenden, later Lincoln's Secretary of Treasury. It illustrates graphically how the comic and the religious come together in Lincoln to form the political man. Sandburg writes:

The good, upright, usually well-tempered Fessenden, it was told over Washington, in a rage over some unjust distribution of patronage turned loose a flood of "intemperate" language on Lincoln one morning. Lincoln took it. He kept cool. The fury of his Maine friend spent itself. Lincoln inquired gently, "you are an Episcopalian, aren't you, Senator?" "Yes, sir. I belong to that church." "I thought so. You Episcopalians all swear alike. Seward is an Episcopalian. But Stanton is a Presbyterian. You ought to hear him swear." (3: 369)

Lincoln, the satyr-statesman, does not become offended at an imagined insult to his dignity or office. He is beyond such petty passions, for his experiences and his philosophy of man combine to allow him a detached and amused view of another's momentary failing. He reacts comically, allowing him an outlet for any resentment or aggressiveness and preserving the political situation. Fessenden is mollified. Lincoln is neither humiliated nor humiliating. And Sandburg relates that after a brief talk about the various styles of profanity, the two men amicably solved their patronage problems.

Comic sense is the balance wheel of Lincoln's politics, and some approximation of this comic quality must be present in every truly political man. The comic sense sums up in its various facets the opposite of dogmatism, fanaticism, self-righteousness, and especially violence. These are the characteristics that are the enemies of the practice of politics. They destroy flexibility and the possibility of compromise. They insist on one true solution to any problem and one party's possession of it. They demand submission to the true believer and his absolute superiority. Finally, they lead to the violence of physical aggression of man against man—the *ultima ratio*—as the necessary means of resolving disputes.

Lincoln's comic sense in politics is typified in his understanding of man's duality, and it starts with a healthy appreciation of his own mixture of motives. His humor at man's flounderings and confusions and their chaotic results enables him to view man sympathetically and constructively. But Lincoln knows that he too is an actor in man's "comedy of errors," and he is not given to violent or officious reactions to political criticisms or partisan attacks on him. He dispels them comically, peacefully, and continues the business of politics—persuasion and compromise in the resolving of social problems.

Lincoln's dispassion and compassion will never be fully comprehended, though their contributions to his comic sense of politics has been shown. Yet, certainly his religious skepticism and ultimate faith would seem to be qualities without which he could not have possessed the quizzical tolerance and gentle mercifulness toward others. In a way, he is the supremely political man of American democracy because he is the exemplar of the anti-authoritarian. He writes:

As I would not be a *slave*, so I would not be a *master*. This expresses my idea of democracy. What ever differs from this, to the extent of the difference, is no democracy.[45]

Again, one must note the resemblance to comic structure in this gemlike definition. Present are contradiction, reverse wording, brevity, and punch line. In another minute masterpiece of comic reasoning, Lincoln's humor leavens an official order to General George B. McClellan:

My Dear Sir:
This morning I felt constrained to order Blenker's divi-

45. Lincoln, *Collected Works*, 2:532.

sion to Fremont, and I write this to assure you that I did so with great pain, understanding that you would wish it otherwise. If you could know the full pressure of the case, I am confident you would justify it, even beyond a mere acknowledgment that the Commander-in-Chief may order what he pleases.

Yours very truly,
Abraham Lincoln (5: 175-6)

One more vital element in Lincoln's comic political philosophy must be broached. In the midst of a vicious civil war, Lincoln's view of man's limitations is matched by a corresponding view of the limits of state. The Chief Executive of the State would have none of a super-organism in which man finds his being and to which he owes selflessness and sacrifice.

Perhaps Lincoln demonstrated his view of man in relation to the State with his "leg cases." These were the appeals to him from sentences for desertion and cowardice. Helen Nicolay says that one of his stories was of the Irish soldier who was asked why he had deserted. "Well, Captain," said he, "it was not me fault. I've a heart in me breast as brave as Julius Caesar; but when the battle begins, somehow or other these cowardly legs of mine will run away wid me!"

Lincoln added, "I have no doubt that is true of many a man who honestly means to do his duty, but is overcome by a physical fear greater than his will." And John Hay recorded in his diary, "Cases of cowardice he was specially averse to punishing with death. He said it would frighten the poor devils too terribly to shoot them."[46]

Lincoln's story of a Negro soldier at the battle of Fort Donaldson challenges episodes in the contemporary *Catch 22* for its comic statement of the value of life versus military heroics. Someone asks the soldier:

"Were you in the fight?"
"Had a little taste of it, sah."
"Stood your ground, did you?"

46. Nicolay, pp. 280-81.

"No, sah—I runs."

"Ran at the first fire, did you?"

"Yes, sah, and I would 'run sooner if I knowed it was a-comin.' "

"That was not very creditable to your courage."

"Dat isn't my line, sah. Cookin' is my perfession."

"But have you no regard for your reputation?"

"Reputations nuffin to me by de side ob life."

"Do you consider your life worth more than other people's?"

"Worth mo to me, sah."

"Do you think your company would have missed you if you had been killed?"

"Maybe not, sah. A dead white man ain' much to dese sojers, let alone a dead nigger. But I'd a' missed myself, and dat's de point wif me." (p. 284)

Lincoln believed in his country and was determined to save it. Death and sacrifice were necessary, but Lincoln never forgot the value of life and the conflict between survival of country and its cost in life. Likewise, Lincoln never wavered in his trust that the North's cause was right and would prevail, but he also never thought the North to be divinely inspired. Thus, he told the Union Governor of Virginia, Pierpont, in early 1863:

If an intelligent angel from heaven would drop down in one corner of this room, and sit there for two weeks hearing all that is said to me, I think that he would come to the conclusion that the war was being prosecuted for the purpose of obtaining cotton from the South for the Northern cotton mills.[47]

Nicolay relates the time when a committee of rich New Yorkers came to Washington. They demanded a gunboat to protect their harbor against depredations of the Confederate ironclad *Merrimac*, which was frightening people all along the Atlantic Coast. Lincoln answered their plea:

47. Sandburg, *The War Years*, 3:338.

Gentlemen, the credit of the Government is at a very low ebb. It is impossible under present conditions to do what you ask. But it seems to me that if I were half as rich as you are reputed to be, and half as badly scared as you appear to be, I would build a gunboat and present it to the government. [48]

Lincoln's comic logic penetrates the weakness of their demand. He refuses the petitioners, yet his humor cushions any aggressive impact. But where Lincoln's balance is most evident is in his "with malice toward none; with charity for all" view of the Civil War. Helen Nicolay reports that Lincoln wished the Confederate leaders would escape after the War: "If you have an elephant on your hands, and he wants to run away—better let him run!" he said (p. 356). A number of his stories had this same gist to them, but an actual incident showed the tenor of his thoughts best of all. Helen Nicolay writes:

On April 11 Lincoln spoke from a window of the White House to a large and joyful crowd, gathered in honor of Lee's surrender. The President's speech was full of conciliation. Senator Harlan followed, and in the course of his remarks, touched on the thought uppermost in everybody's mind. "What shall we do with the rebels?" he asked. A voice answered from the crowd, "Hang them!"
Lincoln's small son was in the room, playing with the pens on the table. Looking up he caught his father's pained expression.
"No, no, Papa," he cried in his childish voice. "Not hang them. Hang on to them!"
"That is it! Tad has got it. We must hang on to them!" the President exclaimed in triumph. (pp. 357-58)

The Humorist-Politician

In the last days of the war, with victory at hand, Lincoln's speech remained "full of conciliation." One of his last

48. Nicolay, p. 266.

official acts was to issue a pardon. He remained true to his comic genius, but, above all, he remained a politician, not a Caesar or a Christ. His comic sense is true to the inner spirit of democratic politics, and it is in the services of their partnership that Lincoln became the First President of the United States.

Lincoln's profession was law, but his constant avocation, occasional vocation, and final full calling was politics. Benjamin Thomas in his biography of Lincoln concludes:

Lincoln had proved himself to be a consummate politician. Except for a few years of retirement, politics had been his life. He had come to his task much better prepared than most people had realized. For during his years in Illinois we have seen him devoting hour upon hour to caucuses, conventions, and legislative sessions, to writing party circulars and making party speeches, to considering requests and weighing recommendations, to devising party strategy and formulating party policies.[49]

In support of this conclusion, Thomas quotes Charles A. Dana, journalist and aid to the President:

"Lincoln was a supreme politician," he observed. "He understood human nature. . . . There was no flabby philanthropy about Abraham Lincoln. He was all solid, hard, keen intelligence combined with goodness." (p. 494)

There is little question among close observers of Lincoln, both contemporary and biographical, that he was a highly accomplished politician. Moreover, a number of them tie his political sense to his humor. Thomas quotes several observers and then, concerning Lincoln's political control, he states, "He owed not a little of this self-mastery to the irrepressible sense of humor that enabled him to recognize the ridiculous and to hold things in true perspective" (pp. 459-61).

49. B. P. Thomas, *Abraham Lincoln* (New York: The Modern Library, 1952-1962), p. 498.

J. G. Randall writes of Lincoln, "He could turn a trick by a good humored story. Your self-important soul, or your strutting dictator, does not often smile. In Lincoln the priceless element of humor was an index to the shape and quality of his mind." In short, Randall states, "it supplied a sense of proportion."[50]

Lincoln's comic genius is an essential element of his political skill and democratic leadership. If the job of the best politician is to allay civil strife through gaining agreement of the people for necessary social action, Lincoln's humor was a major instrument in that task. And his Civil War presidency became the major testing ground in American history for the art of politics. He held together the North in a major war against a military-minded South, despite the North's being split over secession, and by conflicting parties and factions within parties. Yet, in the 1864 election he received a solid majority of the vote. His formula for handling factions was given in a letter of advice to a newly appointed General:

Let your military measures be strong enough to repel the invader, and keep the peace, and not so strong as to unnecessarily harass and persecute the people. It is a difficult role, and so much greater will be the honor if you perform it well. If both factions, or neither shall abuse you, you will probably be about right. Beware of being assailed by one and praised by the other.[51]

Practical, hard-headed advice is given in a humorous statement of balance in politics. Its gist is to seek the mean between extremes, and its spirit is that of compromise.

It is extremely difficult to practice moderation in a civil war. Yet, Lincoln's humor and religious beliefs went hand-in-hand in sustaining a policy of reconciliation toward the South. He understood the mixed motives from which men act in war as well as politics, and his policy toward the South was the same as that toward his political opponents

50. J. G. Randall, *Lincoln The Liberal Statesman* (New York: Dodd, Mead & Co., Apollo Editions, 1947), p. 204.
51. Lincoln, *Collected Works*, 6:234.

after the 1864 election: "I am in favor of a short statute of limitations in politics."[52]

Lincoln's basic understanding of the art of politics matured early. In an 1842 speech to a Springfield Temperance Society, he states its essence in criticizing the traditional temperance approach:

It was *impolitic*, because, it is not much in the nature of man to be driven to anything; still less to be driven about that which is exclusively his own business; and least of all, where such driving is to be submitted to, at the expense of pecuniary interest, or burning appetite. . . .

To have expected them (dram-sellers and drinkers) to do otherwise than as they did—to have expected them not to meet denunciation with denunciation, crimination with crimination, and anathema with anathema, was to expect a reversal of human nature, which is God's decree, and never can be reversed. When the conduct of men is designed to be influenced, *persuasion*, kind, unassuming persuasion, should ever be adopted. It is an old and a true maxim, that a "drop of honey catches more flies than a gallon of gall." So with men. If you would win a man to your cause, *first* convince him that you are his sincere friend. Therein is a drop of honey that catches his heart, which, say what he will, is the great highroad to his reason, and which, when once gained, you will find but little trouble in convincing his judgment of the justice of your cause, if indeed that cause really be a just one. On the contrary, assume to dictate to his judgment, or to command his action, or to mark him as one to be shunned and despised, and he will retreat within himself, close all the avenues to his head and his heart; and though your cause be naked truth itself, transformed to the heaviest lance, harder than steel, and sharper than steel can be made, and though you throw it with more than Herculean force and precision, you shall no more be able to pierce him, than to penetrate the hard shell of a tortoise with a rye straw.

Such is man, and so *must* he be understood by those who would lead him, even to his own best interest.[53]

52. Gross, p. 127.
53. *Abraham Lincoln* (Williams, ed.), pp. 18-19.

In a gentle reprimand to a young officer, Lincoln with a touch of humor summed up his personal code:

Quarrel not at all. No man resolved to make the most of himself, can spare time for personal contention. Still less can he afford to take all the consequences, including the vitiating of his temper, and the loss of self-control. Yield larger things to which you can show no more than equal right; and yield lesser ones, though clearly your own. Better give your path to a dog, than be bitten by him in contesting for the right. Even killing the dog would not cure the bite. (p. 246)

For the political man the display of ego is a wasteful luxury, if not a needless dog bite. Lincoln sublimates the quarreling and viciousness of politics into the comic story or joke.

Lincoln facilitates compromise by channeling his aggression into humor, but he also employs humor as a form of compromise. He tells a story to avoid a slight or evade an impolitic answer. Sandburg relates that a Judge Williams of Indiana asked Lincoln if he recalled a letter that he had sent to General Curtis about the charges of disloyalty against a Reverend Mr. McPheeters in St. Louis. When Lincoln replied that he did, the Judge recounted:

"Well, on the trial of Dr. McPheeters by the General Assembly of the Presbyterian Church, your letter was read. But the curious part of the affair was this: One party read a portion of your letter and claimed the President was on their side, and another part read another portion of the same letter and claimed the President was on their side. So it seems, Mr. President, that it is not so easy to tell where you stand."

Lincoln joined in the laughter and was reminded of an Illinois farmer and his son out in the woods hunting a sow. After a long search they came to a creek branch, where they found hog tracks, and signs of a snout rooting, for some distance on both sides of the branch. The old man said to his boy, "Now, John, you take up on this side of the branch and I'll go up t'other, for I believe the old critter is on both sides."[54]

Lincoln's comic story explains analogically the need for ambiguity in politics, but it also is a parable of the politics of compromise. Often there is truth on both sides of an issue, and the statesman's position should be on neither side, but to cover both sides of them. Time and political bargaining may settle the issue. Otherwise, the statesman as political broker has preserved his freedom and flexibility for negotiating some kind of a political settlement.

Lincoln, the humorist-politician, was a compromiser, and comedy was a part of the compromise. He was also a man of political expedience. Politics and politicians must deal with the here and now. Lincoln had his consistency and basic values, but he did not elevate them into an ideology. He said, "My policy is to have no policy."[55] He meant it in the sense of having no hard and fast rules that would dictate, or constrict the freedom of his action.

An old man from Tennessee was given an audience with President Lincoln. He pleaded for mercy for his son, who was under sentence of death for some military offense. Lincoln said that he would look into the case and give his decision the next day. The old man cried out, "Tomorrow may be too late! My son is under sentence of death! It ought to be decided now!"

Lincoln, in sympathy with the old man, told him a story about General Fisk. The general had once been a colonel in command of a regiment, and he had told his men that he would do all of the swearing for them. The men agreed, and for months there was no known violation. However, the colonel had a teamster who had difficulty controlling his temper when the roads became bad.

The teamster, John Todd, one day was driving his mule team through a series of mudholes, when he let loose with a volley of energetic oaths. The colonel heard of it and

55. Nicolay, p. 350.

called John to account, "John," said he, "didn't you promise to let me do all the swearing of the regiment?"

"Yes, I did, colonel," he replied, "but the fact was, the swearing had to be done then or not at all, and you weren't there to do it."

Lincoln's story relieved the old man, and then the President wrote an order saving his son's life.[56] Humor has served several functions in this instance. It has eased the old man's tension, but, as a comic story, it has also given Lincoln a needed pause for thought about the situation at hand. While he tells the story, he can decide on the issue. Second, in telling the story, he has fastened upon that factor in the issue which is most crucial—its immediacy. Thus, the story reflects his thought processes and reveals what was the decisive element in the issue.

For Lincoln, politics that is concerned with the contingent and calls for ready action cannot be bound by fixed formulas. Often a decision must be made immediately, and in "the leg cases" of Lincoln there is displayed a primary concern for human beings over abstract formulas. In this concern, his politics and religion conjoined. He once told a friend that his religion was like that of an old man named Glenn: "When I do good, I feel good; when I do bad, I feel bad; and that's my religion" (p. 386).

This is not a politics of strong principles or purist ideals. Abraham Lincoln's politics is the typical American politics of compromise and expediency, yet practiced with an honesty and compassion for people that raise it to high statesmanship. The myth of Lincoln's sainthood *above politics* must be resisted, and the comedy of his politics is an excellent antidote to it.

The myth seeks to purge Lincoln's humor of vulgarity and invective. The stories and jokes that have come down to us have been effectively censored, though contemporary witnesses such as the previously quoted Dom Piatt refer to "jests so coarse that they could not be put to record." Sandburg also quotes John W. Forney, "He [Lincoln] would

56. McClure, p. 450.

shout with laughter over a French, German, or Negro anecdote, . . . he seemed to have read the character and to know the peculiarities of every leading man in Congress and the country, and would play off many an innocent joke on them." "Innocent," perhaps, but Forney adds that much of Lincoln's humor could not be revealed without offense to many good men. According to Sandburg, Forney also thought that reporting some of the more hilarious outpourings of Lincoln "would give unnecessary pain."[57]

Democratic politics beyond all other social practices combines antagonistic elements. It centers upon the clash of personalities and ambitions, ideas and issues, but politics requires that in these emotional confrontations of conflicting people the problems be resolved sociably and peacefully. For the thoroughly political man, aggressive humor may be psychologically necessary to relieve his tensions and channel his aggressions into peaceful outlets.

The aggressive humor of politics can be termed comic invective. Invective by itself is abusive denunciation or ridicule, but in politics it is most often salted with humor to maintain the uneasy peace of politics. In his early career, Lincoln almost overstepped the bounds of comic truce. In a series of letters to the editor of a newspaper, he (and Mary Todd, his wife-to-be, and her friend) lampooned a prominent Democratic politician, Shields, as a popinjay. The man took deep offense and challenged Lincoln to a duel that was narrowly averted. Lincoln regretted the incident and may have shouldered much of the blame for the letters on behalf of his female conspirators.[58]

In the settlement of the duel, Lincoln emerges eminently as a man of peace, and in taking offense, Shields appears to have been thin-skinned. Nevertheless, Lincoln did not forgo humorous invective as a political weapon or psychological outlet.

Anthony Gross relates that in Lincoln's first speech as a candidate for the state legislature, he employed comic ag-

57. Sandburg, *The War Years*, 3:308.
58. Randall, 1:61-62. Sandburg, *The Prairie Years*, 1:281-82.

gression to good purpose. In coming to the country town where his opponent lived, he saw on the roof of his rival's house a thin spire of iron. Lincoln inquired about it and was told that it was a lightning rod. When the time for the speech-making arrived, his rival spoke first. He said that he hoped his fellow citizens would not throw him out of office for this unknown man from out of the wilderness. Lincoln rebutted:

Friends, you don't know very much about me. I haven't had all the advantages that some of you have had; but if you did know everything about me that you might know, you would be sure that there was nothing in my character that made it necessary to put on my house a lightning-rod to save me from the just vengeance of Almighty God.[59]

In the debates that took place while Douglas and Lincoln were "stumping" Illinois in the 1858 election, Douglas remarked that his father was a cooper by trade. Lincoln, when his turn came, assented that Douglas's father was a cooper and a very good one at that, "for [here Lincoln gently bowed to Douglas] he has made one of the best whiskey casks I have ever seen."[60]

Another time Douglas told the crowd that when he first knew Lincoln, Lincoln was a grocery-keeper, and sold whiskey and cigars. He added, "Mr. Lincoln was a very good bar-tender." And the audience laughed at Lincoln.

Lincoln replied that he had kept a grocery and sometimes had sold whiskey, and that Mr. Douglas had been one of his best customers. Then he continued his reposte with: "I can also say this; that I have since left my side of the counter, while Mr. Douglas still sticks to his" (p. 444).

Lincoln's most persistent and troublesome political critics during the war were the radical Republicans. One time at the White House Lincoln was attempting to divert Senator Ben Wade of Ohio with a story. Wade shouted at him, "You are on the road to hell, sir, with this government, by your obstinacy, and you are not a mile off this minute."

59. Gross, p. 48.
60. McClure, p. 444.

Lincoln replied, "Senator, that is just about from here to the Capitol, is it not?"

Lincoln managed to remain cool and dignified in the face of a most offensive slight to himself and his office by countering Wade with a telling ridicule of Wade's own bailiwick. He emerges superior, but by comedy has preserved the tenuous peace necessary for any cooperation.

A much more gentle use of comic invective against the radical Republicans is illustrated in the famous Shadrach, Meshach, Abednego story of Lincoln that Sandburg relates:

Late one Sunday afternoon Lincoln was telling his caller, Senator John B. Henderson of Missouri, that Sumner and Senator Wilson, with Thaddeus Stevens, were constantly putting pressure on him to issue an emancipation proclamation. "They are coming and urging me, sometimes alone, sometimes in couples, sometimes all three together, but *constantly* pressing me." And with that Lincoln stepped to a window and preposterously enough, Sumner, Wilson and Stevens were coming toward the White House. Lincoln called to Henderson, pointed to the three approaching figures, and began telling of a school he went to when a boy in Indiana where the Bible was read out loud by the pupils. "One day we were standing up reading the account of the three Hebrew children in the fiery furnace. A little tow-headed fellow who stood beside me had the verse with the unpronounceable names. He mangled up Shadrach and Meshach woefully and finally went all to pieces on Abednego." For this the boy took a licking that made him cry. Then the class reading went on again, each boy in turn till the same tow-headed boy was reached again. As he looked in the Bible and saw the verse he was to read, he let out a pitiful yell. The schoolmaster asked what was the matter. The boy, pointing to the next verse, cried out, "Look there! look! there comes them same damn three fellers again!"[61]

If any single General in the Union Army really treated Lincoln obnoxiously, it was General George B. McClellan. Despite this, Lincoln retained his composure, did not offi-

61. Sandburg, *The War Years*, 1:566.

cially reprimand the General, and even appreciated his good qualities. But his comic aggressiveness manifested itself. He wrote:

Major-General McClellan:
I have just read your dispatch about sore-tongued and fatigued horses. Will you pardon me for asking what the horses of your army have done since the battle of Antietam that fatigues anything?

A. Lincoln[62]

Lincoln has sublimated his aggression and conveyed an unmistakable message at the same time. Along with the army, the constant demands of political patronage burdened the President, and many of his stories and some of his comic invective are directed to the issue. In a telegram in 1863 to two petitioners, he relieved himself thus:

Hon. J. X. Dubois, Hon. O. M. Hatch:
What nation do you desire General Allen to be made Quartermaster-general of? The nation already has a quarter-master-general. A. Lincoln (p. 195)

When Lincoln was pressed to appoint a particular man as Commissioner to the Hawaiian Islands, he replied, "Gentlemen, I am sorry to say that there are eight other applicants for that place, and they are all 'sicker' than your man."[63]

Finally, Lincoln joins mild invective with his sense of democracy in a comic story. Salmon Chase had resigned from the President's Cabinet (subsequently the resignation was rejected), and Lincoln commented:

Now this reminds me of what the Irishman said. His verdict was that "in this country one man is as good as another; and for the matter of that, very often a great deal

62. Lincoln, *Collected Works*, 5:474.
63. McClure, p. 162.

better." No, this Government does not depend upon the
life of any man. (pp. 232-33)

It is very difficult for the highest office-holder in government to use comedy for democratic leveling. But given the
egotism and overweening ambitions of Salmon Chase, and
the comic sense of proportion of Abraham Lincoln, the
deed was done. Lincoln later secured Seward's resignation,
and then he kept both resignations without acting on them,
saying to Senator Harris, "Yes, Judge, I can ride now, I've
got a pumpkin in each end of my bag. (When farmers rode
horseback to market two pumpkins in the bag thrown over
the horse made a balanced load)."[64] Thus, he balanced the
formidable rivals in his Cabinet against each other, maintained Presidential control, and comically expressed an ancient axiom of political balance.

The Popularity of Lincoln's Humor

One final task remains in this interpretation of Abraham
Lincoln. How is it that the supreme humorist of American
politics not only survived but flourished at the polls? In the
introduction to this study, Corwin's law of politics was
stated: "Never make people laugh. If you would succeed in
life, you must be solemn, solemn as an ass." And Richard
Strout was quoted as saying that "a mood of reverent solemnity is the tradition." Lincoln successfully defied the
tradition and may well have profited in popularity from his
political humor.

His storytelling and wit were well known, and his opponents attempted to use his comic reputation against him.
Sandburg has examined the issue. He cites newspaper accounts of a story about Lincoln's humor that the President
regarded as the best story about himself:

Two Quakeresses in a railroad coach were overheard in
conversation.

64. Sandburg, *The War Years*, 1:648.

"I think Jefferson (Davis) will succeed."
"Why does thee think so?"
"Because Jefferson is a praying man."
"And so is Abraham a praying man."
"Yes, but the Lord will think Abraham is joking."

Sandburg continues that Lincoln allowed this story to spread, and "he loved it. Nevertheless, his most deliberate public appearances and utterances encouraged no one to take him for a trifler" (1: 648). Still, a sharp separation between his political performance and his comic asides can not be the answer. We have seen that his comedy often was a part of his political performance. Moreover, a good part of his public reputation was based on his humor, not his performance, which was negative, at least for the first several years of the Civil War.

Sandburg relates that Lincoln's humor became an issue in the 1864 election. Prior to his renomination at the Baltimore convention, *The New York Herald* attempted to smear the President as a jester, "a joke incarnated, his election a very sorry joke, and the idea that such a man as he should be the President of such a country as this a very ridiculous joke." Sandburg states that "the joking habit of the President was considered a vulnerable point by the political opposition," and he quotes some of the news criticisms of Lincoln (3: 303).

Yet, in respect to Lincoln's humor, Sandburg concludes that "this side of him was momentous in one respect at least. It had brought him to folk masses as a reality, a living man who moved and thought and spoke, however rightly or wrongly," and he adds, "an American audience was prepared for Lincoln's humor, was seen in creative bursts of it" (3: 300-302). Several joke books were published in these years, such as *Honest Abe's Jokes* and *Old Abe's Jokes*, and Sandburg believes that the impression conveyed was "of an intensely alive man in the White House, serious though quizzical, close to the plow, with kinship for the common man and 'the folks.' " This impression significantly won "affection for him," and blunted "the edges of war hatred" (3: 316).

Finally, Sandburg holds that the legend woven of all this "played its part toward the end Lincoln wished—that people would say of the White House what the chess player said of the automaton, 'There is a man in there!' " (3: 321). Thus, the chief student of Lincoln's humor implies that the president consciously developed and deliberately courted a political personality of a gentle and common man of common sense, and he did it through his political comedy.

Sandburg believes that the humor of Lincoln was politically successful. He comes to this conclusion because he thinks that the stories and jokes were an intrinsic element of Lincoln's effective political style in dealing with others; because his humor helped create his popular image; and because, as Lincoln said of himself, he had lost only one election by popular vote, and that at the beginning of his political career. The U.S. Senate election in 1858, won by Douglas, was lost in the gerrymandered state legislature by Lincoln, who won the most popular votes.

Yet, the question remains why was Lincoln's humor politically acceptable, even endearing? Why does he stand alone in American history in his public use of humor as a positive instrument of politics? An answer can be attempted along the lines of Lincoln's personality and the functions of his humor.

First, the comic Lincoln was not a role played like that of a clown in a political circus. It was fully a part of his total personality and went along with his almost majestic ugliness. He was an unusually large and powerful man for his day. He is said to have resembled a rangy, rock-hewn, mountain man, or a hardbitten and proud yeoman settler. Then, again, as Sandburg delights in pointing out, his Falstaff is part of his inextricably intertwined Hamlet, and "the American President happened to join comic and mystic elements" (3: 302).

In short, the American people viewed the comic in Lincoln as an integral characteristic of the total man, whom they came to find fully acceptable. His humor was seen as a comely aspect of his homeliness, a graceful acceptance of fate. His humor, viewed in conjunction with his size and strength, appeared as gentleness, not weakness. His humor, when balanced against his seeming deep melancholy, was seen as a permissible safety valve for a man of sadness and concern for others. And the humor of a homespun, rustic man of the vernacular was viewed as the expressive common sense of the people's "Honest Abe."

The people did not consider the comic in Lincoln as condescending to them, or as frivolity with their public affairs. It was truly he himself, and its expression communicated to them a serious but compassionate statesmanship.

Popular communication is the major function of Lincoln's comic storytelling. The story's purpose is not primarily to entertain but to convey a message or make a point, albeit in a pleasing manner. The chief vehicle of Lincoln's public humor was his storytelling, and, again and again, one finds it compared to biblical parables and Aesopian fables. Sandburg begins his chapter on "Lincoln's Laughter—And His Religion" with a quotation from Sir Thomas Browne:

For unspeakable mysteries in the Scriptures are often delivered in a vulgar and illustrative way; and being written unto man, are delivered, not as they truly are, but as they may be understood. (3: 300)

Colonel McClure says of Lincoln's stories, "They contain lessons that could be taught so well in no other way. Every one of them is a sermon. Lincoln, like the Man of Galilee, spoke to the people in parables."[65]

This is the key to the mystery of the popularity of Lincoln's political humor. His story-telling is perceived as his natural and, for that time, authentically American way of popular communication. To a people whose chief, and often only, literary and educational resource was the Bible, Lin-

65. McClure, Preface A, B.

coln's humorous stories have a religious parallel. Their moral points were readily appreciated, and their comedy was taken as but pleasurable frosting.

We have seen that comic story-telling was a natural mode of social communication on the frontier, and Lincoln successfully transferred the method to the larger political arena. With him and the great body of mid-nineteenth-century Americans, it remained a natural and acceptable institution. Yet, it must be emphasized again that the comic function of the stories as political communication is more than frosting. Humor softened hostility as it sublimated aggression. It preserved flexibility in political situations as it riveted attention. Finally, as it eased conflict of issues and personalities, humor moved toward reconciliation amid disunion.

The irony of the popularity of Lincoln's comic storytelling is that it probably received considerable popular sanction from its biblical parallels and its frequent biblical referents and language. Yet, its humor is grounded in a kind of religious skepticism and uncertainty. Certainly, the Bible and its uses have not been considered to further a humorous world view.

The comic story is the heart of Lincoln's political humor and its popular success. Though it has ancient and primitive social antecedents, its political adaptation by Lincoln would seem to be a uniquely American institution. The combination of the conditions of frontier settlement with an advanced civilization produced something akin to an intellectualized saga or fable, clothed in comedy and containing refined analogical reasoning.

Lincoln adapted the mode for political communication, but he also seems to have taken its inner logical structure and transferred it to his serious political thought and expression. Thus, his thoughts on the Constitution and national survival have a kind of comic structure and even a kinship to his story of the Virgin and the Constitution. His second Inaugural Address in all of its solemnity employs word technique, skepticism, and dispassionate tolerance that reflect the philosophy of his humor. At the same time, his comic stories about religion and the punishment of the rebels have previewed the principles of the Address.

There has been little understanding and less use of the story-telling genre in the modern world of politics, despite its persistence and appeal in many forms throughout the history of our civilization. Not only the Socratic myth but also the Aristophanic political satire are kinds of comic storytelling, depending on analogical reasoning and having a good part of their appeal in a comic bemusement with wordplay and an alternative logic to that of social convention.

Yet, the analogical logic of storytelling is deeply conservative in its practical use of "the tried and true" to resolve new issues, for thereby it preserves social continuity and maintains basic values. On the other hand, storytelling may be the most democratic of modes of political education and communication. Its thought processes are the least abstract and are rooted in man's basic speech and sociability. And the comic clothing of the story captures our attention through our childlike wonder at words, our primitive resentment of social authority, and our vicarious sharing in the sublimated aggressions of comedy.

Paradoxically, democracy and its modern companion, science, may have precluded the development of storytelling in politics. Woe be unto the politician who is considered patronizing and less than profoundly serious to the sovereign people who must be treated as fully equal in their political intelligence. At the same time, modern science exalts as the intellectual ideal the purely factual and analytical approach to man's problems.

In our time, Adlai Stevenson cultivated Lincoln's humor, and he fully employed political humor in his own campaigns. His comic style certainly reveals humane values and a sense of the truly political in life. Oddly, his most fervent admirers were not of the people but among the intellectuals. The accident of the fatherly President Eisenhower, a true man of the vernacular, facilitated the overwhelming political rejection of Stevenson, but the latter's humor was not popular with the people. Probably Stevenson's political humor came across as a kind of literary art. When it was combined with his cultivated eloquence and his aristocratic ambience, his political humor well may have been viewed as patronizing and an aspect of the frivolous decadence of the upper classes.

Of course, a sense of humor may have departed from the popular politics of American democracy. Ideologies, moral crusades, and recurring wars take their toll. If so, a politics without humor is but a continuation of war by other means, and democracy itself becomes laughable. However, there are exceptions to this humorless politics in the public arena. The two most notable modern storytellers are Senators Barkley of Kentucky and Ervin of North Carolina. In their Southern and rustic manner they have carried on the frontier humor of an earlier America.

Possibly a political genius or a less harried politics will lead to a rediscovery of comic storytelling. My own recommendation for its political revival will have to follow that of Lincoln's. Not wishing to disappoint a request from a man, he wrote a recommendation to his friend Leonard Swett:

Dear Sir:
This introduces Mr. William Yates, who visits Bloomington on some business matter. He is pecuniarily responsible for anything he will say; and, in fact, for anything he will say on any subject.

Yours very truly,
A. Lincoln[66]

---

66. Lincoln, *Collected Works*, 3:513.

6

Comic Sages of Common Sense

Wherein sagacity clowns politically

Abraham Lincoln has been analyzed as democracy's greatest humorist-politician. Lincoln's comic storytelling was performed in the guise of a man of the people. In telling stories, he was developing a natural talent in a manner common to farm and frontier, but he was also continuing a tradition that extends back to the Bible and into early American history and forward to Will Rogers. Today's journalist-satirists are the heirs of that tradition, though they have a radically changed style.

The tradition of the comic sages cannot contain Lincoln, for he was preeminently a politician and his humor verges on philosophy. Yet, the popular appeal of his comic sagacity and the perception of his common humanity lie in the democratic stamp of this fourth kind of political humorist, the comic sage of common sense.

One student of this comic tradition has dubbed its practitioners "crackerbox philosophers."[1] Another writes of the tradition and its humorists as "Horse Sense in American Humor."[2] The popular image of Lincoln and his humorous style places him in the center of this comic tradition, and his storytelling is a common attribute of the comic sages. These humorists are seen by their audience as plain men of common sense who use their humor as a way of getting to the roots of things, as a practical way of puncturing sophistries and pomposities, and as a manner of conversing with their fellow commoners.

Most of the humorists are writers who create their popular images through their style, but even public personalities project the same qualities. Thus Benjamin Franklin, Davy Crockett, Abe Lincoln, Artemus Ward, Mark Twain, and Will Rogers all have certain traits in common. They were pictured by their contemporaries as plain men of the vernacular who embodied common sense and whose humor merely pointed up the results of the clash of practical wisdom with overrefined social stupidities.

It matters little that Benjamin Franklin was wealthy and a cosmopolitan bon vivant, Abraham Lincoln an affluent lawyer and successful politician, and Artemus Ward and Mark Twain the artfully created characters of professional writers Charles Farrar Browne and Samuel Clemens. Their humorous style and manner of thought were received popularly as authentically common and commonly gifted. The people saw these comic sages as themselves, only more so. To be exact, the people worshiped themselves in typical democratic fashion.

Benjamin Franklin, the first comic sage of historical note, cast himself as the homespun Yankee. His public character was created by his *Poor Richard's Almanac*, which is not much of a repository of political humor. His sallies in the direction of politics were in the form of hoaxes and parodies. His most directly political hoax was an article

1. Jennette Tandy, *Crackerbox Philosophers in American Humor and Satire* (New York: Columbia University Press, 1925).
2. Walter Blair, *Horse Sense in American Humor* (Chicago: University of Chicago Press, 1942).

placed in a London newspaper in 1747 that purported to be "The Speech of Miss Polly Baker." It pretends to be the defense of a woman before a court in Connecticut, on trial for having had a bastard child for the fifth time.

In it Miss Baker says, "I take the Liberty to say, that I think this law, by which I am punished, is both unreasonable in itself, and particularly severe with regard to me, who have always lived an inoffensive life in the neighborhood where I was born, and defy my Enimies (if I have any) to say I ever wrong'd Man, Woman or Child." She continues that she was seduced for the first time by a proposal of marriage that was never fulfilled. Her seducer was "that very person you all know; he is now become a Magistrate of this Country." She had hoped that the Magistrate would appear and aid her defense. She complains that this situation is "unjust and unequal, That my Betrayer and Undoer, the first cause of all my Faults and Miscarriages (if they must be deemed such) should be advanc'd to Honour and Power in the Government, that punishes my Misfortunes with Stripes and Infamy."

Polly Baker asserts that she has raised her children without expense to the community and "would have done it better, if it had not been for the heavy Charges and Fines I have paid." She asks, "Can it be a Crime (in the Nature of Things I mean) to add to the number of King's Subjects, in a new Country that really wants People? I own it, I should think it a Praisworthy, rather than a punishable Action."

She insists, "I have debauched no other Woman's Husband, nor enticed any Youth; these Things I never was charg'd with, nor has any one the least Cause of Complaint against me, unless, perhaps, the Minister, or Justice, because I have had Children without being married, by which they have missed a Wedding Fee." Polly Baker appeals that she would like to be married and has all the qualifications of a good wife. It is the bachelors who will not marry that should be fined:

if you, Gentlemen, must be making Laws, do not turn natural and useful actions into Crimes, by your Prohibitions. But take into your wise Consideration, the great and growing Number of Bachelors in the Country, many of whom from the mean Fear of the Expenses of a Family, have never sincerely and honorably courted a Woman in their Lives; and by their Manner of Living, leave unproduced (which is little better than murder) Hundreds of their Posterity to the Thousandth Generation. Is this not a greater Offence against the Publick Good, than mine? Compel them then, by Law, either to Marriage, or to pay double the Fine of Fornication every Year. What must poor young Women do, whom Custom have forbid to solicit the Men, and whom cannot force themselves upon Husbands, when the Laws take no care to provide them any; and yet severely punish them if they do their Duty without them.

Polly Baker closes by saying that, in carrying out "the duty of the first and great command of nature and nature's God, *Increase and multiply*," she should have a statue erected to her memory.[3] Benjamin Franklin is not playing the role of a crackerbox philosopher here. However, his Polly Baker is of the lower classes, and she does criticize the law and expose its illogic in the language of a plain woman with but sound common sense. The comedy is in the success of the hoax, and then, within the hoax, in the satirizing of the law, its officials, and social convention.

Already, at this time in colonial history, there is the implicit assertion within the comic framework of a natural law against positive laws, of the absurdity of governmental interference with individual welfare, and of the political hypocrisy of governmental officials. Moreover, the prophetic rationality of comic sense is attested to in Polly Baker's speech by the implicit declaration of women's rights.

In a sense, Franklin's Polly Baker hoax took root among the comic sages. Much of their political comedy took the form of letters or articles in newspapers and almanacs purporting to be the observations of simple but shrewd men of the farm or frontier. One of the most popular of such characters was Major Jack Downing, a character created by

3. Leon Harris, *The Fine Art of Political Wit* (New York: E. P. Dutton & Co., Inc., 1964), pp. 41-44.

Seba Smith of Maine. Jennette Tandy writes that this is "the first attempt to presentation of the unlettered philosopher and critic in American literature." Its political humor is in good part occasioned in reaction to the advent of Jacksonian democracy, and she adds:

It was a clever stroke which set this latter argument against unbridled democracy in the mouth of the Yankee hobbledehoy. The comic countryman had by rights the ear of many who were deaf to the ordinary appeals of editor and orator. He could insinuate many things forbidden. The rustic observer could innocently betray official double-dealing. He could poke fun wherever he chose, tell all manner of slighting stories about the great, and satirize the humble Democrat by revealing his own gullibility.[4]

The first letter from Jack Downing appeared in the *Portland Courier* in 1830. In it Jack tells of happenings in the Maine legislature, and he ridicules partisanship with a seemingly innocent indirection. In part of his letter "To Cousin Ephraim Downing, Up in Downingville," he writes:

They kept disputing most all the time the first two days about a poor Mr. Roberts from Waterborough. Some said he shouldn't have a seat because he adjourned the town meeting and wasn't fairly elected. Others said it was no such thing, and that he was elected as fairly as any of 'em. And Mr. Roberts himself said he was, and said he could bring men that would swear to it, and good men too. But, notwithstanding all this when they came to vote, they got three or four majority that he shouldn't have a seat. And I thought it was a needless piece of cruelty for they wasn't crowded and there was a number of seats empty. But they would have it so, and the poor man had to go and stand up in the lobby.
Then they disputed awhile about a Mr. Fowler's having a seat. Some said he shouldn't have a seat, because when he was elected some of his votes were given for his father. But they were more kind to him than they were to Mr. Roberts, for they voted that he should have a seat; and I

4. Tandy, p. 25.

suppose it was because they thought he had a lawful right to inherit whatever was his father's. They all declared there was no party politics about it, and I don't think there was; for I noticed that all who voted that Mr. Roberts *should not* have a seat, voted that Mr. Fowler *should*. So as they all voted both ways, they must have been conscientious, and I don't see how there could be any party about it. (pp. 26-27)

Tandy continues that "Jack, when not furthering his own ambitions, is busy making mountains out of molehills. He is at his best in the exaggeration of some unimportant incident" (p. 28). Seba Smith sets the stage for the political humor of the comic sage, but his own humor is impartially anti-political and his satires of political leaders are droll rather than vicious.

A New Yorker, Charles Augustus Davis, appropriated the Downing character for his own purposes in 1833, and in his hands the political humor became sharper. He continued the vulgarity and rusticism of Smith, but added the homely parable to it. Tandy reprints the parable of "Peleg Bissell's churn, the most famous of them all." In the parable the Major is serving as an advisor to President Andrew Jackson, "the Gineral":

The Gineral was amazingly tickled tother day. Peleg Bissell—(you know, Peleg, who is all the while whittlin, and sawin, makin clocks and apple-parers, and churns, and lives nigh Seth Sprague's school house, down to Downingville) well, Peleg sent the Gineral a new churn of his own invention; and he calls it the "Jackson churn"—and he wants a patent for it. The cute critter says, in his letter to the Gineral, that that 'ere churn is just like his government—it's only got one wheel—and a smasher—and that it will make more butter than any other churn, and out of most anything. The Gineral is so tickled with it, he will set and turn it nearly all day. Says he, "Major, I like this 'ere churn amazingly; that Bissell is a knowin' fellow. If this churn had been made by Congress, it would have more than 50 wheels and springs, and make no more butter arter all. Major, says he, "tell Peleg I thank him, and send him a patent." (p. 33)

One of the most famous of the comic sages is partly literary artifice and partly historical fact. He is Davy Crockett, Tennessee Congressman and frontiersman, who wrote and related some of the stories of himself, but whose public personality was appropriated by professional writers for continuing production. There is little of the Crockett humor that is currently comical. Yet, within his stories, one finds the typical ridicule of politics vulgarly related by a shrewd and somewhat scoundrelly man out of the earthy events of frontier living.

In one of Crockett's best-known stories, "A Useful Coon Skin," he is campaigning in the backwoods for Congress. The story centers on the audience to his speechmaking demanding a liberal dispensing of libations: "They could not listen to me on such a dry subject as the welfare of the nation until they had something to drink, and that I must treat them." Crockett is broke, but by good fortune shoots a coon and trades its skin for whiskey for his audience. He treats the voters and then,

having soon despatched the value of the coon, I went out and mounted the stump without opposition, and a clear majority of the voters followed me to hear what I had to offer for the good of the nation. Before I was halfway through, one of my constituents moved that they would hear the balance of my speech after they had washed down the first part with some more of Job Snelling's extract of cornstalk and molasses. The question being put, it was carried unanimously. We adjourned to the shanty, and on the way I began to reckon that the fate of the nation pretty much depended upon my shooting another coon.[5]

Like Jack Downing, Davy Crockett, in the frontier guise of the commoner, puts down the commoners. They must be politically bribed to think of "the welfare of the nation," and their attention must be kept by continuing the stimulation. In effect, "the fate of the nation" comes to depend on political pay-off to the voters. But Crockett does not pre-

5. Blair, pp. 48-49.

sent himself as a moralist. In the story he is enabled to continue the largess to his constituents through the device of a retrievable coonskin. Through trickery, he keeps reselling the same coonskin to the bar owner. Thus politics taxes business over and over again on what it already owns, to pay off the voters in return for staying in office.

Another comic sage of the ante-bellum period, much more of a literary fabrication than Davy Crockett, was Hosea Biglow, the brain child of James Russell Lowell. Walter Blair titles his commentary on Lowell's creation "A Brahmin Dons Homespun" (pp. 77-101). James Russell Lowell was a scion of the Massachusetts Lowells, as Blair says, "the most exclusive caste in New England, "dating back to the Mayflower, well-to-do, and conservative. Yet when scion James, abolitionist, wishes to become politically influential, he writes:

Fust comes the blackbirds clatt'rin in tall trees, and settlin' things in windy Congresses,—Queer politicians, though, for I'll be skinned ef all on them don't head against the wind.
                         —Hosea Bigelow, Jaalam, Massachusetts

Between 1846 and 1848, James Russell Lowell wrote and published a large number of these sayings in "bumpkin doggerel." Their popularity was immense, and Lowell knew what he was doing. Blair quotes him:

We have got now to that pitch when uneducated men (self-educated they are called) are all the rage, and the only learned animals that continue to be popular are pigs. The public will rush after a paper which they are told is edited by a practical printer . . . [Did he mean Franklin?]. We shall ere long see advertised "easy lessons in Latin by a gentleman who can testify that he knows no more of the language than Mr. Senator Webster." (p. 93)

Blair adds that Lowell commented, "I have struck the old hulk of the Public between wind and water," and years later he said, "The success of my experiment soon began not only to astonish me, but to make me feel the responsibility of knowing that I held in my hand a weapon instead of the fencing-stick I had supposed" (p. 93).

Lowell was abolitionist and against the Mexican War, but his view of politics in general is evident. In "The Pious Editor's Creed," the editor says that he believes in "special ways of praying and converting," and then reveals those ways:

> I mean [I believe] in preyin' till one busts
> On wut the party chooses,
> An' in convartin' public trusts
> To very privit uses. (p. 96)

Lowell had discovered a secret of the dialectic of democracy; it must be in a democratic dialect and, preferably, salted with broad humor. Simple wordplay (praying and preyin') and the spice of comic invective are a part of the formula. In short, the people distrust and resent *their* own politics and government.

One last illustration from Lowell's "What Mr. Robinson Thinks" demonstrates his conservatism and his doubts of the rationality of the sovereign populace. In the poem Bigelow supports the Whig Governor Briggs against Caleb Cushing, a Mexican War general, in the Massachusetts gubernatorial election. Obviously, John P. Robinson is a forerunner of John Q. Public. Several passages from the poem read:

> Guvener B. is a sensible man;
> He stays to his home an' looks arter his folks;
> He draws his furrer ez straight ez he can,
> An' into nobody's tater-patch pokes;
> But John B.
> Robinson he
> Sez he wunt vote for Guvener B.
>
> Gineral C. is a dreffle smart man:
> He's ben on all sides that give places or pelf;

> But consistency was still a part of his plan,—
> He's bin true to *one* party—an' thet is himself;—
> So John B.
> Robinson he
> Sez he shall vote for Gineral C.

And Lowell's Bigelow concludes the poem:

> Parsun Selbur sez *he* never heered in his life
> Thet th' apostles rigged out in their swaller-tail coats,
> An' marched round in front of a drum an' a fife,
> To get some on 'em office, an' some on 'em votes;
> But John B.
> Robinson he
> Sez they didn't know everythin' down in Judee.

> Wal, it's a marcy we've gut folks to tell us
> The rights and the wrongs o' these matters, I vow,—
> God sends country lawyers, and other wise fellers,
> To start the world's team when it gits in a slough;
> Fer John B.
> Robinson he
> Sez the world'll go right, ef he hollers out Gee![6]

Vox populi, vox dei has been rendered comically "the world'll go right, ef he hollers out Gee!" The full poem also ridicules the military and the foreign policy of manifest destiny, perennial targets of American political humor. Finally, in the best manner of the comic twist, it should also be noted that the man of the demos, Bigelow, is anti-democratic. Lowell employs the vulgar against the *vulgus*.

Lowell was democratically conservative and anti-war, besides being an abolitionist. The contradictoriness of these positions may well have lent itself to his comic perspective. But in the Civil War period his abolitionism became dominant, and his writings and opinions became harsh and vindictive. Dogmatic certainty triumphed over comedy, and Lowell's political humor ceased.

6. Kenneth S. Lynn, ed., *The Comic Tradition in America* (Garden City, N.Y.: Doubleday and Co., 1958), pp. 178-81.

There were many comic sages of common sense in the Civil War period, but most of them were afflicted with closed-mind partisanship of the struggle. Their comedy is a victim of that failure of politics. Nevertheless, running through much of their humor is a continuing hostility to government and politicians.

The two comic sages of the period who could be singled out as more broadminded and less politically venomous are Abraham Lincoln and Artemus Ward (Charles Farrar Browne). President Lincoln, a practicing politician, is the man whose humor is most political and most durable. His comic political genius has been explored in the previous chapter, so let us look briefly at Artemus Ward to show that "American political humor as usual" continued throughout the war. In an "Interview with President Lincoln" Ward relates:

I hav no politics. Nary a one. I'm not in the bizniss. If I was I spose I should holler versiffrusly in the streets at nite, and go home to Betsy Jane smellen of coal ile and gin in the mornin. I should go to the Poles arly. I should stay there all day. I should see to it that my nabers was thar. I should git carriges to take the kripples, the infirm and the indignant that. I should be on guard agin frauds and sich. I should be on the look out for the infamous lies of the enemy, got up jest be4 elecshun for perlitical effeck. When all was over, and my candydate was elected, I should move heving & arth—so to speak—until I got orfice, which If I didn't git a orfice I should turn around and abooze the Administration with all my mite and maine. But I'm not in the bizniss. I'm in a far more respectful bizniss nor what pollertics is. I wouldn't giv two cents to be a Congresser. The wus insult I ever received was when sertin citizens of Baldinsville axed me to run fur the Legislater. Sez I, "My frends, dostest think I'd stoop to that there?" They turned as white as a sheet. I spoke in my most orfullest tones, & they knowd I wasn't to be trifled with. They slunked out of site to onct.

In the story, Artemus Ward goes on to visit the new

President, introduces himself, explains that he is not there in search of appointment to public office, and quickly becomes Lincoln's friend against the horde of office-seekers besieging the President. Ward continues:

"Repose in Abraham's Buzzum!" sed one of the orfice seekers, his idee being to git orf a goak at my expense.

"Wall," sez I, "ef all you fellers repose in that there Buzzum thare'll be mity poor nussin for sum of you!" whereupon Old Abe buttoned his weskit clear up and blusht like a maidin of sweet 16. Jest at this pint of the conversation another swarm of orfice-seekers arrove & cum pilin into the parler. Sum wanted post-orfices, sum wanted collectorships, sum wantid furrin missions, and all wanted sumthin. I thought Old Abe would go crazy. He hadn't more than had time to shake hands with 'em, before another tremenjis crowd cum porein onto his premises. His house and dooryard was now perfeckly overflowed with orfice-seekers, all clameruss for a immejit interview with Old Abe. One man from Ohio, who had about seven inches of corn whisky into him, mistook me for Old Abe, and addrest me as "The Prahayrie Flower of the West!" Thinks I, *you* want a offiss putty bad. Another man with a gold heded cane and a red nose, told Old Abe he was "a seckind Washington & the Price of the Boundless West."

Sez I, "Squire, you wouldn't take a small post-offis if you could git it, would you?"

Sez he, "A patrit is abuv them things, sir!"

"There's a putty big crop of patrits this season, aint there, Squire?" sez I, whan *another* crowd of offiss-seekers pored in. The house, dooryard, barn, & woodshed was now all full, and when *another* crowd cum I told 'em not to go away for want of room, as the hog-pen was still empty. One patrit got into the chimney and slid down in the parler where Old Abe was endeverin to keep the hungry pack of orfice-seekers from chawin him up alive without benefit of clergy. The minit he reached the fire-place, he jumpt up, brusht the soot out of his eyes and yelled: "Don't make eny pintment at the Spunkville post-offiss till you've read my papers. All the respectful men in our town is signers to that there dockymint!"

Ward goes into a rage of comic rhetoric at the office-seekers and bullies them out of the President's house. Ward then writes:

"How kin I ever repay you, Mr. Ward, for your kindness?" sed Old Abe, advancin and shakin me warmly by the hand. "How kin I repay you, sir?"

"By givin the whole country a good, sound administration. By poerin ile upon the troubled waturs, North and South. By pursooin a patriotic, firm, and just course, and then, if any State wants to secede, let 'em Sesesh!"

"How 'bout my Cabinit, Mister Ward?" sed Abe.

"Fill it up with Showmen, sir! Showmen is devoid of politics. They hain't got any principles! They know how to cater for the public. They know what the public wants, North and South. Showmen, sir, is honest men. Ef you doubt their literary ability, look at their posters, and see small bills! Ef you want a Cabinit as is a Cabinit, fill it up with showmen, but don't call on me. The moral wax figger perfeshun musn't be permitted to go down while there's a drop of blood in these vains! . Linkin, I wish you well! Ef Powers or Walcutt wus to pick out a model for a beautiful man, I scacely think they'd sculp you; but ef you do the fair thing by your country, you'll make as putty a angel as any of us! A. Linkin, use the talents which Nature has put into you judishusly and firmly, and all will be well! A. Linkin, adoo!"

Ward concludes the story with his and Lincoln's shaking hands and exchanging pictures, so that they could look upon each other's "liniments" from their distant occupations, "he at the hellum of the ship of State, and I at the hellum of the show bizness—admittance only 15 cents."[7] The fictional occupation of Artemus Ward is that of the owner of a traveling waxwork museum. His author, Charles Farrar Browne, was a journalist who did give comic lectures based on his fictional character throughout the United States and in Britain.

7. Arthur P. Dudden, ed., *The Assault of Laughter: A Treasury of American Political Humor* (South Brunswick and New York: Thomas Yoseloff, Publisher, 1962), pp. 94-99.

Artemus Ward in the story displays the usual contempt for politics and draws humor from the popular disrepute in which it is held. He graphically exaggerates, but soundly scores, the problem of public office-holding. In his familiarity with the President, he engages in democratic leveling. Then he draws an interesting parallel between politics and show business and decides on "the hellum of show bizness—admittance only 15 cents." Observing Lincoln and politics, the showman has decided that the cost of admission in the allied industry is too high.

The friendliness of Artemus Ward's sarcasms toward politics is not matched by any of his acquaintances. In fact, the most famous comic sage, Mark Twain (Samuel Clemens), is fully hostile to politics. Twain's mordant wit is not at its best in this field, but it does convey very effectively the American disdain for politics. In a "Letter Read at a Dinner of the Knights of St. Patrick," in 1876, Twain's anti-politics runs rampant:

To the Chairman:
Dear Sir,—I am very sorry that I cannot be with the Knights of St. Patrick to-morrow evening. In this centennial year we ought to find a peculiar pleasure in doing honor to the memory of a man whose good name has endured through fourteen centuries. We ought to find pleasure in it for the reason that at this time we naturally have a fellow-feeling for such a man. He wrought a great work in his day. He found Ireland a prosperous republic, and looked about him to see if he might find some useful thing to turn his hand to. He observed that the president of that republic was in the habit of sheltering his great officials from de-served punishment, so he lifted up his staff and smote him, and he died. He found that the secretary of war had been so unbecomingly economical as to have laid up $12,000 a year out of a salary of $8,000, and he killed him. He found that the secretary of the interior always prayed over every separate and distinct barrel of salt beef that was intended for the unconverted savage, and then kept that beef him-self, so he killed him also. He found that the secretary of

the navy knew more about suspicious claims than he did about handling a ship, and he at once made an end of him. He found that a very foul private secretary had been engineered through a sham trial, so he destroyed him. He discovered that the congress which pretended to prodigious virtue was very anxious to investigate an ambassador who had dishonored the country abroad, but was equally anxious to prevent the appointment of any spotless man to a similar post; that this congress had no God but party; no system of morals but party policy; no vision but a bat's vision, and no reason or excuse for existing anyhow. Therefore, he massacred that congress to the last man.

When he had finished his great work, he said, in his figurative way, "Lo, I have destroyed all the reptiles in Ireland."

St. Patrick had no politics; his sympathies lay with the right—that was politics enough. When he came across a reptile, he forgot to inquire whether he was a democrat or a republican, but simply exalted his staff and "let him have it." Honored be his name—I wish we had him here to trim us up for the centennial. But that cannot be. His staff, which was the symbol of real, not sham reform, is idle. However, we still have with us the symbol of Truth— George Washington's little hatchet—for I know where they've buried it.

Yours truly,
Mark Twain (pp. 211-12)

Mark Twain opposes to politics and partisanship that which is "right"; he opposes to "sham reform," "real reform"; and he proclaims his possession of the "Truth," though politics has buried it. Twain's extremism carries him to the borderline of political humor. He is restrained from outright censoriousness only by the humor in his outrageousness. Comic exaggeration is a constant in American political humor, and Mark Twain, in his bitterness toward life, builds most of his parodies of politics on gross exaggeration. In his "The Facts Concerning the Recent Resignation," he ridicules governmental employment. The parody is in the form of an explanation of the resignation of a clerk of the Senate Committee on Conchology who was employed for a total of six days. In concluding his report, the clerk writes:

I am done with official life for the present. Let those clerks who are willing to be imposed on remain. I know numbers of them, in the Departments, who are never informed when there is to be a Cabinet meeting, whose advice is never asked about war, or finance, or commerce, but the heads of the nation, any more than if they were not connected with Government, and who actually stay in their offices day after day and work! They know their importance to the nation, and they unconsciously show it in their bearing, and the way they order their sustenance at the restaurant—but they work. I know one who has to paste all sorts of little scraps from the newspaper into a scrapbook—sometimes as many as eight or ten scraps a day. He doesn't do it well, but he does it as well as he can. It is very fatiguing. It is exhausting to the intellect. Yet he only gets eighteen hundred dollars a year. With a brain like his, that young man could amass thousands and thousands of dollars in some other pursuit, if he chose to do it. But no—his heart is with his country, and he will serve her as long as she has got a scrap-book left. And I know clerks that don't know how to write very well, but such knowledge as they possess they nobly lay at the feet of their country, and toil on and suffer for twenty-five hundred dollars a year. What they write has to be written over again by other clerks sometimes; but when a man has done his best for his country, should his country complain? Then there are clerks that have no clerkships, and are waiting, and waiting, and waiting, for a vacancy—waiting patiently for a chance to help their country out—and while they are waiting, they only get barely two thousand dollars a year for it. It is sad—it is very, very sad. When a member of Congress has a friend who is gifted, but has no employment wherein his great powers may be brought to bear, he confers him upon his country, and gives him a clerkship in a department. And there that man has to slave his life out, fighting documents for the benefit of a nation that never thinks of him, never sympathizes with him—and all for two thousand or three thousand dollars a year. When I shall have completed my list of all the clerks in the several departments, with my statement of what they have to do, and what they get for it, you will see that there are not half enough clerks, and that what there are do not get half enough pay. (pp. 209-10)

Many of Mark Twain's comments on politics were in the form of bitter witticisms. He seems to have had little enjoyment or understanding of politics as a kind of drama. On the contrary, the journalist Finley Peter Dunne, creator of Mr. Dooley, has a full appreciation of the comic exaggeration and dramatic make-believe of politics. His Mr. Dooley is well situated to convey this attitude. He is the cynical, philosophic saloonkeeper of Archey Road in Chicago at the turn of the century. Mr. Dooley and his clients represent the new citizenry of the United States and their urban habitat. Appropriately, they also represent the most naturally political of ethnic groups succeeding the English in settling in the United States—the Irish. And Dunne writes their dialogue in a phonetic approximation of an Irish brogue.

Perhaps the most comically exaggerated of the Mr. Dooley dialogues is "Troubles of a Candidate" on the election of 1900. In it, Mr. Hennessy, a saloon patron, laments to Mr. Dooley the dullness of the campaign. Dooley replies:

I begin to see signs iv th' good times comin' again. 'Twas on'y th' other day me frind Tiddy Rosenfelt opened th' battle mildly by insinuatin' that all dimmycrats was liars, horse thieves an' arnychists. 'Tis thrue he apologized fr that be explainin' that he didn't mean all dimmycrats but on'y those that wudden't vote fr Mack but I think he'll take th' copper off befure manny weeks. A ladin' dimmycratic rayformer has suggested that Mack though a good man fr an idjiot is surrounded be th' vilest scoundhrels iver seen in public life since th' days iv Joolyus Caesar. Th' Sicrety iv th' Threeasury has declared, that Mr. Bryan in sayin' that silver is not convartible be th' terms iv th' Slatthry bankin' law iv 1870,

an' th' sicond clause iv th' threaty iv Gansville, has committed th' onpard'nable pollytical sin iv so consthructin' th'
facts as to open up th' possibility iv wan not knowin' thrue
position iv affairs, misundhersthandin' intirely. If he had
him outside he'd call him a liar. Th' raypublicans have
proved that Willum Jennings Bryan is a thraitor be th'
letther written be Dr. Lem Stoggins, th' cillybrated anti-
thought agytator iv Spootne Duyvil to Aggynaldoo in which
he calls upon him to do nawthin' till he hears fr'm th' doc.
Th' letther was sint through th' postal authorities an' as they
have established no post-office in Aggynaldoo's hat they
cudden't deliver it an' they opened it. Upon r-readin' th'
letther Horace Plog iv White Horse, Minnesota, has wrote
to Willum Jennings Bryan declarin' that if he (Plog) iver
went to th' Ph'lippeens, which he wud've done but fr th'
way th' oats was sproutin' in th' stack, an' had been hit with
a bullet he'd ixpict th' Coroner to hold Bryan to th' gran'
jury. This was followed be th' publication iv a letther fr'm
Oscar L. Swub iv East Persepalis, Ohio, declarin' that his
sister heerd a cousin iv th' man that wash'd buggies in a
livery stable in Canton say Mack's hired man tol' him
Mack'd be hanged befure he'd withdraw th' ar-rmy fr'm
Cuba.

Oh, I guess th' campaign is goin' as well as cud be ix-
picted. I see be th' raypublican pa-apers that Andhrew
Carnegie has come out fr Bryan an' has conthributed wan
half iv his income or five hundhred millyon dollars to th'
campaign fund. In th' dimmycratic pa-apers I r-read that
Chairman Jim Jones has interciptied a letther fr'm the Prince iv Wales to Mack congratulatin' him on his appintmint
as gineltman-in-waitin' to th' queen. A dillygation iv Mor-
mons has started fr'm dimmycratic headquarthers to thank
Mack fr his manly stand in favor iv polygamy an' th'
raypublican comity has undher con-sideration a letther fr'm
long term criminals advisin' their colleagues at large to vote
fr Willum Jennings Bryan, th' frind iv crime.

Mr. Dooley continues with examples of the flagrant charges
and countercharges that can be expected in the campaign.
He then pictures the candidates' dramatization of their personalities:

I tell ye, Hinnissy, th' candydate is kept movin'. Whin he sees a dillygation pikin' up th' lawn he must be r-ready. He makes a flyin' leap fr th' chairman, seizes him by th' throat an' says: 'I thank ye fr th' kind sintimints you ye have conveyed. I am, indeed, as ye have remarked, th' riprisintative iv th' party iv manhood, honor, courage, liberality an' American Thraditions. Take that back to Jimmy Jones an' tell him to put it in his pipe an' smoke it.' With which he bounds into th' house an' locks the dure while th' baffled conspirators goes down to a costumer an' changes their disguise. If th' future prisidint hadn't been quick on th' dhraw he'd been committed to a policy iv sthranglin' all the girl babies at birth.

No, 'tis no aisy job bein' a candydate, an' 'twud be no easy job if th' game iv photygraphs was th' on'y wan th' candydates had to play. Willum Jennings Bryan is photygraphed smilin' back at his smilin' corn fields, in a pair iv blue overalls with a scythe in his hand borrid fr'm th' company that's playin' "Th' Ol' Homestead," at th' Lincoln Gran' Opry House. Th' nex' day Mack is seen mendin' a rustic chair with a monkey wrinch, Bryan has a pitcher took in th' act iv puttin' on a shirt marked with th' union label, an' they'se another photygraph iv Mack carryin' a scuttle iv coal up th' cellar stairs. An' did ye iver notice how much th' candydates look alike, an' how much both iv thim looks like Lydia Pinkham? Thim wondherful boardhin'-house smiles that our gifted leaders wears, did ye iver see annythin' so entrancin'? Whin th' las' photygrapher has packed his ar-rms homeward I can see th' gr-reat men retirin' to their rooms an' lettin' their faces down fr a few minyits befure puttin' thim up again in curl-pa-apers fr th' nex' day display. Glory be, what a relief 'twill be fr wan iv thim to raysume permanently th' savage or fam'ly breakfast face th' mornin' afther iliction! What a raylief 'twill be to no fr sure that th' man at th' dure bell is on'y th' gas collector an' isn't loaded with a speech iv thanks in behalf iv th' Spanish Gover'mint! What a relief to snarl at wife an' frinds wanst more, to smoke a seegar with th' thrust magnate that owns th' cider facthry near th' station, to take ye'er nap in th' afthernoon undisthurbed be th' chirp iv th' snap-shot! 'Tis th' day afther iliction I'd like f'r to be a candydate, Hinnissy, no matther how it wint.[8]

Finley Peter Dunne's ability to caricature a candidate and the humor of democratic leveling are joyously present in the comic classic of all book reviews. Mr. Dooley discusses with Mr. Hennessy Theodor Roosevelt's book on his adventures in Cuba in the Spanish-American War. Mr. Dooley says:

'Tis "Th' Biography iv a Hero be Wan who Knows," 'Tis "Th' Darin' Exploits iv a Brave Man be an Actual Eye Witness." 'Tis "Th' Account iv th' Desthruction iv Spanish Power in th' Ant Hills," as it fell fr'm th' lips iv Tiddy Rosenfelt an' was took down be his own hands. Ye see 'twas this way, Hinnissy, as I r-read th' book. Whin Tiddy was blowed up in th' harbor iv Havana he instantly con-cluded they must be war. He debated th' question long an' earnestly an' fin'lly passed a jint resolution declarin' war. So far so good. But there was no wan to carry it on. What shud he do? I will lave th' janial author tell th' story in his own wurruds.

Mr. Dooley goes on to recount, supposedly in Roosevelt's words, the most ridiculously egotistical and self-serving account of the latter's heroics in taking San Juan Hill and conquering Cuba. Dunne concludes Mr. Dooley's review this way:

"I have thried, Hinnissy," Mr. Dooley continued, "to give you a fair idee iv th' contints iv this remarkable book, but what I've tol' ye is on'y what Hogan calls an outline iv th' principal pints. Ye'll have to r-read th' book ye'ersilf to get a thrue conciption. I haven't time f'r to tell ye th' wurruk Tiddy did in ar-rmin' an' equippin' himself, how he fed himsilf, how he steadied himsilf in battle an' encouraged himsilf with a few well-chosen wurruds whin th' sky was

8. Finley Peter Dunne, *Mr. Dooley's Philosophy* (New York and London: Harper & Brothers, 1906), pp. 229-34.

darkest. Ye'll have to take a squint into th' book ye'ersilf to l'arn thim things."

"I won't do it," said Mr. Hennessy. "I think Tiddy Rosenfelt is all r-right an' if he wants to blow his hor-rn lave him do it."

"Thrue f'r ye," said Mr. Dooley, "an' if his valliant deeds didn't get into this book 'twud be a long time befure they appeared in Shafter's histhry iv th' war. No man that bears a gredge again' himsilf 'll iver be governor iv a state. An' if Tiddy done it all he ought to say so an' relieve th' suspinse. But if I was him I'd call th' book 'Alone in Cubia.'" (pp. 13-18)

There is far more than ridicule in Dunne's perception of politics. His understanding of the necessary egotism and self-dramatization of politics allows him to ridicule Roosevelt without malice and with some good nature. His use of Mr. Hennessy as Dooley's foil permits Dunne to show the popularity of the very politics he is comically ridiculing.

Probably the prime target for the ridicule of high office in the United States is the vice-presidency. Aside from succeeding to the presidency in case of the incumbent's death or severe disability, constitutionally the Vice-President has the relatively unimportant job of presiding over the Senate. He may also do odd assignments for the President at the latter's pleasure. Consequently, the vice-presidency is the favored butt for jokes about politicians, and Mr. Dooley has a glorious time with it, as can be seen in these excerpts from "The Vice-President."

"It's sthrange about th' vice-prisidincy," said Mr. Dooley. "Th' prisidincy is th' highest office in th' gift iv th' people. Th' vice-prisidincy is th' next highest an' th' lowest. It isn't a crime exactly. Ye can't be sint to jail f'r it, but it's a kind iv a disgrace. It's like writin' anonymous letters. At a convintion nearly all th' dillygates lave as soon as they've nommynated th' prisidint f'r fear was iv thim will be nommynated f'r vice-prisidint. They offered it to me frind Joe

Cannon, and th' language he used brought th' blush iv shame to th' cheeks iv a naygur dillygate fr'm Allybamy. They thried to hand it to Hinnery Cabin Lodge, an' he wept bitterly. They found a man fr'm Wisconsin, who was in dhrink, an' had almost nommynated him whin his wife came in an' dhragged him away fr'm timptation. Th' way they got Sinitor Fairbanks to accipt was be showin' him a pitcher iv our gr-reat an' noble prisidint thryin' to jump a horse over a six-foot fence. An' they on'y prevailed upon Hinnery Davis to take this almost onequalled honor be tellin' him that th' raison th' Sage iv Esoopus didn't speak earlier was because he has weak lungs."

And Mr. Dooley comically covers the constitutional duties of the second highest office in the land:

"Th' feelin' iv th' vice-prisidint about th' prisidint's well-bein' is very deep. On rainy days he calls at th' White House an' begs th' prisidint not to go out without his rubbers. He has Mrs. Vice-Prisidint knit him a shawl to protect his throat again' th' night air. If th' prisidint has a touch iv fever th' vice-prisidint gets a touch iv fever himself. He has th' doctor on th' 'phone durin' th' night. 'Doc, I hear th' prisidint is onwell,' he says. 'Cud I do annything fr him,—anything like dhrawin' his salary or appintin' th' postmasther at Injynnapolis?' It is princip'lly Hinnissy, because iv th' vice-prisidint that most iv our prisidints have enjoyed such rugged health. Th' vice-prisidint guards th' prisidint, an' th' prisidint, afther sizin' up th' vice-prisidint, concludes that it wud be betther fr th' counthry if he shud live yet awhile. 'D'ye know,' says th' prisidint to th' vice-prisidint, 'ivry time I see you I feel tin years younger?' 'Ye'er kind wurruds,' says th' vice-prisidint, 'brings tears to me eyes. My wife was sayin' on'y this mornin' how comfortable we ar-re in our little flat.' Some vice-prisidints have been so anxious fr th' prisidints safety that they've had to be warned off th' White House grounds.

"Aside fr'm th' arjoos duties iv lookin' afther th' prisidint's health, it is th' business iv th' vice-prisidint to preside over th' dliberations iv th' Sinit. Ivry mornin' between ten an' twelve, he swings his hammock in th' palachial Sinit chamber an' sinks off into dhreamless sleep. He may be awakened by Sinitor Tillman pokin' Sinitor Beveridge in th' eye. This is wan way th' Sinit has iv deliberatin'. If so, th' vice-prisidint rises fr'm his hammock an' says: 'Th' Sinitor will come to ordher.' 'He won't,' says th' Sinitor. 'Oh, very well,' says th' presidin' officer; 'he won't,' an' drops off again. It is his jooty to rigorously enforce th' rules iv th' Sinit. There ar-re none. Th' Sinit is ruled by courtesy, like th' longshoreman's union."[9]

Finley Peter Dunne does not gain his comic insights from an ideal of politics that he contrasts to the sordid reality. Rather, true to his Chicago origins and Irish heritage, his humor is based on political realism and the absurd incongruities of actual politics. In "Reform Administration," his Mr. Dooley examines the public attitude toward political reform:

In th' first place 'tis a gr-reat mistake to think that annywan ra-aly wants to rayform. Ye niver heerd iv a man rayformin' himsilf. He'll rayform other people gladly. He likes to do it. But a healthy man'll niver rayform while he has th' strenth. A man doesn't rayform till his will has been impaired so he hasn't power to resist what th' pa-apers calls th' blandishments iv th' timpter. An' that's thruer in politics thin anywhere else.

But a rayformer don't see it. A rayformer thinks he was ilicted because he was a rayformer, whin th' thruth iv th' matther is he was ilicted because no wan knew him. Ye can always ilict a man in this counthry on that platform. If I was runnin' fr office, I'd change me name, an' have printed on me cards: 'Give him a chnst; he can't be worse.' He's ilicted because th' people don't know him an' do know th' other la-ad; because Mrs. Casey's oldest boy was clubbed by a polisman, because we cudden't get wather above th' third story wan day, because th' sthreet car didn't stop fr us, because th' Flannigans bought a pianny, because we was near run over by a mail wagon, because th' saloons are open

9. Finley Peter Dunne, *Dissertations* (New York: Harper & Bros., 1906), pp. 115-23.

Sundah night, because they're not open all day an' because we're tired seein' th' same face at th' window whin we go down to pay th' wather taxes. Th' rayformer don't know this. He thinks you an' me, Hinnissy, has been watchin' his spotless career f'r twinty years, that we've read all he had to say on th' evils iv pop'lar sufferage befure th' Society f'r the Bewildermint iv the Poor, an' that we're achin' in ivry joint to have him dhrag us be th' hair iv th' head fr'm th' flow'rs' bowl and th' short card game, make good citizens iv us an' sind us to th' pinitinchry. So th' minyit he gets into th' job he begins a furyous attimpt to convart us into what we've been thryin' not to be iver since we come into th' wurruld.

Mr. Dooley concludes by examining the mentality of the reformer and of political idealists in general. In so doing, he comically captures another of the major features in the anti-politics of America. Mr. Dooley says that the reformer "thinks business and honesty is the same thing." He adds:

I don't want Father Kelly to hear me, but I'd rather have a competint man who wud steal if I give him a chanst, but I won't, do me plumbin' thin a person that wud scorn to help himsilf but didn't know how to wipe a joint. Ivry man ought to be honest to start with, but to give a man an office jus' because he's honest is like ilictin' him to Congress because he's a pathrite, because he don't bate his wife or because he always wears a right boot on th' right foot. A man ought to be honest to start with an' afther that he ought to be crafty. A pollytician who's on'y honest is jus' th' same as bein' out in a winther storm without anny clothes on."[10]

Last, some of the most perceptive of Dunne's comic dialogues had to do with American imperialism. Benjamin Franklin parodied British imperialism in the American Revolution. James Russell Lowell's bumpkin, Hosea Bigelow, ridiculed the Mexican War. Lincoln too condemned the Mexican War, and he humorously ridiculed military preten-

10. Finley Peter Dunne, *Observations* (New York: R. H. Russell, 1902), pp. 165-73.

sions. American political humor is anti-militaristic, and it is consistent with the comic ethic of debunking authority and leveling one's superiors. Dunne's Dooley not only comically ridicules the American imperialism of the Spanish-American War, he also lampoons the ignorance of the people on foreign affairs. In "On the Philippines," Dunne writes:

"I know what I'd do if I was Mack," said Mr. Hennessy. "I'd hist a flag over th' Ph'lippeens, an' I'd take in th' whole lot iv thim."

"An' yet," said Mr. Dooley, "tis not more thin two months since ye larned whether they were islands or canned goods. Ye'er back yard is so small that ye'er cow can't turn r-round without buttin' th' woodshed off th' premises, an' ye wudden't go out to th' stock yards without takin' out a policy on yer life. Suppose ye was standin' at th' corner iv State Sthreet an' Archey R-road, wud ye know what car to take to get to th' Ph'lippeens? If yer son Packy was to ask ye where th' Ph'lippeens is, cud ye give him anny good idea whether they was in Rooshia or jus' west iv th' tracks?"

"Mebbe I cudden't," said Mr. Hennessy, haughtily, "but I'm f'r takin' thim in, annyhow."

And Mr. Dooley asks himself:

Will I annex Cubia or lave it to the Cubians? Will I take Porther Ricky or put it by? An' what shud I do with the Ph'lippeens? Oh, what shud I do with thim? I can't annex thim because I don't know where they ar-re. I can't let go iv thim because some wan else'll take thim if I do. They are eight thoudan' iv thim islands, with a popylation iv wan hundherd millyon naked savages; an' me bedroom's crowded now with me an' th' bed. How can I take thim in, an' how on earth am I goin' to cover th' nakedness iv thim savages with me wan shoot iv clothes? An' yet 'twud break me heart to think iv givin' people I niver see or heerd tell iv back to other people I don't know. An', if I don't take thim, Schwartzmeister down th' sthreet, that has half me thrade already, will grab thim sure.[11]

11. Finley Peter Dunne, *Mr. Dooley in Peace and in War* (New York: Small, Maynard & Co., 1898), pp. 43-48.

In "Expansion," Dunne, well in advance of most scholarly analyses of the confusions of American foreign policy,
comically reveals the schizophrenia of American attitudes
toward foreign involvement. In the following excerpts,
idealism is constantly spilling over into aggression:

"Whin we plant what Hogan calls th' starry banner iv
Freedom in th' Ph'lippeens," said Mr. Dooley, "an' give th'
sacred blessin' iv liberty to the poor, down-trodden people
iv thim unfortunate isles,—dam thim!—we'll larn thim a
lesson."

"Sure," said Mr. Hennessy, sadly, "we have a thing or
two to larn oursilves."

"But it isn't f'r thim to larn us," said Mr. Dooley. " 'Tis
not f'r thim wretched an' degraded crathers, without a mind
or a shirt iv their own, f'r to give lessons in politeness an'
liberty to a nation that manny-facthers more dhressed beef
than anny other imperyal nation in th' wurruld. We say to
thim: 'Naygurs, we say, 'poor, dissolute, uncovered
wretches,' says we, 'whin th' crool hand iv Spain forged
man'cles f'r ye'er limbs, as Hogan says, who was it crossed
th' say an' sthruck off th' comealongs? We did,—by dad, we
did. An' now, ye mis'rable, childish-minded apes, we propose f'r to larn ye th' uses iv liberty. In ivry city in this un-
fair land we will erect school-houses an' packin' houses an'
houses iv correction; an' we'll larn ye our language, because
'tis aisier to larn ye ours than to larn oursilves yours. An'
we'll give ye clothes, if ye pay f'r thim; an' if ye don't ye
can go without. An', whin ye're hungry, ye can go to th'
morgue—we mane th' resth'rant—an' ate a good square
meal iv ar-rmy beef. An' we'll sind th' gr-reat Gin'ral Eagan
over f'r to larn ye pathriteism with blow-holes into it, an'
Gin'ral Alger to larn ye to hould onto a job; an', whin ye've
become edycated an' have all th' blessins's iv civilization
that we don't want, that'll count ye one. We can't give ye
anny votes, because we haven't more thin enough to go
round now; but we'll threat ye th' way a father shud threat
his childher if we have to break ivry bone in ye'er bodies.
So come to our ar-rms, says we."

Mr. Dooley then explains to Hennessy:

"An' there it stands, Hinnissy, with th' indulgent parent kneelin' on th' stomach iv his adopted child, while a dillygation fr'm Boston bastes him with an umbrella. There it stands, an' how will it come out I dinnaw. I'm not much iv an expansionist mesilf. F'r th' las' tin years I've been thryin' to decide whether 'twud be good policy an' thrue to me thraditions to make this here bar two or three feet longer, an manny's th' night I've laid wake tryin' to puzzle it out. But I don't know what to do with th' Ph'lippeens anny more thin I did las' summer, befure I heerd tell iv thim. We can't give thim to anny wan without makin' th' wan that gets thim feel th' way Doherty felt to Clancy whin Clancy med a frindly call an' give Doherty's Childher th' measles. We can't sell thim, we can't ate thim, an' we can't throw thim into th' alley whin no wan is lookin'. An' 'twud be a disgrace f r to lave befure we've pounded these frindless an' ongrateful people into insinsibility. So I suppose, Hinnissy, we'll have to stay an' do th' best we can, an' lave Andhrew Carnegie secede fr'm th' Union. They'se wan consolation; an' that is, if th' American people can govern thimsilves, they can govern annything that walks."[12]

Again, the comic sense has revealed an enduring problem of democratic politics. Moreover, Mr. Dooley, in making the primary need of the American people governing "thimsilves," forecasts the war protest on Viet Nam three-quarters of a century later; America should stop trying to police the world and begin policing itself.

Finley Peter Dunne is unique among American comic sages. He is urban, and his dialect is ethnic. With the exception of Lincoln, an actual politician, he is the most politically knowledgeable and tolerant of the humorists. The rhetorical exaggerations of the politicians, the ignorance of the public, the idealistic illusions of the reformers, the mock warfare of political parties, the ethnic prejudices and rivalries of politics, the political venality of big business, all come under his sharp and amused gaze. The politics that he ridicules is twentieth-century politics, only now a little

12. Finley Peter Dunne, *Mr. Dooley in the Hearts of His Countrymen* (New York: Small, Maynard & Co., 1899), pp. 3-8.

more aged and complex. Above all, Dunne doesn't condemn politics from a utopian vantage point. His comic ridicule focuses on its incongruities and contradictions, and his standard is a rational one with amused allowance for man's fallibility and selfishness.

The last of the great comic sages of common sense in political humor reverts to kind, and his comic insights are the worse for it. Yet, in all probability, Will Rogers was the most popular and widely read of the entire breed, barring not even Lincoln. After all, Lincoln was a politician, a Republican, and a Northerner in a Civil War. Will Rogers, the cowboy humorist, was a Broadway musical star, a radio commentator, and a newspaper columnist.

Will Rogers had little formal education and no actual political experience. Only after he became renowned as a humorist with a news column and a radio program does it seem that he became a close observer of politics. He himself said that all he knew was just what he read in the papers. Thus, his humor, both in his own perceptions of politics and in the popular reception of him, provides a good approximation of the democratic political temperament. And, Will Rogers's political humor is blatantly anti-political.

Will Rogers, the lovable cowboy-humorist, is famed for his remark "I never met a man I didn't like." Yet, any student of his political humor could counter that Will Rogers never met a political man he didn't dislike. Even if he was able to separate the political role from the total man, his contempt is testimony to a regard for politics as a parasitical barnacle on man's natural hull. In commenting on the presidential election during the depression, the depth of Rogers's negativism is clear:

There should be a moratorium called on candidates speeches. They have both called each other everything in the world they can think of. From now on they are just talking themselves out of votes. The high office of President of the United States has degenerated into two ordinarily fine men being goaded on by their political leeches into saying things that if they were in their right minds, they wouldn't think of saying. Imagine Mr. Hoover last night "any change of policies will bring disaster to every fireside in America." Of all the conceit. This country is a thousand times bigger than any two men in it, or any two parties in it. These big politicians are so serious about themselves and their parties. This country has gotten where it is in spite of politics, not by the aid of it. That we have carried as much political bunk as we have and still survived shows we are a super nation. If by some divine act of Providence we could get rid of both these parties and hired some good man, like any other big business does, why that would be sitting pretty. This calamity was brought on by the actions of the people of the whole world and its weight will be lifted off by the actions of the people of the whole world, and not by a Republican or a Democrat. So you two boys just get the weight of the world off your shoulders and go fishing. Both of you claim you like to fish, now instead of calling each other names till next Tuesday, why you can do everybody a big favor by going fishing, and you will be surprised but the old U.S. will keep right on running while you boys are sitting on the bank. Then come back next Wednesday and we will let you know which one is the lesser of the two evils of you.[13]

As do most anti-political men, Will Rogers reveals a mystic faith in some "unseen hand" for his supernation. At the same time, he speaks of running government like a big business. Yet he was scathing about the business connections of the Republican party:

There is an epidemic of towns trying to claim the birth of the Republican Party.

All they have to do to find where the Republican Party was formed is find where the first corporation was formed. It was incorporated for the sole purpose of taking over the management and finances of the United States.

Its slogan is: "Stay with us, we can afford to pay more than our competitors." (p. 452)

Rogers was a Democrat but he was nonpartisan in his dislike of both parties as political organizations. In an article

on corruption as a national issue, he relates it to both parties and finds it endemic to their politics. In several of the
passages, Rogers comments:

The Democrats were supposed to have started it (corruption) in what was called Tammany Hall. But a good thing
can't be restricted and is bound to spread. So the Republicans had their eyes open for all new wrinkles that would
help them stay on the U.S. Pension list. So like everything
else they took it and improved on it and brought corruption
up to the high standard that it is today.

He distinguishes between Democratic and Republican
graft:

The Democratic graft was mostly confined to sorter
rounding the Saloon keepers into line with a Campaign collection every year. They thought that was just about the
height of "Big Business." I guess it was because they didn't
know there was any other business. They dident know that
a man that was owner of some mines, or lumber or coal,
might also dig up something for the pot. (If promised a little break in the Tariff, or Railroad rates, or suppressed opposition.) But their mind was on a Saloon and that's as high
as they could elevate it. So the Republicans just was wise
enough to see that the same principal applied to one business as to the other. . . .
While the Democrat was still fooling his time away with
the "Jitney" fellow the Republicans said, "There is only one
way to be in Politics and thats to be in a big way. Whats
the use of being a Piker?" So instead of getting a couple of
hundred dollars from some poor little Guy, they grabbed
off a couple of thousand from the big fellow that was looking for something worthwhile, and they just kept working
and building their business right up, till, look what it is today.

Rogers's conclusion on corruption in politics follows:

But the parties will never be changed as long as we live,
for you can't change human nature. You can't broaden a

mans vision if he wasent born with one. And another thing, its hard to get people to believe a thing as Corruption, when its something that has always been going on. These things gradually come under the heading of legitimate Campaign business. (pp. 443-45)

Rogers also opined, "You take a Democrat and a Republican and you keep them both out of office and I bet they will turn out to be good friends and maybe make useful Citizens and devote their time to some work instead of 'lectioneering all the time" (p. 426). At the same time, he said "If I was running I would be ashamed to let anybody know which one of those Parties I belonged to," and "the only way in the World to make either one look half decent is to keep them out" (p. 425).

In the 1924 election when Coolidge announced that his policy would be Common Sense, Rogers retorted, "Common Sense is not an Issue in Politics; its an affliction." Coolidge's opponent, John W. Davis, announced that his policy would be Honesty, and Rogers added, "neither is that an issue in Politics; it's a Miracle, and can he get enough people that believes in Miracles to elect him?" He summed up the election by saying that the only division between the two major parties is on the question, "Who will get the Post Offices?" and, "no matter how many Parties you have they are all fighting for the same thing—Salary. You abolish salaries and you will abolish Politics and Taxes" (p. 429).

For Will Rogers, politics was the sham competition, false promises, and public fraud that he associated with the political parties. In turn, parties and their politics taint government and its officials, and he wrote:

No wonder Hoover can't get a Cabinet.
Big men won't take it for they won't take a chance on a Senate insult. If he has ever earned more than a Senator, he is in league with big business. If he ever drove a Standard Oil truck, or was a bookkeeper in a Morgan bank, he is in league with monopolies. If he is independently rich, he is in league with the devil.

But if he has never done anything, and been a financial failure at that, he will pass the Senate as a brother, and every time Hoover finds a man of that type he is a Democrat.

And that's another stanch rule. You can't use even an able man from the other party. That would revert to democracy, and not politics. (p. 452)

Political parties are politics, not democracy, and they interfere with ability in government. Rogers relies on a democratic ideal when he says, "on account of us being a democracy and run by the people, we are the only nation in the world that has to keep a government for four years, no matter what it does" (p. 453).

In a 1925 essay on Americanism, Will Rogers verges on seriousness in his adulation of the "Normal Majority" against politics and politicians. The essay points to a rather naive populism (probably a product of his Oklahoma origins) as the source of his comic invective against politics. In fact, in the following passages the political humorist almost seems to parody himself:

We lost Roosevelt TR, a tough blow. But here we are still kicking. So, if we can spare men like Roosevelt and Wilson there is no use in any other Politician ever taking himself serious.

. . . *Even when our next War comes we will through our shortsightedness not be prepared, but that won't be fatal. The real energy and minds of the Normal Majority will step in and handle it and fight it through to a successful conclusion.* A war didn't change it before. Its just the same as it was, and always will be, because its founded on right and even if everybody in Public Life tried to ruin it they couldn't. This country is not where it is today because of any man. It is here on account of the real common sense of the big Normal Majority. A Politician is just like a Necktie Salesman in a big Department Store. If he decides to give all the Ties away, or decided to pocket all the receipts, it don't affect the Store. It don't close. He closes, as soon as he is found out. (p. 434)

Will Rogers seems to hold out the millennialist hope that the "country" Store will some day close out the Politician Salesman when he is found out. Rogers is not a comic political realist like Finley Peter Dunne. He is a populist-idealist in his humor, rooted in America's rural past and uncomprehending of the necessity of politics in the urban present.

In this analysis, most of the comic sages are not only anti-political, but their humor is likely to be informed by some disappointed idealism. The very posture that the comic sage adopts suggests that idealism. In his popularity, he poses as a common man of no-nonsense common sense who speaks to the people in their language. Most often, he is ridiculing the conventional wisdom and its authorities. In good part his popular appeal will be based upon the assumption that his comic intelligence is a reflection of, or at best, a refinement of popular intelligence.

The comic sage may be Democratic, like Rogers, Republican like Lincoln, Anti-Jacksonian Democrat like Smith and Dorrs's Major Downing, or abolitionist and pacifist like Lowell. Yet all share a kind of populism—the good sense of the people against the abstract knowledge and power of government. Some of them can be populist and, at the same time, anti-democratic in their humor, for they are essentially against government—and so are the people. In the United States the popular morality has been individualistic and anti-government even while being democratic. Traditionally, democracy has been taken to mean the people running their own lives and spending their own money with minimal governmental interference. A democratic government is not so much for the people's use, as it is to prevent its misuse against them.[14]

The comic sages, conservative or democratic, have been

14. The best explanation for this American "democracy" as antigovernmental in contrast to European democracies of a Rousseauist type can be found in Hannah Arendt, *On Revolution*. Essentially, the gist of his thesis is that in the United States the people revolted for political freedom and had already achieved substantially material plenty, whereas in France the people revolted to take over the government to use it to overcome poverty and attain plenty. Cf. also David Potter, *The People of Plenty*.

n agreement with the people in their comic aggression
against government and politics. With them, despite their
populist traits, as with other great political humorists of the
past, the underlying thrust of their intellectual influence is
conservative. In the case of the comic sages that conservatism is peculiarly American, anti-political and antigovernmental.

One feature of Will Rogers's political humor should be
noticed in passing. Along with Brown's Artemus Ward, Rogers noticed the show-business quality of politics. As Brown
was a showman, so also was Rogers, and their grasp of the
drama of politics probably resulted from their professional
affiliations. Rogers said, "Politics is the best show in
America." Another time, when his remarks were objected
to by a Congressman as those of a professional joke maker,
he retorted:

Now can you beat that for jealously among people in the
same line? Calling me a Professional Joke Maker! He is
right about everything but the Professional. *They* are the
Professional Joke Makers. Read some of the Bills that they
have passed, if you think they ain't Joke Makers.[15]

Another time when Will Rogers discussed being a political candidate, he concluded, "I have looked politics and the
movies both over and while they have much in common I
believe politics is the most common, so I will stay with the
movies" (p. 457). Rogers saw the analogy and played with it
for many of his witticisms, but he never followed it
through. Moreover, his own anti-political sense made him
twist the relationship into an insult, instead of a good-
humored recognition of the attributes of make-believe.

Will Rogers is the last of these great populist-political
humorists. They have gone out of style. Their only re-
placement would seem to be the journalist-satirists of the
daily newspapers. Blair, in his *Horse Sense in American
Humor*, thinks that the demise of the comic sages is due to
our changing way of life, the decline of rural America, the

15. Dudden, pp. 421, 435.

rise of higher education, and increasing skepticism abou
traditional verities.[16]

Satirical Journalists

The journalists of political humor may fill the place of the
comic sages of common sense, but their styles are no
populist. They don't employ the vernacular, misspelling
crackerbox philosophers, or appeals to common sense. Mos
often, they employ satire and parody to ridicule curren
political events and personalities. Quite often, their humo
demands from their audiences considerable political know
ledge and subtle imagination. It would seem that their ap
peal is necessarily to a qualitatively different citizenship
from that of the comic sages.

A brief sampling of the political humor of several of the
best known of the satirical journalists will illustrate the
sophisticated contrast of their styles to their rusticlike pre
decessors. Though the popularity of the latter can not be
measured, academic studies of newspaper readers would
indicate that the audience of their successors must be very
limited. However, their influence may be disproportion
ately great as an opinion elite.

Russell Baker of the *New York Times* is a former politica
reporter in Washington. His political knowledge is as un
questionable as is the quality of his newspaper and it
readership. In 1962 Baker took on the matinee idol of the
Democrats in "A first reader on Washington for children c
the space age":

Look, Jerry, look. See the New Frontiersman. Look an
see the New Frontiersman run. He is running to th
Capitol to serve the program. Be careful. Do not get in hi
way or he will have to step on you. Why does the Nev
Frontiersman have to step on people who get in his way?

Because, little children, he is pragmatic. He is tough
minded. He is hard-nosed. Look at his hard nose. See hi

16. Blair, pp. 308-10.

tough mind. Is he not a splendid sight? He will soon teach
Senator Robert S. Kerr to leave the program alone. It is
lucky that you are not Senator Robert S. Kerr or you would
have to look the New Frontiersman in the eye and feel his
hard nose.

But what is this? Senator Robert S. Kerr is throwing the
program out of the window. See the medicare bill fly away.
See the trade bill scattered on the air. This will make the
New Frontiersman very cross, will it not? Poor Senator
Robert S. Kerr.

Look, the New Frontiersman is advancing. Why is the
Senator not running? Why is he smiling? Why is he tweak-
ing the New Frontiersman's nose? Look, he is giving the
New Frontiersman a new program. It is the Senator Robert
S. Kerr program. The New Frontiersman is accepting it.
He is smiling at the Senator and shaking the Senator's
hand. What a splendid sight. This is democracy in action.

Why did the New Frontiersman not stop the Senator
from throwing the President's program out of the window?
Children, you have much to learn. Remember, the New
Frontiersman is pragmatic. Stand back! Stand back! He is
leaving for the White House. You must not smile at him or
he will ask if you think there is something funny about trying to run a country.[17]

In the same column Russell Baker goes on to ridicule the
political bombast of Senator Goldwater and the ideological
chaos of the Democratic Party, all in a parody of a children's primer. Baker, even more than Finely Peter Dunne,
satirizes politics in full awareness of its complexities. He
ridicules President Kennedy and the slogans and posturing
of his administration. He builds on the separation of powers
between the President and Congress and the actual veto
powers of Congressional leaders over presidential programs.
Above all, the language and charades of politics are the
targets of Baker's comic ridicule.

In 1966, in "Yet Another Post-Election Analysis," Baker
satirizes another enduring peculiarity of American politics:

17. Russell Baker, "Observer," *New York Times*, Sept. 6, 1962.

Political analysts agree that Governor George Romney would make a good Presidential Candidate if he knew something about foreign affairs and something about domestic affairs. This is like saying Rock Hudson would make a good surgeon if he knew something about surgery.

The difference is that nobody in his right mind would let Mr. Hudson suture a cut toe without ten more years of education, while a national majority, according to the last Gallop poll, is already willing to let Mr. Romney take charge of the Government.

What we are faced with, at least in politics, is a deepening distrust of professionalism. The recent elections tell the story. In Alabama, the voters gave the Governorship to an inexperienced housewife. In California, to an actor. In Georgia, they seem to favor a restaurateur.

PRESIDENTIAL POTENTIAL

Illinois has sent a camera-maker to the Senate. He and the actor Governor-elect of California, perhaps because neither has yet served a day in public office, are already seriously discussed as men of Presidential weight.

What accounts for this public swing to the amateurs? There are sundry explanations. Mr. Romney "looks like a President" and is very moral. Alabama admires its housewife-Governor's husband. California and Illinois were tired of their professional Governor and Senator, and besides the actor and camera-maker are young and telegenic. Georgia likes its restaurateur because he is opposed to letting Negroes eat chicken with white folks.[18]

Baker points out that high political skills are far more intricate than those of a plumber, surgeon, or space-flight director. He then parodies the amateurism of politics by projecting it onto the practice of several prosaic skills and envisioning the absurd results.

Interestingly, Baker contributes to the phenomenon that he ridicules. Politics is distrusted because it is feared and misunderstood. A politician practices politics and is regarded as the criminal to his crime. Ergo, the less political

18. *Ibid.*, Nov. 29, 1966.

the political candidate, the more he is to be trusted and the more he deserves political office. And the comic (or alternativate) logic is that the amateur is more likely to be politically incompetent and thus less able to use political power. The amateur is the anti-political citizen's candidate against politics.

Popular humor reflects this logic in several witticisms: *Politician* is the one title that a successful politician will reject. A good politician is never a politician; he is a statesman. President Truman defined the latter thus: "a statesman is a dead politician."

Probably one of the deepest reasons for the distrust of politicians is the popular misunderstanding of their roles as brokers of opinion among competing and conflicting groups in a pluralistic society. The less homogeneous the constituency of the politician, the greater is the pressure on him to corrupt the clarity of language and bend the facts of history in order to conciliate the clash of faction and forge political unity from social diversity. In short, that's where the votes are. But it is also one of the richest veins to mine for political satire. In "From the History-For-Nixon Committee" Baker writes, "A Nixonian History of America":

America was discovered in 1492 by a hard-working ethnic named Columbus, following in the wonderful American tradition of that magnificent Scandinavian Leif Ericson.

Neither of them as Abraham Lincoln later commented on his way to prayer, could have done the job, however, without the inspiration of that great citizen of Poland, Pulaski, who never allowed the word "abortion" to be spoken at his dinner table. As soon as the discovery had been given saturation media exposure, the Americans began moving out of Europe to escape the horrors of religious persecution, which was the Communism of that period.

Polls soon showed that there would have to be a revolution to preserve what was right about America. For years Americans had been working hard to buy themselves a small home and send their children to a decent school, while some people far away in London were spending the

American taxpayers' money on idle loafing around Pall Mall and four-day week-ends at Chequers.

Americans were sick and tired of supporting these spongers, who laughed when George Washington told them there was nothing undignified in taking honest but menial jobs.

In the resulting revolution everyone commented favorably upon the Americans' strict adherence to the rules of fair play. America had given the world a beautiful example of how to conduct a revolution without making a nuisance of yourself, as do some small countries today.

The Founding Fathers, thanks to the help of millions of Americans of Irish and Greek ancestry, then established the United States of America and created the Federal system of Government which is based upon a delicate balance of power among the President, the Department of Defense and the Lockheed Aircraft Corporation.

In the peaceful years that followed, the Democratic party governed so well that the Republican party saw no reason to come into existence. By today's standards these magnificent old Democrats—Jefferson, Madison, Monroe, Jackson—would be called Republicans; for in those days the Democratic party had not yet been seized by dangerous radicals feared by every honest hard-working American in the land. . . .

In the meantime, of course, America was going from strength to strength. The tax haven was invented, and the hamburger, and Southern California and the thirty-second TV campaign spot commercial.

America soon became the great friend and champion of freedom everywhere in the world. This made Americans proud and happy. Today they have no problems worth speaking of, except for the presence of a few congenital malcontents of the sort who can never see the doughnut for staring at the hole.

Their present leader, President Nixon, has many good friends who are Catholic.[19]

The language of politics has another comical side to it. If conciliation through the obscuring and softening of issues

19. *Ibid.*

and facts burdens the literal-minded and true believers in society, the exaggerated and aggressive rhetoric of politics is even more offensive to most people. This author remembers the shock with which he read a letter of congratulations from Senator Taft to President Truman in the aftermath of the 1948 presidential election. In the particularly vicious campaigning of that election, Taft as Mr. Republican had led in the battle of political invective against Truman, who was one of the coarsest and most caustic of modern presidents. Yet, wonder of wonders, the campaign at an end, congratulations were in order, and they remained friends.

Much of the time the battles of grossly exaggerated rhetoric and low political invective pass the bounds of good taste. Sometimes the verbal attacks verge on incitement to physical violence, and once in a great while they have occasioned it. There appear to be rules of battle (charges of treason and disloyalty violate them), and the people in their distrust of politics make proper discounts for the inflated rhetoric of politics. Nevertheless, they derive pleasure from it; their political attention is captured and the stimulation of competition increases their participation; and last, their real aggressions are exercised and relieved in the mock warfare of words. Thereby, political rhetoric parallels comedy in function and technique. No wonder that it provides such humor for the political satirist; in this sense, politics is comedy itself.

Art Buchwald, one of the most widely read satirical journalists, has parodied the rhetoric of the 1964 presidential election in "That's Friendship." That election, in which Senator Goldwater ran against President Johnson and Vice-presidential candidate Senator Humphrey, was characterized by vicious smears on both sides. Buchwald first quotes Goldwater in a post-election speech:

I have served in the United States Senate for the last twelve years and I have had some of the most hair-pulling debates I ever want to have with Hubert Humphrey, but I don't think two people in this country are closer together as friends. And with Lyndon Johnson I have argued, fought, and debated on the floor, in his office and my office, but we can still call each other friends. It is only when we allow disagreement to overrun and overrule good judgment that we forget our basic goodness and decency in this country.

Buchwald then poses a friendly get-together of President Johnson and Senator Goldwater in the White House after the election:

Mr. Goldwater sits down. "Well, how's the old faker and phony?"

President Johnson chortles, "That was a bit rough, you trigger-happy maverick."

Mr. Goldwater slaps his sides. "You sure got mileage out of that one. I swear everyone in the country thought I was going to push the button as soon as I got in."

"I can't say you helped me much when you said I was soft on Communism," Mr. Johnson says, wagging his finger.

"Heck, Lyndon, I figured I'd run it up the flagpole and see who saluted. And by the way, what was all this stuff during the campaign about me being against Social Security?"

Mr. Johnson roars with laughter. "I knew that would get under your skin. You never did have much sense about the old folks' vote."

Mr. Goldwater says, "Well, you might have thought that was funny, but I didn't see you laughing when I brought up Bobby Baker, Billie Sol Estes, and Matt McCloskey."

Both Johnson and Goldwater accept each other's election rhetoric as normal and continue to address each other with the campaign smears while having a drink together. When Vice-President Humphrey comes in, Goldwater warmly welcomes him as he calls Humphrey a radical left-winger. In turn, Humphrey responds in warm friendship to Goldwater, terming the latter an extremist reactionary. Finally, the conversation ends with a toast of mutual friendship.[20]

20. Art Buchwald, *And Then I Told The President* (New York: Fawcett World Library, Crest Book, 1964, 1968), pp. 13-14. This is a republication in book form of Buchwald's newspaper articles.

Art Buchwald's political humor is highly topical in its satirizing the day-to-day events of politics. Interestingly, his humor often consists of escalating the almost comic exaggerations of politics itself into such absurd hyperbole that it becomes recognizably laughable while exposing its intrinsic political nonsense.

Buchwald catches another nuance of political rhetoric when he satirizes the empty eloquence of the politician of great repute. In "Bobby Saves the Day," he recounts the role of U.S. Senator Robert Kennedy of New York in the settlement of that city's subway strike. He begins with the actual facts of the Senator's flying to the city in the midst of a paralyzing strike, making a grand entrance, briefly conferring with the Mayor, and then holding a press conference. Buchwald continues:

> With Mayor Lindsay standing at his side, Senator Kennedy said, "This is an intolerable situation."
>
> There was a gasp from the press. No one had put it that way before. Mr. Kennedy continued. He called on men of goodwill to reach a settlement and he said, "It is no longer a question of principle. It is now a question of protecting the city and the poor people this strike has hurt the most."
>
> One reporter said to another reporter standing next to him, "He makes a lot of sense."
>
> The other reporter said, "If he had only said it at the beginning of the strike everyone would have been willing to listen to reason."
>
> Mr. Kennedy described the strike as a "catastrophe." You could see the look of gratitude on Mayor Lindsay's face as the Senator spoke.
>
> Then Senator Kennedy dropped his blockbuster. He said, "The difference between the parties is not so great. In fact it is relatively small. There must be give and take on both sides."
>
> As the Senator spoke, negotiators for both the Transit Workers and the Transit Authority watched in their suites at the Americana Hotel.
>
> "That's it," cried one of the members of the Transit Authority. "There must be give and take on both sides. Why didn't we think of that?"

A transit labor union leader said, "He said the strike was a catastrophe to the city. No one told us that before."

One of the three mediators of the strike who had averaged two hours' sleep for the past twelve days said, "I don't think anyone has a better grasp of the picture than he has. What would we have done without him?"

Mr. Kennedy revealed that he had sent a telegram to the panel and the Mayor urging the Transit Authority, as well as the union, to accept the findings of the mediation board.

No one knows if it was the telegram or Mr. Kennedy's appearance in New York that turned the tide. But the next day the strike was settled. Sources close to Mayor Lindsay say the Mayor's warmth and gratitude to Senator Kennedy for coming in at the end of the strike have never been higher. The Mayor just has no words to express it.[21]

"Nothing" was said impressively, but it was said by a "somebody." In the rhetoric of politics the who and the how are more important than the what—a triumph of form over substance. Certainly it is a fitting target for comic ridicule. At the same time, the people are reminded of their unseemly hero worship; the hero is pricked in his platitudes and reduced to life size; and rationality is asserted against rhetoric. Yet, have not the personality and his platitudes contributed something to the settlement and, thereby, served politics?

In democratic politics, however undesirable, the personality of the politician is a chief reference point of the voters. By the appearance of the tree, they judge its fruits. The politician who lends his prestige to a political settlement facilitates its popular acceptance on the basis of his popular acceptance. The prestige may precede the product, but if the latter often proves wanting, the former will prove as illusory as its etymological origins. In politics, image must finally reckon with identity.

And the platitudes of politics are not intended to impart new knowledge or impose final truths in a clash of opinions.

21. Art Buchwald, *Son of the Great Society* (New York: G. P. Putnam's Sons, 1965, 1966), pp. 230-31. This is also a collection of Buchwald's newspaper articles.

They are intended to soothe partisan tempers and reassert ancient verities. Platitudes restore psychological equilibrium between opposing parties and permit compromise without surrender or loss of face. In turn, political compromise becomes stuff for the comedy of political invective. But comic invective too releases harmlessly the aggressions of frustration and disappointed expectation on the part of would-be true believers.

Art Buchwald also uses the show-business analogy to politics. In the following excerpts from "Running for Show Business," he ridicules politics by comically reversing the situation of actors becoming politicians:

I spoke to one such politician who said, "I think it's the duty of every citizen, no matter what his profession, to become an actor."

"But what do you know about show business?" I asked him.

"What does Ronald Reagan know about politics?" he replied.

"That doesn't answer the question."

"Look, I can introduce *Death Valley Days* or the *General Electric Theater* as well as Reagan can, if not better. If he is going to take the bread out of my mouth, I'm going to take it out of his."

"But the reason Ronald Reagan is going into politics is not to take the bread out of your mouth. He's personable and people like him and he's always played a good guy. That's all you need to run for office these days. But show business requires talent."

The politician demonstrates his acting ability and Buchwald advises him:

"Sir, I don't want to be a spoilsport, but it's much easier for a person in show business to become a politician than it is for a politician to become a show business personality. People pay good money to see someone in the entertainment world, while they get their politicians for free. They expect to be disappointed when they hear a politician, but if you fail in show business the public gets angry."

Buchwald ends the satirical dialogue with a comic twist that brings the ridicule full circle. The politician complains:

"The trouble with you guys is that you just think because a guy has been a politician all his life he doesn't know anything. We care about things, too."
"I'm not doubting you," I said. "But I want to ask you a question. Suppose you don't make it in show business. Suppose there is nowhere for you to go. What will you do then?"
"I'll probably run for Governor of California." (p. 122)

Buchwald ridicules politicians for being actors, actors for becoming politicians, and the people for their perverted values with regard to politics. However, underlying the entire satire is the real resemblance of politics to show business. Politicians are public actors, and the "show business personality" is already a "personality" who merely has to play to a new public.

Arthur Hoppe, a San Francisco comic columnist, casts his caricature of the public personality in the role of the comic strip's Superman. In "Gary Boldwater, Boy American!" Hoppe sharply ridicules Senator Barry Goldwater in his campaigning for the 1964 Republican presidential nomination. But his comic strip parody is so imaginative, and his exaggerations remain so true in their magnifying of actual characteristics, that the humor rises above malice. Hoppe announces:

Hi there, boys and girls out there in front of your TV sets. Comfy? Well hold on to our hats 'cause here we go—off on a brand-new thrilling adventure series with a brand-new thrilling adventure hero . . . Gary Boldwater, Boy American!
(Theme: "The Stars and Stripes Forever.")
Faster than the speed of sound, stronger than the Chase

National Bank, able to bound over tall issues in a single leap . . . Gary Boldwater, Boy American!

Who will save us from the Communists? Who will save us from the Keynsians? Who will save us from ourselves? Gary Boldwater, Boy American!

So c'mon, kids, let's join Gary today for "The Thrilling Adventure of the Phony Treaty." There he is in his disguise as a stuffy old senator with his stuffy old horn-rimmed glasses and stuffy old double-breasted suit. That's his pretty secretary, Lotus Lane (who doesn't know who he really is either), handing him a document.

* * *

Lotus: Here's a copy of that nuclear test ban treaty, Senator Boldwater. Shall I read it to you?

Gary (who always pretends he can't read): Well, now, Miss Lane, I don't see much sense in that. The way I hear, it's just another simple old treaty. Nothing to get het up about.

Lotus (vexed): But Senator, look, it's written in two languages!

Gary: Now, now, Miss Lane. Heaps of things are written in two languages. Like . . . Well, like heaps of things.

Lotus (angrily): Oh, Senator, you're just like so many Americans. You're sweet, but you're so naive!

(She stomps out and Gary whips off his glasses and suit to reveal the uniform of a general in the U.S. Air Force Reserve! The uniform of . . . Gary Boldwater, Boy American! Leaping in the cockpit of his very own jet plane, he zooms into the sky and circles over the Washington Monument.)

Gary (musing as he flies in circles): There! Now I am able to think more clearly with my 100 IQ brain. Could Lotus be correct? Wait! I shall scan this document with my 20-20 vision. "The government of . . ." Hmmm. ". . . discontinuance of all test explosions . . ." Hmmm. "In witness whereof the undersigned . . ." Leaping lizards! Lotus was right! Our nation is in peril! Oh, that I shall but be in time to save the day!

(We shift to the Capitol where our beaming senators are about to ratify the treaty. Suddenly, through the skylight, crashes a parachutist. Could it be? Yes, it is! Gary Boldwater, Boy American!)

* * *

Gary: Gentlemen, before voting you should know that one of the signatures on this pact is that of an "Andrei Gromyko," who is a proven card-carrying member of the Communist Party!

(There are shocked cries of "Oh, no!" and "Egad, sir. he's right!" The treaty is torn up. The senators give Gary a Big Six before he can modestly slip away. Later, once again in disguise, Gary greets a breathless Lotus Lane in his office.)

Lotus (glowingly): Oh, senator, I wish you'd been there to see him. If only you could be more like that.

Gary (winking at the camera): Well, Lotus, I guess we can't all be Gary Boldwater, Boy American! (turning serious): But it sure would be a great country if we could.[22]

Even though Hoppe's political parody is in the context of the miraculous-hero comic strip, the ridicule of the politician-actor as a fictitious character in a public drama is unmistakable. His private and real character is comically contrasted to his public and artificial personality as a superman possessed of miraculous powers. Political issues are reduced to ultimate absurdity in terms of public prejudice and ignorance, and the ideological hero, superman-simplicissimus, solves them with either-or decisiveness.

Of course, comic ridicule casts a wide net in Hoppe's

22. Arthur Hoppe, "Our Man Hoppe," *Detroit News*, Aug. 26, 1963.

parody: ideological thinking and hero-worship, political oversimplification, patriotism as jingoism, and the limited average man with excessive political power. Humor pleasurably camouflages the sharpest political criticism, and the parody becomes educational as a kind of analogical reasoning. Politics and its characteristics are removed from their accustomed setting and placed in a fully apparent foreign context, but one with credible similarities to the original setting. The stupidities of the burlesqued politics are made manifest by their transferral. The familiar, placed in the foreign, is seen with new insight. The humorist's choice of the foreign setting for the once-familiar factors provides a new perspective for his audience.

The pleasure in the humor comes from the ridicule occasioned by reducing the subjects of the parody to more human proportions; it comes from the wonder of discovery in seeing that two things that appeared to be totally alien (politics and the comic strip) having amazing similarities; and, last, the pleasure comes from learning new information about politics. Man is Aristotle's learning animal, and political humor is one side of the rational faculty of man whereby he may learn about his governance.

One last example of the political humor of the journalist-satirists is drawn from Jules Feiffer. Feiffer's work appears in cartoon form, but the substance of his humor is in the story line, with the drawings merely adding illustration to it. Back in 1965 he satirized the politics of President Johnson's grandiose claims to bring about the Great Society. In a series of cartoons he pictures a crowd of people gazing heavenward and questioning a pair of boot-clad feet, suspended from the clouds, and the feet respond to the people. The dialogue runs as follows:

Q. What do you see, Mr. President-of-all-the-People?
A. I see a land where love reigns. I see great farms and great cities. I see men at work, children at play, women at peace.
Q. What else do you see, Mr. President-of-all-the-People?

A. I see the end of divisiveness and contrariness. I see small men growing large and closed minds opening wide. I see a rich harvest of book-learning and the arts.

Q. Tell us more Mr. President-of-all-the-People?

A. I see Black and White in final harmony. Rich and poor, old and young, big and little, small and large.

Q. But what of our enemies, Mr. President-of-all-the-People?

A. I see love entering their hearts. I see understanding and good will. I see peace, sound and strong, hewn out of the rock of give and take.

Q. Is there nothing more that you see, Mr. President-of-all-the-People?

A. I see a mandate for happiness. I see the determined faces of millions—fat and skinny, tall and short, bold and shy—crying as one: "Onward to the Great Society!"

Q. And how will all this come about, Mr. President-of-all-the-People?

A. I shall wheel and deal.[23]

Feiffer artfully mixes the particular with the general in his comic invective against politics. Immediately, the cartoon story is directed against the inflated rhetoric of the programs of President Johnson's administration in contrast to the reputation of the President as an unscrupulous and ruthless political manipulator—a wheeler-dealer. The cartoon's drawing accentuates the contrast. The cloud-suspended boots and the voice from the heavens address the supplicant masses. The President is godlike and his vision millennial, but, finally, his powers for effecting heaven-on-earth are purely political, devilish, "wheel and deal."

Johnson's "Great Society" has here been ridiculed as rhetorically millennialist and practically politics-as-usual. He has been exposed as a god-posturing political operator, just another wheeler-dealer. However, in Feiffer's bill of particulars he has comically leveled a general charge against

23. Jules Feiffer, *Detroit Free Press*, Jan. 14, 1965.

politics. In politics the word is contradicted by the deed; the end is nullified by the means; the promises of politics are made lies by politics itself.

Finally, the comic function of democratic leveling is implicit in both story line and drawing. The people gaze upward at a contrived illusion. The promises are empty. The reality is a politician and his sordid machinations.

At core, the comic criticism is accurate. The promissory language of politics is at odds with its actualities. Political idealism is countered by the reality of political manipulation. A moral politician is oxymoronic—a contradiction of terms. The shell game of politics diverts the attention of the people toward the clouds and away from muddy reality.

Yet, comic negativism overlooks the positive side of these political characteristics. The language of politics is affective, not primarily denotative, and, purposefully, a kind of double-talk. Ideals precede a political system, and their derivative values contribute within politics to its sustenance, but issues over ideals cannot be a part of any stable politics. A politician is a manipulator, but his manipulation of egotistical men is a brokering of their special interests and maintains a tolerable consensus among politically diverse elements.

Of course, the function of political humor is not positive. Nevertheless, the persistent themes of its negativism reveal deep-seated traits of American anti-politics. Thus, major targets of the comic invective of the journalist-satirists appear to be the connotative language of politics, the personality-posturing of politicians, and the manipulations of broker-politicians. But these features of politics are intrinsic to politics as a system of representative government. At the same time, comic invective acts as a healthy purgative of the political system. Political humor is Janus-headed.

7

American Politics, Comic Warfare

Wherein words war—and make peace

He is a man of splendid abilities, but utterly corrupt. Like
rotten mackerel by moonlight, he shines and stinks.
—John Randolph of Roanoke
on Edward Livingston

The earthy storytelling of the comic sages is the most na-
tive of American political humor, but it is not the most
common or continuous kind. That honor belongs to the
least honorable and most dubious of candidates, namely,
comic invective. From a knowledge of Aristophanes to a
nodding acquaintance with British parliamentary humor,
and with an understanding of the sublimation of overt aggression in both politics and humor, comic invective appears to be the most universal form of political humor.

Invective is verbal abuse or ridicule. Comic invective
couches the abuse in humor. Oftentimes the dividing line
between sheer vituperation and humor becomes indiscerni-
ble. Nevertheless, comic invective is our most common

246

form of political humor, and it will be maintained here that this is due to a necessary function that comic invective performs in democratic politics—to sublimate warfare.

Here we will attempt to understand American political humor as a function of American politics. The gist of the argument is typified by comic invective; American political humor is basically negative. It is anti-political and anti-partisan; it ridicules and derides government and officialdom; and, last, political humor even completes the circle by attacking the people themselves. Yet, true to the genius of comedy, the negative serves the positive. Negative political humor supports politics and democracy, and the existence of the former is a sure sign of the health of the latter.

The Uncivil War of Politicians

The two-faced nature of political humor extends to the comic villains themselves. On the one hand, many politicians are fully aware and proud of their role in society's peace and progress. On the other, they remain fully representative of the attitudes of their constituents. Thus, politicians are the source of much of the comic invective against each other, against themselves as self-deprecation, and against parties and politics.

It is not surprising that politicians are their own worst comic enemies. I have presented politics as a kind of sublimated warfare; in that warfare, politicians are the soldiers who do verbal battle against each other. Though they come to have a protective cynicism and a professional toleration of political excesses, they too remain subject to all the passions and foibles of mankind. They are a part of an anti-political society, based on politics, even while they practice the profession more suspect than the oldest one.

Moreover, while they engage in what most of them know to be "a game of politics," the competition of mock battle is there to excite the emotions; the egos become deeply involved in the struggle for popularity and power, and these egos are caught up in the very illusions of ideology and history-making that they have created. When livelihood, ego, and ideals are at stake, political humor as comic invective is often the escape valve for the anxieties and aggressions that result.

Invective is the personal abuse or insulting of someone verbally. In politics, it becomes tolerable, or even an art, through its comic camouflage. Generally the humor in the insult lies in its wordplay. The wordplay diffuses the direct aggression of the personal insult into a game of wits, something like the vicious but verbally dexterous "dozens" played by ghetto blacks.

Comic invective excites the admiration of an audience for its wit, despite any sympathy for a party to a dispute. The invective may utilize pun, parody, irony, exaggeration, or ridicule, but its target, instead of feeling physically threatened or challenged, is confronted with a humorous situation in which the onlookers enjoy the verbal pyrotechnics. Possibly, they also vicariously join in the "kill" and displace some of their own aggressions. The victim must respond in kind, join in the laughter, or gracefully remain silent. Otherwise, whether the victim responds physically or with humorless anger, he is branded a poor loser. In effect, comic invective shifts the battleground from the muscular to the mental arena, and one must play according to new rules.

In a sense, the acceptance of comic invective is a tribute to rationality over the *ultima ratio*, but its success requires a stable society with a rough political consensus. When deep issues rend a society and enflame its passions, there is little dispassion for the appreciation of wit. Fanatics are humorless. Political humor demands the luxury of uncertainty, suspension of belief, or the appreciation of civilized graces, such as the cultivation of language. Concern for salvation or survival does not permit such indulgence.

In the early years of the Republic and into the Civil War period, the comic temper in politics was short-fused. Invective had narrow limits, and duels were fought over imagined excesses. Among others, both Henry Clay and Abraham Lincoln were involved in duels growing out of invective. High stakes incite high passions. Yet, since the Civil War, comic invective has remained biting and become more humorous without recourse to violence. It has become domesticated, but so has politics. Domesticated politics demands sublimation of aggression; comic invective fills the demand.

As early as the American Revolution, comic invective was delightfully present, despite great issues and high passions. Possibly the possession of a common culture by rival rebels and Tories, and the presence of a large, uncommitted, middle group contributed to the humorous style of insult. Most of the examples that remain are the literary hoaxes of Franklin or the comic poems of the verbal warriors. One of the latter is of interest because it joins battle with Thomas Paine explicitly on the grounds of invective. Newspapers were political instrumentalities and the Tory *New York Gazette* of James Rivington in 1779, took issue with Paine:

Hail mighty Thomas! in whose works are seen
A mangled Morris and distorted Deane;
Whose splendid periods flash for Lee's defense,—
Replete with everything but Common Sense.
You, by whose labors no man e'er was wiser,
You, of invective great monopolizer;
O say, what name shall dignify the lays
Which now I consecrate to sing your praise!
In pity tell by what exalted name
Thou would'st be damned to an eternal flame:
Shall Common Sense or Comus greet thine ear,
A piddling poet, or puffed pamphleteer?[1]

Poetry and rhyming are forms of wordplay and, combined with invective intent, they become humorous. Poetic invective was used against leading political personalities on both sides in the Revolution. Philip Freneau, a genuine poet,

1. Carl Holliday, *The Wit and Humor of Colonial Days, 1607-1800*. (Philadelphia and London: J. P. Lippincott Co., 1912), p. 112.

devoted his talents to reviling the British and Loyalists during the Revolution. Afterwards he was subsidized by the Jeffersonians against the Federalists, and he displayed invective viciousness in his partisan poetry (pp. 145-70).

Not until the early nineteenth century does politics appear to become stabilized enough for direct comic invective among politicians to become a matter of record. The first, and still the most famous, political artist of comic invective was John Randolph of Roanoke. An interesting and eccentric character, he served as Congressman, Senator, and later as Ambassador to Russia. He is quoted in the introduction of this chapter in his classic insult to Edward Livingston.

Randolph was a beardless bachelor, possessed of a high voice. As a conservative of the Virginia aristocracy, he spoke from on high but directed his words below the belt of his many victims. In a famous exchange of invective in Congress with Tristam Burges of Rhode Island, the verbal viciousness began with the latter's reference to Randolph's reputed impotence:

Burges: Sir, Divine Providence takes care of his own universe. Moral monsters cannot propagate. Impotent of everything except malevolence of purpose, they can not otherwise multiply miseries than by blaspheming all that is pure and prosperous and happy. Could demon propagate demon, the universe might become a pandemonium; but I rejoice that the Father of Lies can never become the Father of Liars. One adversary of God and man is enough for one universe.
Randolph: You pride yourself on an animal faculty, in respect to which the slave is your equal and the jackass infinitely your superior.[2]

Randolph's telling counter is rightfully admired and often quoted, but Burges's initial invective deserves high praise. It is cruelly personal, grossly extravagant, and metaphorically superb. "The Father of Lies can never become the

2. Harris, pp. 53-54.

Father of Liars," by itself is poetic wordplay on the germ of truth.

Yet, all citations of the exchange give the victory to Randolph. Why? Certainly, if both invectives are considered separately, Burges's is technically superior. And the answer is that they are not isolated, but shots in a verbal duel. The very superiority of Burges's opening shot enhances Randolph's return fire. Burges has the advantage of premeditation and, possibly, advance preparation. Under the fire of his withering insult Randolph does not wilt; he counterattacks tersely, tellingly, and in kind. He has played the word game according to the rules, responded rationally under extreme provocation, and he wins an early accolade for demonstrating how to keep politics political through humor.

John Randolph was probably the first Congressman to use a famous historical allusion for political ridicule. He said of Richard Rush's selection as Secretary of the Treasury: "Never were abilities so much below mediocrity so well rewarded; no, not when Caligula's horse was made consul" (p. 53). A century later, U.S. Senator Carter Glass, another Virginian also in its aristocratic tradition, improved on the Caligula invective. When the populist and demagogic Huey Long was admitted to the U.S. Senate, Senator Glass remarked that the Senate of the United States had surpassed Caligula in making his horse a consul; it had made the posterior of a horse a U.S. Senator.

John Randolph was so good at being comically bad that there was some danger of his overusing his invective. However, several of his most pointed sarcasms are notable because of the fame of their targets. Randolph said of Thomas Jefferson:

I cannot live in this miserable, undone country, where as the Turks follow their sacred standard, which is a pair of Mahomet's green breeches, we are governed by the old red breeches of that prince of projectors, St. Thomas of Cantingbury; and surely Becket himself never had more pilgrims at his shrine than the saint of Monticello.

Because of John Calhoun's early involvement with the War Hawks in the agitation for the War of 1812, Randolph, the epitome of Southern conservatism, disliked and distrusted the philosopher and statesman of states' rights. Randolph addressed Calhoun in the U.S. Senate, "Mr. Speaker! I mean Mr. President of the Senate and would-be President of the United States, which God in His infinite mercy avert."

Randolph said, concerning the reputation of Martin Van Buren for deviousness, "He rowed to his object with muffled oars," and of Henry Clay, "Clay's eye is on the Presidency, and my eye is on him." Randolph was opposed to Henry Clay's Missouri Compromise and filibustered relentlessly against it. He was being constantly interrupted by Congressman Beecher of Ohio who, whenever Randolph paused, would arise and seek to move "the Previous Question." Finally, Randolph addressed the Chair:

Mr. Speaker, in the Netherlands, a man of small capacity, with bits of wood and leather, will, in a few moments, construct a toy that, with the pressure of thumb, will cry "Cuckoo! Cuckoo!" With less ingenuity, and with inferior materials, the people of Ohio have made a toy that will without much pressure, cry, "Previous Question, Mr. Speaker!" (pp. 56-59)

It is said of Beecher that after the enormous laughter at his expense, he never crossed swords with Randolph again.

John Quincy Adams who, along with his father, the second President, had been bitterly attacked by Randolph, quoted Ovid against the latter:

His face is ashen, gaunt his whole body
His breath is green with gall; his tongue drips poison.

Adams, the son, also pilloried Daniel Webster, saying, "the gigantic intellect, the envious temper, the ravenous ambition and the rotten heart of Daniel Webster." In the same vein Calhoun described Henry Clay: "he prefers the specious to the solid, and the plausible to the true. . . . He is a bad man, an imposter, a creator of wicked schemes." Clay retorted to Calhoun that he was a rigid, fanatic, ambitious, selfishly partisan and sectional "turncoat" with "too much genius and too little common sense," who would die either a traitor or a turncoat. In political debate Calhoun boasted of being Clay's master and Clay responded, "Sir, I would not own him as a slave" (pp. 52-54).

Much of this is so vindictive that it almost ceases to be humorous. Almost, not quite; for a rule of comic invective seems to be that the sheer extravagance of an insult has a comic effect when coupled with imaginative wordplay. The very extravagance of an outburst of invective permits the release of excess emotions. At the same time, the flagrance of the exaggeration diminishes its seriousness through the obvious distortion of fact. The insult becomes laughable and, in true comic spirit, disruptive invective serves political tranquillity.

Nevertheless, less of insult and more of wordplay makes for easier humor. Little Alexander Stephens, Representative from Georgia and later Vice-President of the Confederacy, was ridiculed in Congress by a gigantic Western representative. He shouted in debate, "You little shrimp! Why I could swallow you whole!" Stephens countered, "If you did, you'd have more brains in your belly than you ever had in your head."[3]

One of the great humorists of Congress was Representative Samuel "Sunset" Cox, who salted his comic invective with poetry. He badly needed the gift of laughter, for he was a House Democrat in the Civil War and a leader of the Democrats in the House in the many years of "bloody flag waving" after the war. Boykin relates that when Representative Owen Lovejoy of Illinois berated Cox in this manner and referred to his small size, Cox proposed an epitaph for the bulky Lovejoy:

3. Edward Boykin, *The Wit and Wisdom of Congress* (New York: Funk & Wagnalls Co., 1961), p. 159.

Beneath this stone *Owen Lovejoy* lies,
Little in everything—except in size; (laughter)
What though his burly body fills this hole,
Yet through hell's keyhole crept his little soul. (p. 158)

Many years later, in 1880, in a debate on a Harbor and River Bill, Cox was needled by Representative Hoar of Michigan as "my genial little friend." Cox retaliated by mercilessly ridiculing the corpulency of the 250-pound Horr and concluded with:

I fear my friend's end will come sooner than he knows. Corpulence is a disease. I am tired of making obituaries here. But if I am called on to speak his eulogy I would draw on two eminent poets who will combine for such an occasion. One is the sweet singer of Michigan and the other Byron. Over his grave let there be inscribed:

Here lies the body
of
Congressman *Horr*;
'Tis Greece,
But
Living Grease
no more!
Requiescat!

But for once Cox met his match, and in one of the most remarkable *ad hominem* exchanges in the history of Congress, Horr replied:

I wish to say in defense of myself that those words, "genial little friend," were used in the heat of debate. (Laughter) And had I known the sensitiveness of the gentleman from New York, had I known the poetry of his nature, I certainly never should have used the language I did at the time. I should have addressed him in the language of one of our modern poets, "Dear little Buttercup, sweet little Buttercup, I."

Horr continued by recalling that Cox had stated that he would have been President if he had been six inches taller. Horr said that he had no doubts of it, if the six inches were added to his upper story. Horr concluded that he, unlike Cox, was not a highly literary man, nor a poet, but a friend had furnished him with an epitaph for Cox:

Beneath this slab lies the great SAM COX,
He was as wise as an owl and grave as an ox;
Think it not strange his turning to dust,
For he swelled and he swelled till he finally "bust."
Just where he's gone and how he fares
Nobody knows and nobody cares.
But wherever he is, be he angel or elf,
Be sure, dear reader, he's puffing himself.[4]

It will be noted that much comic invective is highly personal. To the contrary of the rules for argument, it is directed at *the man*, not the facts or the issue at hand. Possibly to argue *comically* about the man is far easier than to extract humor in argument from ideologies and issues, which immediately divide people into opposing camps. Even when the comic argument is centered on the man using it, it may be that he has a greater attachment to his passionate beliefs or partisan interests than to features of his personality, which are so distorted in ridicule or comic invective that he feels little real threat to his ego.

Obviously, there must be bite, and there will be hurt in comic invective, otherwise it could not serve as a release for aggression. The question is one of degree. Too much hurt or personal involvement and aggressive retaliation would follow. Humor as a safety valve would fail. The personal attack directly involves only the victim. The ideological (or issues) attack necessarily brings others in. Because much of ideology and the framing of issues is already sym-

---

4. *Ibid.*, pp. 68-69. Cox himself has written an account of American humor available in reissue, *Why We Laugh* (New York and London: Benjamin Bloom, Inc., 1876, 1969).

bolical (imaginatively exaggerated and nonfactual), it is more difficult to exaggerate so grossly that the victims will perceive the presence of comedy, relax their defensiveness, and enjoy or at least nonviolently tolerate, the pseudo-aggression.

As we shall see, political parties do not fall inside the restraint that comic invective exercises toward issues and ideologies. They are not considered by either the politicians or most people to be ideological or a real issue in an election. In fact, because of their make-believe character, they are even more prone to political humor. Likewise, there are issues that become so stereotyped or so much political fictions that they too become ideal targets.

The key to political humor is reserve, or dispassion, or critical neutrality. Anything, however subject to invective, can be cruelly humorous for one group as long as it is directed to outsiders. But for comic invective to serve its function as political humor, it must relieve tensions within the body politic and promote its political stability. For, to the extent that it enflames violent reactions or hardens partisan prejudices, it diminishes as humorous and as political.

The element of party warfare is often present in the personal comic invective of politics, but seldom are the two combined so masterfully as in an example from the Southern hustings. Representative Sergeant S. Prentiss of Mississippi in the 1830s was debating the Governor, M'Nutt. The latter alluded to Prentiss's love of whiskey. Prentiss rejoined by depicting the joys in liquor, and then he pounced:

Now, fellow-citizens, during this ardent campaign, which has been so fatiguing, I have only been drunk once. Over in Simpson County, I was compelled to sleep in the same bed with this distinguished nominee, this delight of his party, this wonderful exponent of the principles and practices of the unwashed Democracy, and in the morning I found myself drunk on corn whiskey. I had lain too close to his soaked mass of Democracy and I was drunk from absorption.[5]

Here is a "whopper" in the comic-story tradition of the South, and it is the more humorous and politically effective for it. Prentiss has diverted the charges of his own drunkenness. He has ridiculed his opponent's party affiliation. And in the comic exuberance of his wordplay he has bested M'Nutt with good feeling and without actually threatening his reputation or ego.

The great Senator Thomas Benton of Missouri, after he lost his Senate seat because of his anti-secession stand, ran for Governor in 1856 against Trusten Polk. Once, in campaigning throughout the State, Benton began his speech meditatively, "T-r-u-s-t-e-n Polk! T-r-u-s-t-e-n Polk! A man that nobody trusts; a knave in politics and a hypocrite in religion."[6]

When Benton, who was a fierce nationalist, was asked shortly after Calhoun's death if he would continue to pursue Calhoun beyond the grave, Benton replied, "No, sir" When God Almighty lays His hand upon a man, sir, I take mine off, sir" (p. 165).

A natural target for ridicule and invective was Senator Charles Summer of Massachusetts. He was a radical Republican in the Civil War era, dogmatic, pompously learned, and a bombastic orator. In 1866 he opposed a bill to employ Vinnie Ream, a sculptress, to carve a statue of Abraham Lincoln (the famed statue in the Rotunda of the Capitol). A debate waged for weeks over the bill. Summer made a plea not to pass the bill on the grounds of economy, the sake of art, the lack of talent of the sculptress, and the greatness of the martyred Lincoln. Senator Nesmith of Oregon rebutted him and said, in part:

The Senator from Massachusetts has pandered so long to

5. Boykin, p. 49.
6. *The Wit and Humor of American Statesmen* (Philadelphia: George W. Jacobs & Co., Publishers, 1902), p. 164.

European aristocracy that he cannot speak of anything that originates in America with common respect.

If this young lady and the works she has produced had been brought to his notice by some near-sighted, frog-eating Frenchman, with a pair of green spectacles on his nose, the Senator would have said that she was deserving of commendation. If she could have spoken three or four different languages that nobody else could have understood, or, perhaps, that neither she nor the Senator could understand, he would vote her fifty thousand dollars. (Laughter). He is a great patron of art, but not of domestic art. He is a patron of foreign art; he is a patron of those who copy and ape European aristocracy, and he does not propose to patronize or encourage the genius which grows up in our own great country, particularly in the wilds of the West.[7]

Summer and his foreign airs of learnedness were being ridiculed by that sense of "Americanism" noted by so many in our history. All he could do was retreat, and he did. At another time, President Grant took a crack at his education, saying, "The reason Summer doesn't believe in the Bible is because he didn't write it himself."[8]

The xenophobic element in American humor is not precisely political. Ridicule of the foreigner may serve to solidify the home country, but it is not directed toward the peace and stability of relationships between competing groups within society. However, because of the mixed elements in the United States, ethnic political humor has xenophobic elements and does serve a comic political function. Each national grouping that has come to the United States has been ridiculed in one way or another, but the Irish, because of their high politicization, have been most often used for political humor.

A late-nineteenth-century example based on fact has to do with the campaign speech of the Honorable Tim Campbell of Brooklyn given against his Italian opponent, Dago Rinaldo:

7. Boykin, pp. 224-26.
8. *The Wit and Humor of American Statesmen*, p. 122.

There is two bills before the country—the Mills bill and the McKinley bill. The Mills bill is for free trade, with everything free; the McKinley bill is for protection, with noththing free. Do you want everything free, or do you want to pay for everything? Having thus disposed of the national issue, I will now devote myself to the local issue, which is the Dago Rinaldo. He is from Italy. I am from Ireland. Are you in favor of Italy or Ireland? Having thus disposed of the local issue, and thanking you for your attention, I will now retire. (pp. 23-24)

The extreme simplification of the speech is an example of the humorous *reductio ad absurdum*. Though not intended by the candidate to be humorous, its acceptance into the folklore of political humor constitutes its appreciation as humor. As such, it is a laugh at the sovereign populace as well as their ethnic prejudices. A most complicated technical issue is reduced by word associations into a blatantly false deduction. Then, the choice of candidates is presented as a choice between their ethnic origins on the grounds of one's own ethnic affiliation and prejudice.

Like comic invective in general, ethnic political humor is overtly hostile but covertly serves stability and the assimilation of out-groups. Hostility couched in humor retains sting but loses fear through the enjoyment of it. At the same time, that which is being aggressively ridiculed becomes familiar through its pleasurable exposure. It becomes subject to rational criticism, rather than prejudiced hostility. A feared "trait" of a rival ethnic group is treated as a laughable foible and, thereby, the in-group becomes understanding of the foreign. In turn, the ethnic target of the humor is more acceptable in the larger society, and the minority group comes to see itself and the objectionable features of its behavior in light of the standards of the larger society.

Generally, the best political invective is aimed at a personality, though it may have ethnic or partisan overtones. Boykin, in his collection of Congressional wit, writes, "Nothing ever uttered in the American Congress quite matches James G. Blaine's plastering of Roscoe Conkling of New

York before an enthralled House in 1866." Boykin says that Conkling had been needling Blaine for days in his arrogant, swaggering manner. Suddenly Blaine retaliated and used the metaphor of a strutting turkeycock, which dogged Conkling in cartoons for the rest of his life. Blaine said:

As to the gentleman's cruel sarcasm, I hope he will not be too severe. The contempt of that large-minded gentleman is so wilting, his haughty disdain, his grandiloquent swell, his majestic, supereminent, overpowering turkey-gobbler strut, has been so crushing to myself and all the members of the House, that I know it was an act of the greatest temerity for me to venture upon a controversy with him.

But, sir, I know who is responsible for this, I know that within the last five weeks, as members of this House will recollect, an extra strut has characterized the gentleman's bearing. It is the fault of another. That gifted satirical writer, Theodore Tilton of the *New York Independent*, spent some weeks recently in this city. His letters as published in that paper embraced, with many serious statements, a little jocose satire, a part of which was the statement that the mantle of the late Henry Davis Winter had fallen on the member from New York.

The gentleman took it seriously, and it has given his strut additional pomposity. The resemblance is great; it is striking. Hyperion to Satyr; Thersites to Hercules; mud to marble; dunghill to diamond; a singed cat to a Bengal tiger; a whining puppy to a roaring lion! Shade of the mighty Davis! Forgive the almost profanation of the jocose satire![9]

It is difficult to exceed this venomous personal invective, comically camouflaged in the most brilliant wordplay. Conkling is attacked as a stupidly egotistical and overbearing man by comparing him with a very stupid and proud-of-bearing bird, the very image of which becomes laughable. Conkling's egotism is called so great that he takes satire for compliment, and to this is added a string of metaphorical contrasts, the viciousness of which is only exceeded by their

9. Boykin, pp. 47-48.

comic extravagance. Yet, however brilliant the invective in isolation, its bite for Conkling lies in his vulnerability to it. The most effective political humor always has a large germ of truth in it.

A number of years later Blaine ran against Grover Cleveland for President of the United States. This time he became the victim of a classic one-line campaign slogan of comic invective: "James G. Blaine, James G. Blaine, Continental Liar from the State of Maine." In his political career he had told less than the full truth concerning some political corruption involving the railroads, and the catchy comic slogan served to remind the voters of it laughingly. When a serious candidate for office can successfully be made the object of ridicule, obviously his credibility for that office is damaged. Blaine lost.

However, his opponent, Cleveland, had poetic invective leveled at him in the same campaign, and he won. Cleveland, many years before and when he was a bachelor, had fathered an illegitimate child by his boardinghouse-keeper. The rhymed invective went:

Maw, Maw, where's my Paw
Gone to the White House, haw, haw, haw.

It was said of the result of the contest in political invective that the American people would take for public office a scoundrel in private life who was publicly upright over a man of scrupulous private conduct and public chicanery (Blaine).

In the administration of FDR, Harold Ickes was the invective hatchet man in the presidential campaigns. He called the Republican candidate, Wendell Wilkie, in the 1940 election "the rich man's Roosevelt; the simple, barefoot boy from Wall Street." In the 1944 election he said of Roosevelt's rival, the youthful Thomas Dewey, "Dewey has thrown his diaper in the ring." And he ridiculed the formality of Dewey's appearance, saying Dewey looked "like the little man on top of the wedding cake."[10] The only compar-

10. Harris, p. 142.

able recent presidential election invective is the question posed of the Republican candidate, Richard Nixon, in the 1960 campaign: "Would you buy a used car from this man?"

Politicians in public can be highly partisan in their invective, depending on relative party strengths in elections. However, they cannot afford to appear to be poor sports, poor losers, or disloyal to their party teammates. They do not play according to the public's rules of the game, but the public does not have quite the same rules as the players. Often the egos and incomes of politicians are at stake, and between themselves they may resort to vicious comic invective. Thus, George Allen, Truman's Clown Prince of the White House, tells of Senator Thomas Gore of Oklahoma describing his opponent in an election. Gore conceded, "I don't want to be hard on him, because anybody has a right to aspire to a place in the Senate, even my place. I would say of this fellow that he has every attribute of a dog except loyalty."[11]

George Allen also tells of Senator Pat Harrison of Mississippi getting a job in the Agriculture Department for his former Governor, Theodore Bilbo. He feared that Bilbo coveted his Senate seat, and Bilbo was a vicious but masterful Southern demagogue whom he wished to keep out of his way with a job in Washington. He talked the Secretary of Agriculture George Peek into giving Bilbo a job on grounds of party, and of agricultural expertise, but warned against allowing Bilbo to give political speeches, to control government money, or to be left alone with pretty stenographers. Peek replied, "In other words, Senator, this good Democrat, Bilbo, will be fine for us if we muzzle him, tie his hand, and lock up the petty cash."

Senator Harrison agreed. Peek gave Bilbo the job. Bilbo served till the next senatorial election when he ran against Harrison's colleague, defeated him, and then tried to eliminate Harrison by sponsoring opposition to him in the next election (pp. 68-69).

11. George Allen, *Presidents Who Have Known Me* (New York: Simon & Schuster, 1950), p. 52.

Some of the best political humor, particularly comic invective, does not become a part of the public spectacle. Politicians fear being considered clowns or poor sports. But in the more secluded confines of the legislative arena, the battle of wits is not so restrained. At the turn of the century, Speaker Reed of the House of Representatives not only ruled the House with dictatorial efficiency, but he also exercised a cutting wit to keep members in hand. One morning the House Beau Brummel took exception to a news story on himself. He addressed the Chair:

"Mr. Speaker, I rise to a question of personal privilege. I have here a copy of this morning's *New York Sun* in which I am referred to as a thing of beauty and a joy forever."
Reed: "The point is well taken, It should have been a thing of beauty and a jaw forever."

Another day, Speaker Reed was annoyed by the insistent chatter of two members. He turned to the Sergeant-at-Arms and said in a voice audible to all: "They never open their mouths without subtracting from the sum of human knowledge."

Another member, to emphasize his stand on a point under debate, paraphrased Clay's famous remark, saying, "I'm right. I know I'm right so I say, with Henry Clay, sir, I would rather be right than President." Reed responded *sotto voce*, but fully audibly, "The gentleman need not worry for he will never be either."[12] The play on the word "right" and Clay's epigram were effectively employed in a more recent comic invective against Dewey's presidential candidacy. It was said that Dewey had written a book, "I'd Rather Be President."

There are few other professions in which this invective repartee would not be considered excessively harsh. In politics, among politicians themselves, there is broad tolerance of and admiration for comic invective as long as it is sufficiently witty. Politics is talk; legislation is the drafting

12. Boykin, pp. 165-66.

of words; and politicians (often lawyers) are verbal craftsmen. When they use ambigously or imprecisely words that can be given another meaning or twisted into humor or invective, their vulnerability is a reflection of their poor craftsmanship or political insensitivity. Comic invective is political warfare, but it is also a measure of political skill.

Huey Long was a master of the art of political ridicule. He came to dislike President Franklin Roosevelt and considered the president and his policies a threat to his own political ambitions. He mercilessly ridiculed Roosevelt's policy of limiting farm crops in a Congressional speech:

A man came in to see me the other day and said to me, "I ask you to consider what good I have done for this country. I am the man who taught two trees to grow where one used to grow before." I said, "You are the worst citizen we have in this state under our system of things. You are the man who ought to be condemned and hung tomorrow morning. The idea of your coming in here and asking for consideration because you taught two trees to grow where one used to grow. We want a man who fixes it so that none can grow. We want a man who can teach the people how none could be raised. That is what we want in this year of our Lord 1935, of Franklin Delano Roosevelt the little." (p. 182)

George Allen related Roosevelt's reaction to one of Long's speeches against him as follows:

Although capable of vindictiveness, Roosevelt was curiously detached in his attitude toward strictly political enemies. Once I listened to a speech in the Senate by Huey Long ripping Roosevelt to pieces with sarcastic fury. I described some of the Louisiana Kingfish's anti-Roosevelt histrionics to McIntyre, who insisted that I tell the President about them. Roosevelt listened fascinated. He didn't behave as one being attacked personally; there was no resentment. He was simply interested in the technique of a rival, as an actor might be interested in the performance of another actor.[13]

"The play's the thing," and one might add, to paraphrase Shakespeare, wherein the wit may catch the conscience of populus-king. The politicians play for their relief and pleasure, but the final consideration must always be the effect of the comedy of politics on the spectators; are they laughing with you or at you?

Politicians against Themselves

I have remarked that politicians must be considered a part of their culture. In the United States there is the seeming anomaly of an anti-political culture within a society based on politics. Yet, the politician is a representative in politics of the people who are anti-political. To be elected and succeed as a representative, the politician must be eminently political, but he must conceal his politicization from his constituents, and perhaps from himself. To appear to be a politician, or to like politics, is to become suspect by the anti-political electorate.

President Franklin Delano Roosevelt, superbly the dramatic artist in the "play" of politics, could use ironic humor for self-deprecation while, at the same time, it indirectly ridiculed his opponents. His favorite story told of a commuter from Republican Westchester County in New York. Every morning the man walked into the train station, handed the paper boy a quarter, picked up the paper, glanced at the front page, returned the paper, and rushed out to his train. Finally, the newsboy, overcome with curiosity, asked the customer why he glanced only at the front page.

"I'm interested in the obituary notices," said the man.

"But they're way over on page twenty-four, and you never look at them," the boy objected.

13. Allen, p. 156.

"Boy, the son of a bitch I'm interested in will be on page one" (p. 238).

Roosevelt made fun of himself, but he conveyed to his audience the type of people (Westchester County) who opposed him. At the same time, their bitter invective demonstrates Roosevelt's championship of the common people.

Two stories of the late President Kennedy ridicule Irish "traits" of machine politics and political Catholicism. Kennedy, himself Irish and Catholic, shows in his use of humor both an understanding of the implicit criticism and his own superiority over the "traits" (at least rhetorically). One of Kennedy's stories was about a powerful ward boss among the old Boston Irish:

A man named Finnegan moved into Lomasney's ward and soon walked up to Lomasney and asked to be an officer in the Hendricks Club of the ward. Lomasney liked his spirit and consented. Then, Finnegan asked Lomasney to back him for the Boston Common Council. Lomasney was a little surprised, but he did. Of course, Finnegan won. Then, Finnegan asked for backing for the Great and General Court (State Legislature). Though slightly annoyed, Lomasney complied. Next, Finnegan pestered him for a seat in the State Senate. But he still wasn't satisfied. He came back to Lomasney. "And what on earth is it you want this time?" Lomasney asked. "Please, Mr. Lomasney," said the new State Senator, "will you help me get my citizenship papers?"[14]

The ingredients of this story are common to much political humor, but all of it points to the unscrupulous power of the political machine. In another story Kennedy makes light of the strong Catholicism of the Irish and the consequent reputed power of the Pope over Irish politicians. Here he embellishes an old joke of Al Smith's. The occasion was his opposition to Federal aid to parochial schools, for which he

14. Booton Herndon, ed., *The Humor of JFK* (Greenwich, Conn.: Fawcett Publications, A Gold Medal Book, 1964), pp. 21-22.

was heavily criticized by fellow Catholics. Kennedy commented:

As you all know, some circles invented the myth that after Al Smith's defeat in 1928 he sent a one-word telegram to the Pope: "Unpack." After my press conference on the school bill, I received a one-word wire from the Pope myself: "Pack." (p. 48)

Kennedy not only ridicules his supposed Irish flaws and thereby counters them as political liabilities, but he engages in self-deprecation and counters a constant charge against politicians, their egotism. Egotism, so necessary to political drive and durability, must be liberally possessed by the politician, but any outward display of it exposes a representative of the people to harsh ridicule for being better than they are.

Kennedy, an heir to one of the great American fortunes, had to counter not only popular fear of political power but also envy of his family fortune. At the Gridiron Club in Washington, he related: "I just received the following wire from my generous Daddy—'Dear Jack—Don't buy a single more vote than necessary. I'll be damned if I'm going to pay for a landslide' " (p. 50).

Kennedy, perhaps because of his all too obvious assets, was a master of self-deprecatory humor. Just as leveling humor seeks to reduce political leaders and social personages to the equality of simple humanity, comic self-deprecation counters potential hostility at apparent superiority by humorous exposure of one's common human plight. Thus, after President Kennedy's fashionable wife received a great social reception in Paris, the President ironically introduced himself to the French press. He said, "I do not think it altogether inappropriate to introduce myself to this audience. I am the man who accompanied Jacqueline Kennedy to Paris, and I have enjoyed it" (p. 68).

Kennedy's successor as President, Lyndon B. Johnson, had a reputation as a ruthless manipulator of political power. A superb politician, he knew the uses of humor for disarming suspicion; that which can be laughed at is less to be feared. Moreover, the politician who can make fun of himself in respect to the deepest criticisms concerning him appears in his awareness and acceptance of the criticisms to rise above them. One of Johnson's favorite stories meets his reputation for unscrupulousness head-on:

A graduate of a teacher's college was sent to a town in East Texas for a job interview with its school board. The chairman of the school board informed the applicant that the town was rent over a crucial issue—whether the earth was round or flat. He asked the young teacher which way he taught about the shape of the earth. The teacher replied, "Either way you want it, either way you want it."

Johnson humorously admits that a politican doesn't decide issues; he represents the opinion of a dominant majority. The comic story laughs at the popular prejudice that a politician should know the truth and proclaim it, regardless of its effects on his constituents. In a representative democracy the politician has some flexibility between opposing sides in an issue, but he is always bound by the limitations of the people. So be it.

Johnson won his election to the U.S. Senate in 1948 by very few votes and, of course, the inevitable charges of rigged election were made. Humorously, he was dubbed Landslide Lyndon, and he countered with this tale: A citizen was walking through the streets of San Antonio when he observed a little Mexican boy, whom he knew, sitting on the curb and crying. He went up to him and asked, "José, why are you crying?" José replied, "My daddy doesn't like me." The citizen said, "But José, your daddy is dead." José responded, "But he came back to vote for Lyndon Johnson, and he didn't see me."

President Johnson's Republican opponent in the 1964 Presidential election was Senator Barry Goldwater of Arizona, an outspoken conservative who had been attacked as a dangerous reactionary. Adlai Stevenson quipped of him that he is the kind of man who looks forward to the rear future. Senator Humphrey, in the 1964 campaign, ridiculed Goldwater's opposition to welfare legislation, saying "he was sitting under the no-no tree in the shade of his own indifference."

However, Senator Goldwater demonstrated his political temper and disproved charges of right-wing fanatacism by making fun of his own conservatism. Through the comic technique of grossly exaggerating the political criticisms, he made them unreal to the public while showing his casual disdain for their lack of truth. Speaking at a convention of editorial cartoonists, Goldwater talked about a possible new career:

The theatre kind of appeals to me too. When my contract with 18th-Century-Fox runs out I shouldn't have too much trouble. I've been offered a job as a consultant on the Flintstones' TV show. Thanks to some cartoons depicting my political philosophy, the producers got the idea that I am America's foremost authority on the Stone Age.[15]

In 1962 when Senator Goldwater was campaigning for the Republican Party nomination for presidential candidate, he spoke before the Alfalfa Club in Washington, receiving a humorous award. In part, he said:

Emotion chokes me when I think that you have chosen a bare-foot boy from the Arizona "valley of fear" to lead this underprivileged, under-nourished, underhoused, under-clothed and over-Kennedied nation of under one hundred and ninety million underlings back to the Old Frontier of McKinley's day. The UNDERtaking, naturally, overwhelms me. It takes my breath away even though I feel the White House is ready for me since Jacqueline remodeled it in an Eighteenth Century decor, and I feel this is a double honor since I've never even been to Harvard. . . .

Now right at the beginning let me scotch one bit of campaign slander the opposition has come up with. It is perfectly true that during the heat of the pre-convention maneuvering, I said that if nominated I would not accept, and if

15. Harris, p. 269.

elected, I would not serve. But that statement was lifted out of context and deliberately distorted.

In the first place, when I said it, things didn't look so good. But do they tell you that? Of course not. They claim that I meant it. What I really said was that Sherman had said it first. Eisenhower had said it in 1948, Adlai had said it in 1952 (and wishes to God he'd stuck to it), and Nixon is saying it now. It beats me how they can take a clear-cut sentence like that and distort it. Why even Pravda garbled it in translation, and they usually get things right. . . .

Now I must take note of the fact that my opponents call me a conservative. If I understand the word correctly, it means to "conserve"—well, then, I'm just trying to live up to my name and conserve two things that most need conserving in this country—gold and water.

I don't apologize for being a conservative, I can remember when "conservative" and "mother" were clean words.

Now let me turn to my campaign platform. As you all know, I have argued for some time that we should do away with the cumbersome and lengthy, unmeaningful and platitudinous promises that the platforms of both parties have become. We need bold, brief statements that all Americans can understand. . . .

The first plank fits neatly on one page, but I think it's basically sound and honest. It will mean the same thing to you whether you live in the North or South, whether you're a farmer in Maine or an industrial worker in California. It says, and I ask you to pay close attention: ELECT GOLDWATER. . . .

The other two planks deal with labor, education, foreign policy, and the farm problem. Here's Plank Number Two—ELECT GOLDWATER. Now you may notice a certain similarity between the first plank and the second, and I want you to know that that was deliberate. It has been my experience that the public is confused if you offer too many issues. The thing to do is to get hold of one good one and stick to it. Hammer it home. Repetition is the way Madison Avenue sells toothpaste and soap, and it's the way the New Frontier stays in the limelight. But when repetition occurs at the White House—and it has since 1932—it's not a sales pitch, it's a giveaway. You don't even have to guess the price.

And now for the final plank—Plank Number Three. This is the bell-ringer and it's even shorter. It just says DIT-TO.[16]

Goldwater is not content to merely ridicule the ideological issue of conservativism; he cuts through to the realities of politics. First he ridicules himself for having said at one time that he wouldn't accept presidential nomination or office. He recognizes the changing contingencies of politics and comically regrets his own stupidity. Second, he disposes of all the ideological pretense of campaign platforms and admits to the main chance in all its guises—"Elect Goldwater." In inimitable comic duality, Goldwater has made light of himself even as he proclaims the self-centeredness of politics, thereby protecting himself against the criticism.

Adlai Stevenson, twice-defeated presidential candidate, demonstrated the same protective technique with ironic humor. One of the most humorous and articulate of all modern politicians, Stevenson was always vulnerable to criticisms of his wordiness. One witticism about Stevenson in the 1952 campaign had to do with his opponent for the Democratic nomination, rustic-appearing, hand-shaking Senator Kefauver of Tennessee: "Stevenson had better not discount Senator Kefauver in the primary contests. After every Stevenson speech, Kefauver can shake hands with the crowd and admit that he didn't understand it all either."

Stevenson may well have been too literary for the common taste, but much of his humor was of the common anti-political bent. He said, "a politician is a statesman who approaches everything with an open mouth." And he commented on his humor, "that kind of thing tickles the fancy of ordinary people because they've all heard the saying, 'I approach everything with an open mind,' and I was talking about these politicians who talk about everything as if they

16. Lewin, pp. 91-92.

know all the answers."[17] He doesn't add that his quip served as a protective screen against his own popular image.

It might be noted that the open mouth-open mind political joke is a natural one when directed to the talk merchants of politics. It was used as invective by Senator Connally of Texas against Senator Styles Bridges: "If the Senator from New Hampshire would approach these matters with an open mind instead of an open mouth, he could understand these matters" (p. 222).

In 1940 Representative Luther Patrick of Alabama submitted to the House a set of "Rules for a Congressman." All of the rules are humorous, but they are also serious; that is, they are a reliable guide to the proper conduct for a Congressman. Yet, they involve impossibility in some instances and contradiction in others. In short, the rules reflect what we demand of politicians, what they can never achieve, and, consequently, what we will always criticize about them. Two of the Rules are excellent examples of this comic contradictoriness:

> 5. Be a cultured gentleman, a teller of ribald stories, a profound philosopher, preserve a store of "Confucius say" gags; be a ladies' man, a man's man, a he-man, a diplomat, a Democrat with a Republican slant, a Republican with a Democratic viewpoint, an admirer of the Roosevelt way, a hater of the New Deal, a new dealer, an old dealer, and a quick dealer. . . .

> 7. Have the dope on hot spots in town, with choice telephone numbers for the gay boys from back home, and help to contact all local moral organizations and uplift societies in Washington[18]

The ambivalent attitude of the electorate toward their representatives finds its match in their representatives'

17. Harris, p. 252. In his anthology of humor Harris included an interesting discussion with Stevenson on the latter's understanding of humor in relation to politics.
18. Boykin, pp. 387-88.

views of their own status in politics. Senator Nesmith's humorous awareness of this failing is revealed in this story of the Senator from Oregon:

> Some two years after he had taken his seat he was recounting to Senator Wade his wonder upon first seeing the Capitol and especially the still great wonder that he should have been honored by being elected a member of so august a body.
> "Well," said Senator Wade, "you have been here a couple of years; what do you think of it now?"
> "Think," replied Nesmith, "why the wonder to me now is how you and so many other fellows ever managed to get here."[19]

The mysterious alchemy of the exercise of political power transforms the honor of representing the people into the egotism of ruling over them. Ironic humor of politicians serves to remind them of this temptation. Another nineteenth-century Senator, Vest, recounted:

> I once met a good old lady out West who evinced great surprise of a not very complimentary sort when she met me.
> "And so you're Senator Vest, the great Senator?" she asked.
> "I'm Senator Vest," I replied, bowing.
> "Well, well," she exclaimed contemptuously, "after all I've heard about you, I'd never'd a thought it." (p. 104)

A Congressional tale displays the same leveling humor but with a different moral to it. A Congressman was campaigning in one of the back counties of his district, and he came upon a woman sitting on the roadside watching her man split rails up on a hill. He greeted the woman, and she inquired of him his business in the locality. In doing so, she guessed at his occupation, ruling out preaching because "preachers don't pack their bottles in their outside pockets."

19. *Wit and Humor of American Statesmen*, pp. 206-7.

At this the Congressman took the bottle out and offered her a drink. She, in turn, called the railsplitter, and renewed her query to the politician: "What do you do for a living?" And he concludes the story:

"I'm a member of Congress," I said, blushing at my own greatness.
She gave a long, low whistle.
"Bill," she called, to the man up on the hill, "he don't do nothin' for a livin'; he's a member of Congress." William came down from the hill and there were three less drinks in the bottle as I rode on. (pp. 76-77)

The Congressman's self-estimation is sharply contradicted by an earthy remark, "he don't do nothin' for a livin'." Its elemental truth in a country based on the work ethic and economic productivity restores a sense of proportion to politics, and the Congressman is more of a representative for it.

J. Proctor Knott, a Representative from Kentucky in the post-civil war era, once addressed the Speaker on the split personality of the representative-ruler:

Mr. Speaker, I have been satisfied for a long time that the affection of a young mother for her first-born bears no sort of comparison to the love which gentlemen on this floor entertain for the people. To do anything like justice to the depth of that sentiment would bankrupt all the resources of the most pathetic eloquence or the most stirring poetry. If we speak of the law, it is "the people's law"; if we speak of ourselves it is as "the people's Representatives"; if we allude to the Constitution, it is "the people's Constitution"; if we have anything to say about the government, it is "the people's government." Everything belongs to them, and their interests are paramount to every other consideration. Gentlemen love them—love them as they do the apple of their eyes. They would undergo any sacrifice for them. There is not an office, from President down, that any of us would not relieve the people of the trouble of holding, and of which we would not heroically shoulder the emoluments.[20]

20. Boykin, p. 41.

Knott repeats all the political clichés of respect for the people, and then, abruptly terminates the sentiment with a comic twist as to the politicians' more banal motivations. Much of the politician's self-deprecatory humor serves to remind him not to become too serious about himself or his importance. George Allen tells a political story of how one Senator humorously was recalled to the tenuousness of political rule:

Henry Ashurst, the great former Senator from Arizona, once made a tremendously impressive fight for a cause he believed in and thought dear to the hearts of his constituents. He invoked the prophets, Shakespeare, Dante, and a score of lesser thinkers to make his oratorical points. But when the roll call came, he quietly voted against the cause he had defended. One of the Senators who had opposed him in the debate grasped his hand and congratulated him on his shift. "Thank God, Henry, you have seen the light," said his colleague. "Oh, no," Ashurst replied, "I didn't see the light. I felt the heat."[21]

Allen comments that the Senator, who frequently boasted that the clammy hand of consistency never rested long upon his shoulder, didn't hesitate to vote against his own opinion when confronted with the heat of home opinion. At times in the life of every politician, the philosophical issue over the proper role of a representative must yield to the practical necessity of votes. A live politician must then forgo the illusions of statesmanship, and be content with the humor of political paradox.

Politicians and the People against Parties

The mock warfare of political humor finds ample materials in the stuff of American political parties. Like so much of politics, parties are built upon contradictions. In fact, legions of political scientists have spent innumerable hours try-

21. Allen, p. 218.

ing to define what they are, if they are at all. Perhaps, the best definition is such because it is the least definite— American political parties are states of mind. As Will Rogers once said:

"I belong to no organized political party; I'm a Democrat."

But politicians organize and campaign under the ephemeral banners of political parties. They associate themselves with one and against the other. In the battle of words that political warfare wages, the nebulousness of political parties provides a perfect framework for partisan attack and comic invective. They are the ghost armies that can be verbally made to be all things, and then ridiculed for being none of them.

Though political party affiliation may be in the final reality but a state of mind, attitudes affect behavior and influence politics. A favorite tale of one politician has to do with the advice of an older Senate page to the new pages. He said:

It's sometimes difficult to tell the difference between a Republican Senator and a Democratic Senator. Nearly all Senators—Republicans and Democrats alike—look prosperous and distinguished and carry themselves with dignity. But if you really want to tell whether a particular Senator is a Republican or a Democrat, observe how he comes into a room. A Republican Senator struts into a room just as if he owns the place. On the other hand, a Democratic Senator swaggers in as though he doesn't give a damn who owns it. [22]

A much earlier partisan assessment of the difference between Democrats and Whigs (the predecessor of the Republican Party) reveals a certain consistency in the unconscious comedy of partisan politics. Boykin relates that in 1846 a Congressional representative from the Ohio backwoods, nicknamed "Sausage" Sawyer, rose to protest in the House.

22. F. Hodge O'Neal and Annie Laurie O'Neal, eds., *Humor, The Politician's Tool* (New York: Vantage Press, 1964), p. 134.

He was angered that his party, the Democrats, had won the presidency with Polk, but the Whigs still held 235 of the 730 federal clerkships. He was interrupted in his speech:

A Member. How do you know they are Whigs?
Sawyer. Don't I know a Whig from a Democrat as far as I can see him? (The House in a roar).
A Member. How can you tell one from the other?
Sawyer. Just as easy as you can tell one of your sheep from the others; or just as well as you can tell a racehorse from a workhorse. A Whig always dresses up fine, or better than Democrats do, and looks like he thought he knew more and was a great deal better than a Democrat. They ain't plain folks like we are.[23]

The reality of political parties may be evasive, and certainly the politicians are aware of their shifting and confused nature. Yet, their rivalry and successes are influenced by their partisan identities, and the people's evaluation of them is bound up with the people's partisanship. In turn, popular partisan attachments are determined by social class status, regionalism, and historic circumstances. The proper-tied propriety of Republicans versus the equalitarianism of the Democrats comes through in the two above comic tales. Regional partisanship spurs the humor of the following:

A crowd of Democrats was setting one day on the porch of a hotel in New Hampshire during the Grant-Seymour campaign of 1868. An old traveler, ragged, dirty, rusty, unshaven and unshorn, ambled up and stared vacantly at the crowd which began to question him. Finally, someone asked, "You're a Seymour man, aren't you, old fellow?" Straightening up he answered, "Fom my present appearance you would probably take me for a Democrat, but I ain't. I learned my politics before I took to drink." (p. 305)

Again, Republican propriety is contrasted to Democratic "liberality." But regional partisanship is more directly present in a story of Senator McIntyre of New Hampshire. He tells of a Democratic candidate for the U.S. Senate campaigning in a densely rural and Republican part of northern New England. Everywhere he was coolly received by people, who had never seen, let alone voted for, a Democrat. In one general store, amid the usual chilliness, an old man sitting in the corner suddenly hollered at him, "I voted for a Democrat once."

The candidate smiled broadly, strode over to the oldster with his hand outstretched, and began to introduce himself. But before he could get a word out, the old man broke in:

"Yes, I voted for a Democrat about twenty-five years ago, and I've regretted it ever since."[24]

The social class representation of Republicans is the butt of this terse description by Representative Beall of Texas in 1910:

The Payne tariff bill has shown that the Republicans are expert mathematicians. They can add, subtract, multiply, and divide all in one operation. They can add to the wealth of the rich, subtract from the substance of the poor, multiply millionaires, and divide themselves—all in one bill.[25]

The same Representative Beall elaborated on the division of the Republicans at another time:

The doom of Cannonism and czarism, of Aldrichism and bossism has been sounded. The Republican party has been dismembered. Like Gaul of old, it is divided into three parts—regular Republicans, insurgent Republicans, and chameleon Republicans. The regular Republicans ride the elephant all the time; the insurgent Republicans ride some and walk some, occasionally giving the poor old beast a savage kick, but always taking care to hold on to the tail as evidence of their allegiance. The chameleon Republicans walk with the insurgents when it is popular and ride with the regulars when it is profitable. (p. 304)

24. O'Neal, p. 140
25. Boykin, p. 259.

Note what an apt characterization this metaphor is of either party at any time. Change the party symbol and fill in the current terms for the party divisions and one has instant political humor. The comedy lies in the continuing nature of the parties, not in any particular malaise.

But political parties change in their stands on issues, and there is constant change in their appearances. Thus, Senator Mills of Texas told a story during a tariff debate in 1894 to illustrate how the parties verbally champion some element of their constituencies as a symbol of their virtue. In his story a man fell asleep and dreamed he went to hell:

A politician asked him, "Did you see any Democrats down there?" He said, "Oh, yes, there were a few, not many, but there were a few around." "What were they doing?" "They were talking about reducing taxation and things of that sort, trying to do something for the public good." "Did you see any Populists down there?" "Yes, there were a few Populists." "What were they talking about?" "They were talking about having a good time in hell by issuing greenback money, $150 for every individual in hell." "Did you see any Republicans down there?" "Oh, yes." "What were they doing?" "Everyone of them was holding a Negro between him and the fire." (p. 303)

Another variation on the same story was told in the same political period by Representative Talbert of South Carolina. He said that the way some of our Republican friends treat the colored man is amusing and reminded him of an old Republican who went up to Heaven:

He knocked on the gates and a Saint came and asked him if he was riding. When the good old Republican answered, "No," the saint told him that he couldn't enter. The sorrow-stricken old Republican then went down the hill. At the bottom he met an old Uncle Sambo and asked him where he was going. "I'm going to Heaven," replied Uncle Sambo.

"Well," said the old Republican, "you can't get in unless you ride in."

"What are we to do?" asked Uncle Sambo.

"I will tell you, Uncle. Just let me get up on your back, and you carry me up to the gate. I will knock and they will ask me if I'm riding. I will say 'yes,' and then they will open the door, and I will just ride in on your back and we will both get in that way."

The punch line (and the moral) is apparent. The black agrees to the scheme. They ride up to the gate, and the saint tells the Republican, "Well, just hitch your horse outside and come right in" (pp. 9-10). A political party rides into office on the back of groups or issues that it champions for purely self-serving reasons while it leaves the causes of injustice unaffected—out in the cold. Political humor warns against "full faith and credit" for political parties; parties are confidence games, and too much confidence in promises is a guarantee of too little reality in performance.

Aside from the humor of the two stories on racial politics, the most interesting feature of them for present-day politics is that today the Democrats would have to be substituted for the Republicans. Of course, the racial terms would also have to be replaced. The O'Neals recount a modern comic tale in which the black man emerges clearly superior:

A handsome Black was selected to run for office as a Republican against the white Democratic nominee in a Southern state. This was the first time since Reconstruction days that a Black had run for office, and some whites were upset. At the Black's first political speech, a white bigot heckled him as he began to speak, "What have you got to say for yourself, you black Republican bastard?"

Without blinking an eye or showing any emotion, the Black replied, "I'm Black and I can't help it; I'm Republican and I'm proud of it; and if the last is true, it's because my mother was too darn Democratic."[26]

Many examples of partisan comic invective are purely witty insults without reference to distinguishing characteris-

26. O'Neal, p. 139.

tics of either party. Thus, in the nineteenth-century Congress, Representative John P. Hale, when accused of a prejudiced remark, replied, "I never said that all the Democrats were rascals; only that all rascals were Democrats.[27] Representative Emory Speer said, "The Democratic party is like a mule[,] without pride of ancestry or hope of posterity," and Senator McLauren opined, "The basic principle that will ultimately get the Republican party together is the cohesive power of public plunder."[28]

These witticisms can easily be reversed and used on the other party as the occasion demands or the circumstances warrant it. The constant is their invective quality and its political appeal to the American democracy. In the Harris anthology, he tells of how President Theodore Roosevelt was once bested by a heckler. He was being constantly interrupted by a drunk, who kept shouting, "I'm a Democrat." Roosevelt finally addressed the drunk, "May I ask the gentleman why he is a Democrat?" The drunk replied, "My grandfather was a Democrat; my father was a Democrat; and I am a Democrat." Roosevelt retorted, "My friend, suppose your grandfather had been a jackass, and your father had been a jackass, what would you be?" The drunk replied, "A Republican!"[29]

The same story is repeated in the O'Neals' anthology as Congressman Broomfield's favorite story. Only it is told of an old farmer interrupting a Democratic orator, and the punch line is, "I'd be a Democrat."[30] Broomfield is a Michigan Republican who uses the story for partisan reinforcement of his supporters. Roosevelt was an aggressive egotist who used the humor in protective self-deprecation.

Few stories are strictly factual, and their humor becomes part of political folklore to be drawn upon and adapted to various political needs. The humor, like the political parties themselves, is always undergoing superficial verbal reconstruction, but the constant elements in it remain. Senator

27. Cox, p. 310.
28. Boykin, p. 31.
29. Harris, pp. 236-37.
30. O'Neal, pp. 140-41.

Drake once replied to his fellow U.S. Senator from Missouri, Carl Schurz:

My colleague says, "I firmly believe that the Republican party does contain the seeds of its own regeneration." He also says, "The only way to preserve the vitality of the Republican party is to make it the party of the progressive reforms; in other words, the new party which is bound to come in one form or another." He further says, "I think therefore, the Republican party has the stuff in it to become the new party." From these expressions I gather this threefold proposition; first, that a new party must come; second, that the Republican party needs to be born anew; and thirdly, that, on the whole, maybe it contains the proper ingredients out of which to make the coming new party. Sir, I deny my colleague's claim to originality in this proposition. I hold him up as a plagiarist. It is identically the proposition of a certain county tribunal, which, having determined to build a new jail, passed three resolutions on the subject: first, that they would build a new jail; second, they would build it out of the materials composing the old one; and third, that the old one should stand until the new one was built.[31]

Here, the logic of analogue in comedy demonstrates an analytic rationality and decisively punctures the "new-party-out-of-old-party" claim of political reform. Nevertheless, every several years, the same claim is made by one or the other of the parties. The political need to appear as new, reformed, or progressive is constant in party politics, while the basic elements of successful party organization (or lack of it) remain just as constant. The appearance of change is the response to popular idealism; politics can be pure and build a better world. However, idealism is anti-political, a single-minded crusade not adaptive to the diversity of a pluralistic society. Idealism crashes into social reality, and the constant elements of party heterogeneity crush reform. But humor triumphs; the old jail will have to stand until we can build a new one out of it.

31. Boykin, p. 314.

Political parties always disappoint their militant partisans; yet, however great their disillusion within a party, their illusions persist as to its superiority over the other party. Even the politicians, despite frequent professional cynicism, become caught up in the partisan charades. After all, that's the way the game is played. Is the gamesman likely to publicly violate its rules? One man's party organization is another's political machine. Substitute *machine* for *combine* in Representative Galusha Grow of Pennsylvania's explanation in 1896 of the partisan attitude to the House of Representatives:

Mr. Speaker, by the remarks which have been made here in reference to political "combines", I am reminded of the witty clergyman who said that his "doxy" was orthodoxy and that all other "doxies" were heterodoxy. We all believe in the "combine" that we ourselves belong to, and the bad fellows are all in the other "combine." (p. 25)

The political distortions of the partisan "doxy" were used with invective by Adlai Stevenson against his rival for presidential office in 1952, General Eisenhower. He said, "General Eisenhower employs the three monkeys' standard of campaign morality: see no evil—if it's Republican; hear no evil—unless it is Democratic; and speak no evil—unless Senator Taft says it's all right."[32] Taft had been the party stalwarts' candidate against Eisenhower for the Republican presidential nomination, and it was widely reputed that Eisenhower, to gain the support of the party orthodoxists, capitulated to Taft on party policy.

One of the classic comic stories of partisan bias is based on historic fact. George Allen's version of it is as follows: A party of men from Utah set out on a gold-prospecting expedition in December of 1873. After suffering extreme winter hardships, some stayed in an Indian camp to wait for spring, but six others pressed on to the gold fields. Six weeks later, one of them, Alfred Packer, turned up alone,

32. Harris, p. 239.

saying that his companions had deserted him. Despite his saying that he had subsisted on roots and small game, he was quite healthy and requested whiskey first. After nourishment, he set out for the town of Sauguache where he arrived with money for drinking and gambling.

In the spring, after the snows had melted, the remains of five men were discovered along Packer's trail. Their skulls had been crushed and their bodies partially stripped of flesh. When Packer was confronted with the evidence, he explained that he had been forced to kill one of the five who had become insane and killed the other four. He had not related the episode afterwards because of its shock to him.

Packer was not believed, but he escaped and was not re-captured till ten years later. He was returned for trial. By that time the two-party system had become established in the area, and all the jurymen were Republicans; but the Judge, M. B. Gerry, was a Democrat. Packer's trial was conducted with bipartisan efficiency, and he was sentenced to be hanged. The Democratic Judge Gerry pronounced sentence:

"Alfred Packer, you man-eating son of a bitch, stand up." When Packer obeyed, the Judge went on: "Alfred Packer, you depraved Republican cannibal, I hereby sentence you to hang by the neck until you are dead. There were only six Democrats in Hinsdale County, and, by God, you've et five of them."[33]

The Governor of Colorado, John A. Love, gives an embellished version of the anecdote. He recounts that he had been sent a book on the Packer story. After a news conference the book was sitting on top of his desk and a reporter spied it. He asked the Governor, "Do you think Packer really ate those Democrats?" Governor Love replied, "Oh, I doubt it very much. Did you ever try to clean one?"[34]

33. Allen, pp. 232-34. Allen credits Palmer Hoyt of the *Denver Post* with the original story.
34. O'Neal, p. 138.

The stories recall Lincoln's remark that much American humor is grim and gruesome. Moreover, the expressions of partisanship portrayed in political humor are extreme in their invective, and our enjoyment is generally proportionate to their extremeness. Another of Allen's historic tales relates that in the early mining days in Butte, Montana, the Socialists had been strong. They once elected a mayor who, in turn, hired an all-Socialist police force. When the Democrats regained power, their mayor appointed a fellow partisan chief of police. The latter was asked what he intended to do about the Socialist cops. He replied, "We will give them all a fair and impartial trial and then fire the sons of bitches."[35]

Allen comments that politics is a rough game, and can be played only by rugged men. He overlooks its gamesmanship and the humor that is part of it. The verbal extravagance of partisan and other political invective is appreciated just because of its extravagance. It shockingly exceeds our normal expectations and offends our propriety. It may also confirm our suspicions—be fair and then fire them—of our fellow man's aggressive intent or inherent depravity. We can say, "I knew it all along," with a sense of superiority, but without personally being threatened. The game element of the humor must always be present, or, in the case of a suspense joke, shortly made manifest.

And, of course, with political humor the extravagance and exaggeration add to the thrills of pseudo-warfare. The closer to the border of actual violence the verbal battle can skirt, the greater the thrill of emotions and relief of tensions through the release of aggressive impulses. However, the political game can become strained when partisanship becomes too serious.

Religious claims of partisan righteousness push beyond the pale of politics. Partisan invective was used in 1906 to counter the claim to God's sponsorship of the Republican party. During a debate in the House of Representatives over the fortification of the Philippines, Representative

35. Allen, p. 144.

James of Kentucky sparred with Representative Sibley of Pennsylvania:

Mr. James. I believe that you said that the Republican party and God are in partnership; that would be joining light with darkness; corruption with incorruption.
Mr. Sibley. Whenever you talk about the Republicans and God, and it comes in a slurring way from that side often, if the Republican party has been attempting to act in accordance with the will of God the Democratic party had better reverse its policy and its way, instead of standing against the Lord Almighty and all the facts of history, and survey the marvelous victories that have been accomplished by the Republican party following such leadership—the great good it has accomplished in the elevation of moral sentiment and the higher ideals of national life and national honor. Gentlemen talking about God and the Republican party must not endeavor to get away from the meaning of what they say.
Mr. James. Then you were away from God when you were with the Democratic party?
Mr. Sibley. Now, my friend, do you want me to enter a plea of guilty? If I enter a plea of guilty will that suffice?
Mr. James. I want to know whether, during the time you were serving the Democratic party, God was on that side, or whether you discovered God when you found the Republican party?[36]

Comic rationality has reduced the pious arrogance of partisan Godliness to the either-or humor of "you're damned if you do, and you're damned if you don't." Mr. Sibley, posing as a religious man in politics, has been exposed as an egotistical ass. As was said in the introduction, religious pretensions in politics are most safely countered and publicly ridiculed through the logic of humor.

Perhaps William Faulkner in *The Rievers* should have the last word on partisan invective. He demonstrates that partisanship of any kind is an invitation to ridicule. In the pluralism of politics, when one proclaims the superiority of his factional difference, the others join in the comic attack

36. Boykin, p. 160.

on him to expose his inferiority and to remove the preten-
der to the crown that must belong to all. Faulkner wrote:

A Republican is a man who made his money;
A Liberal is a man who inherited his;
A Democrat is a barefooted Liberal in a cross country race;
A Conservative is a Republican who has learned to read and
write.

The People against Politics

During the McCarthy period of the 1950s, Walt Kelley's
comic-strip character Pogo said, "We have met the enemy
and they is us." A most encouraging aspect of political
humor is that its negativism extends to the sovereign
people. If the people were exempt from the comic criticism
that pervades politics, then democracy might be a much
greater threat.

Representative democracy in America holds that the
people are the ultimate sovereign, but that their power
must be exercised through a structure of government that
contains and limits them. It must be expressed through
elected representatives who refine the popular views with
knowledge and experience, and who are themselves limited. And even majority rule in both popular voting and
the voting of representative bodies has its limits; in politically extraordinary situations, extraordinary majorities are
required.

Ambrose Bierce, one of the most bitter of American
humorists and anti-political in every way, in his *The Devil's
Dictionary*, defines *vote*, n., as "The instrument and symbol
of a freeman's power to make a fool of himself and a wreck
of his country." He defines *referendum*, n., as "a law for
submission of proposed legislation to a popular vote to learn
the nonsensus of public opinion."[37] In another work Bierce
recounts the fable of *The Humble Peasant*:

37. Lewin, pp. 212-13.

An office Seeker whom the President had ordered out of Washington was watering the homeward highway with his tears.

"Ah," he said, "how disastrous is ambition! How unsatisfying its rewards! How terrible its disappointments! Behold yonder peasant tilling his field in peace and contentment! He rises with the lark, passes the day in wholesome toil and lies down at night to pleasant dreams. In the mad struggle for place and power he has no part; the roar of the strife reaches his ear like the distant murmur of the ocean. Happy, thrice happy man! I will approach him and bask in the sunshine of his humble felicity. Peasant, hail!"

Leaning upon his rake, the Peasant returned his salutation with a nod, but said nothing.

"My friend," said the Office Seeker, "you see before you the wreck of an ambitious man—ruined by the pursuit of place and power. This morning when I set out from the national capitol—"

"Stranger," the Peasant interrupted, "if you're going back there soon maybe you wouldn't mind using your influence to make me Postmaster at Smith's Corners."

The traveler passed on. (p. 183)

Could Reinhold Neibuhr's Christian realism be illustrated more succinctly? Could Rousseau's peasant democracy be ridiculed more tellingly? There is no purity in politics or populace; the only distinction is between those who have office and those who covet it. There can be no politics of perfection; there must be a politics of limits, of "save us from ourselves."

In a "Self-Interview" in 1962, Samuel Brightman, then an official of the Democratic National Committee, ridicules another facet of the people's politics. He asks himself why the Democrats had their "brains beaten out in 1952 and 1956":

A: Circumstances beyond our control.
Q: You mean—
A: I mean our candidate. We had insurmountable handicaps. In the first place Stevenson was trained for the

public service. Not only that, but he promised to talk sense to the American people.

Q: Well—

A: It was all right to promise to talk sense, but Stevenson kept his promise.

Q: But I still don't understand—

A: This poor misguided man was talking to an audience conditioned by TV commercials. People who won't buy a ball-point pen unless it will write on butter and who insist upon a shaving-cream that will soften sandpaper are unable to accept a believable proposition. Our opponent's promise to cut taxes and provide more government services was as unbelievable as a TV commercial and the voters flocked right down to their corner voting booth and bought the giant economy size. (p. 88)

In comic sarcasm Brightman indicts the people on two counts: they do not want trained professionals in politics; popular voting is not an act of rational choice. Further, he implies that campaigning and popular voting have kinship with the wish-fulfillment psychology of advertising. The humor lies in the metaphor of the TV commercials and in blatantly stating the reality of popular politics, both of which contradict the conventional shibboleths of democratic ideology. Thus, there is shock, recognition of reality, and the enjoyment of learning and of defying tradition.

This same comic recognition of the reality of popular politics is apparent in two political stories: When Representative Martin Dies of Texas was thinking of running for Congress, he asked the advice of the Governor of his state. The Governor told him to campaign for most of the then popular spending policies, farmers' subsidies, veterans' aid, aid for the aged, and so on. Then, he added, "Oh, yes, Martin, don't forget to have a strong plank for economy in your platform." Dies protested, "But Governor, if I advocate all of those spending measures and at the same time call for economy, don't you think the people will consider me inconsistent?"

The Governor replied, "Martin, the people don't think, and if they ever started, they wouldn't elect you to Congress anyway."[38]

These harsh strictures on popular elections, though comically exaggerated, are rendered palatable to our democratic sensibilities only by their humorous camouflage. Our defenses are lowered and a thought about political reality has been smuggled into our consciousness. Less bitter and more lightly humorous because the contradiction is more flagrant is the comic favorite of Henry Maier, former Mayor of Milwaukee. He likes to repeat the campaign slogan of a nameless politician, "I'm for lower taxes and better municipal services—no matter how much it costs to get them" (p. 165).

This comic contradictoriness that appeals to the people so strongly led Will Rogers to remark, "The South is dry and will vote dry. That is, everyone who is sober enough to stagger to the polls will."[39] And a comic story related in Congress touches on the political ambivalence behind the contradictoriness. A political candidate, in New York when the question of the Maine liquor law was before the people, declared:

> Fellow citizens: I am in favor of the Maine liquor law; I believe it is a good law. I believe it would promote temperance; but, fellow citizens, I am opposed to the enforcement of the Maine liquor law because it interferes with personal liberty.[40]

There is a confused reasoning behind much of the comic contradictoriness of politics, and the politician's ambiguity in his response to it. The people wish to vote morality for their fellows, but they have a deep sense of the limits of government and of their own freedom. Politics is a kind of psychodrama for them, but government is power. They can vote on way in politics, but government had better act another in carrying out the policies.

38. O'Neal, p. 98.
39. Dudden, p. 438.
40. Boykin, p. 338.

The sense of popular unconcern about any underlying reality in politics is conveyed in many political cartoons. Back in the Cold War period, one cartoon depicted two stout matrons leaving an auditorium after a lecture on foreign affairs. One remarks to the other, "I'm glad we have that six month's breather on the Berlin situation—what with our bridge tournament coming up." Another cartoon, from "Berry's World" in 1968, show two old people rocking on a porch, and one says with a smile, "For Pinkos, them Ruskies sure know how to handle liberals."

Both cartoons employ the stock ingredients of political humor, contradiction and shock, but it is the shock of reality. The people do see themselves as politically ridiculous. Pictorial caricature and humorous exaggeration make apparent irrational political traits that are so common they are considered normal. The criticism is acceptable because it is implicit and comically cushioned.

A political cartoon that would be a pertinent illustration in many texts of American political theory or in histories of American politics shows two drunks, deep in their cups, at a bar. One drunk is leaning toward the other and saying belligerently, "Whash thish guvment tryin' to do? Run the country?"

Here is seemingly the ultimate in political contradiction. One smiles at its sheer nonsense, and then is shocked by it into an awareness of the reality of popular attitudes. Historically and constitutionally we are profoundly distrustful of government while admitting its minimal necessity. After all, the famed axiom, "Government is a necessary evil," has an element of comic contradiction in it.

Yet, the other side of the coin is that the cartoon and the axiom express a logic of the limits of government and political power. The people are depicted as politically irrational. Yet, they are conceded ultimate sovereignty. Then their exercise of that sovereignty must ultimately be limited to the scope of popular competence. If the government is theirs, it had better not "run the country" in any full sense of the term.

The same counter-logic is present in a current witticism

reported from Washington: A constant refrain in the criticism of Nixon's presidency is his lack of moral leadership. One wag retorts, "Nonsense, if the American people wanted moral leadership, Nixon would give it to them." Overtly, the political humor constitutes a clever invective against Nixon's opportunism and, thus, lack of principles. However, with a moment's reflection, the comment becomes but a restatement of the politician's proper role in our constitutional system, and of the popular confusion over positive government versus social freedom.

Oftentimes, popular humor expresses an innate sense of the limits of people's politics, and, therefore, their government. One news item reported: "A little old New England lady felt very strongly about NOT going to the polls and expressing a preference for candidates." She stated, "I never vote; it only encourages them." The lady in her seeming stupidity directly flaunts the democratic ideal, and she enjoyably shocks us by her perverse irrationality and our consequent superiority to her. Yet, in the humor is there not another message, however unintentional—when ignorant people vote, it does encourage politicians to respond to their ignorance with ignorant government.

Former Representative Charles Weltner of Georgia tells a campaign story of comic popular wisdom. He relates that when he was campaigning in a rural area, he ran across a gnarled, weatherbeaten old farmer in faded overalls. Weltner asked him for his vote, and the old man replied that he was not a voter. Since most country folk vote, Weltman was surprised and inquired why. "Well," he said, "I voted once. In nineteen and twenty-eight I voted for Herbert Hoover. After that, I decided I just don't have any business voting."[41]

Again, a seemingly irrational response, counter to the democratic ethic, is the humorous gist of the story. But, perhaps the old man sensed the full extent of his political incompetence in the original irrationality of his vote for Hoover. For him, the consequences of that vote were the Great Depression and an incompetent government. Cer-

41. O'Neal, p. 140.

tainly that his particular vote brought on the depression is comic nonsense, but to generalize his comic reasoning is possibly to realize a truth of democracy—its limits.

James Reston of the *New York Times* addressed himself to our confusions by recounting the favorite folk story of the late Sam Rayburn, famed Speaker of the House of Representatives. The story follows:

Way back yonder in the beginnin' of the world, ole Adam and Miss Eve was livin' on fawty acres of good bottom lan' the Lord had give 'em. They didn't have no boll weevil nor neither high water an' they made a good crop every year.

They had 'em two good cows; a heap of shoats an' they et they own fryin' chickens because it wasn't no preachers there to eat 'em. They had a fine garden full o' mustard greens an' rosen-ears an' a house which didn't never leak. Ole Adam had the best mules in the county; two bran'-new Studebaker wagons; an' a pack of fine rabbit dawgs.

Miss Eve, she he'ped ole Adam make the crop. She done the cookin', washin', and ironin', an' they got along mighty good.

There wa'nt but one thing twixt 'em. Old Adam he was a man that liked to hunt and fish, and ever'time he could sneak off, there he was chasin' rabbits, or lookin' after his troutlines.

But that vexed Miss Eve 'cause when ole Adam was away, she got kin o' lonesome, it not bein' no foks for her to talk to. So one day she say, "Adam, don't you git some folks for me to talk to whilst yo 'way, I ain't gwine let you hunt an' fish."

Ole Adam he didn't like that 'cause he loved to hunt and fish mo' than anything in the world. So he went off down the big road studdin' what could he do 'bout hit, when here come the Lawd. The Lawd He give Adam hi-dy, and Adam he give the Lawd hi-dy.

"Lawd," say ole Adam, "You sho' been good to me. You gi'e me fawty acres of good bottom lan' an' us makes a good crop all the time. You gi'e me Miss Eve and she sho' is a good woman. She he'ps make the crop, an' does all the cookin', ironin', an' washin'.

"But Lawd, You knows I'm a man that'd druther hunt an'

fish than anything in this world o' Yourn, but Miss Eve say don't I git some folks for her to talk to wilst I'm 'way she ain't gwine lemme hunt an' fish. Lawd, please Suh, can't You make some folks to keep that woman company?"

The Lawd say, "Adam, when does you want them folks made?" And ole Adam he say, "Please suh, could You make 'em this evenin'?"

So the Lawd got out his almanac—the one with the quarterin's of the moon in it—to see did he have anything to do that evenin', and when he see he didn't, he tole ole Adam to meet him twarge sundown by the creek that got that good clay bank an' he would make the folks.

Well, ole Adam he was right there when the Lawd come up on his good saddlehorse, got off, and hitched him to a little persimmon tree. Adam handed the Lawd a heap o' clay. He started kneadin' it to make the folks, and ole Adam he cut some fresh green saplings for the framin' work.

The Lawd he made some Hebrew chillun an' some Christian chillun, some white chillun an' some colored chillun, some A-rabs an' some Chinermans. Then he put 'em all by the fence rail and say, "Now, Adam, you meet me right here soon after sun-up in the mawning! I'll be back then to put the brains in these folks."

Ole Adam he was right there at first day. But it wa'nt nothin' there. All them folks without brains had already walked off before the Lawd come back, an' they been multiplyin' and replenishin' the Earth ever since.[42]

Reston headlined his column containing the story, "Antidote For Going Nuts." Appropriately, humor rescues us from the frustrations and pessimism of dealing with the human plight when we are faced with the limitations of the human intellect. The same problem is confronted in a biting aphorism of the Reverend Milton Richardson, Dean of Christchurch Cathedral in Houston, Texas, which appeared in the *New York Times*:

Government is the organization of the general human av-

42. James Reston, "Walk-Off Folks Are Gaining," *New York Times* (reprinted in *Detroit Free Press*), February 9, 1963. Reston attributes the written story to David Cohn of Mississippi.

erage into the machinery of power. It makes those above the average live down to it or suffer the consequences.

The humor of the statement lies in its reversal of the conventional wisdom, and in its shockingly stark pessimism about the effect of government on human excellence. Burke could have penned it on the French Revolution, for its relevance to a democracy is penetrating. Beyond the immediate humor, the conclusion is inescapable as to the limits of politics in popular government.

Popular humor does not neglect the opposite problem of politics—its total rejection by those who become radically disillusioned by its narrow limits. Jules Feiffer in a brilliant story-cartoon sketches the steps in political alienation. The cartoon shows a hippie-type character, long-haired and without socks, sitting and slouching on the ground. In each pose he utters a statement:

"Politics is a lie."
"So I dropped out of politics."
"Politics uses history."
"So I quit studying history."
"History is printed in books."
"So I quit reading books."
"Books are made up of words."
"So I quit knowing words."

In the last panel the hippie sits with his mouth taped and dark glasses on him. He bears a sign "Give to the Pure."[43]

Politics in contrast to purity is a lie, but to reject politics is to reject life itself in its most human endeavors—action, thought, speech. Purity is symbolized by muteness and blindness; purity is a loss of humanness. Feiffer's logic is Aristotelian and points to the doctrine of the mean. His comedy employs exaggeration and contradiction. Essentially, the hippie in search of a pure humanity rejects politics as inhuman because of corruption, and ends by having rejected humanness; for corruption, like politics, is fully human.

43. Jules Feiffer, *Detroit Free Press*, Nov. 12, 1967.

Popular political humor is seldom perfectionist. General-ly, it is earthy and proceeds from the acknowledgment of flawed humanity to a comic criticism of its flaws. Realistic but critical, political humor draws delight from a kind of disillusionment.

Perhaps a comic switch in one last humorous anecdote of politics can sum up the chief point of the people against their own politics. In 1859 Representative Alexander H. Stephens of Georgia, friend of Lincoln and future Vice-President of the Confederacy, concluded a speech in the House on the admission of Oregon as a state to the Union. His closing words were "the very voice of the Almighty— *Vox Populi, vox Dei.*"

With applause for the magnificent speech ringing in his ears, he left the chamber. Walking along the corridor, he overheard a gentleman enthusiastically remark to a friend, "You should have been there and seen him, his slight form quivering, yet erect, his shrill voice ringing through the hushed hall in that grand climax—*Vox populi, vox Dei.*"

His friend, somewhat bored, replied, "Yes, no doubt, but I'll bet you ten dollars you can't tell what *vox populi, vox Dei* means." The bet was quickly accepted with "I'll bet I can. Put up your money."

The money was wagered and the Stephens enthusiast said, "Why, it means, 'My God, My God! Why hast thou forsaken me?' "

"That's right," agreed the challenger. "The money is yours. I didn't think you knew."[44]

The immediate humor lies in the mutual ignorance of the friends. Second, humor is derived from the contradiction in the specific misunderstanding of the term. The speech's apotheosis of the voice of the people is understood by the good citizens as a cry of desperation. The implicit rational-ity of the comic logic seems to be that if the voice of the people is the voice of God, God has indeed forsaken man. Perhaps as long as the people in the wisdom of their ignor-ance can not recognize *Vox populi, vox Dei*, their God will not forsake them.

44. Boykin, pp. 395-96.

8

Positive Negativity, the Comic Political Drama

Wherein nay is yea—and drama man's reality

This study began with contemporary observations of the decline of humor in politics. It now seems that these observations were too narrowly confined to the direct humor of the hustings. We have seen that humor permeates politics: politicians against politicians, politicians and people against the political parties, and the politicians and people against politics, government, and the sovereign people themselves. Above all, the dominant note of political humor is its negativity, and therein is its positive contribution to politics.

An article by Elliot Carlson, "Wanted: A Bit of Campaign Humor," alleges a loss of the sense of political humor related to "deep, long-term changes in the country's society and manners." Carlson cites scholars who attribute the trend toward political sobriety to the rise of a solemn middle class, the bland requirements of a mass-media TV, and changing life-styles of the younger generation. Yet he also cites the psychology of political humor, such as its therapeutic effects and the reducing of the great tensions of politics.[1]

If there has been a psychological need for political humor, no one has shown how that need has diminished or what other mechanism has supplanted the need. We have seen that humor in politics springs from deep social sources: the sublimation of aggression, the resentment of social authority, the necessary repressions of civilized society, the leveling impulse for democratic equality, and even the creative impulse in man. Moreover, humor and laughter in men are believed by many authorities to be distinctive characteristics of his human nature.

This study accepts the psychological theories of the functions of humor, but it analyzes humor at its rational apex in Western civilization—in a political regime. A political regime, understood as a social order in which free men govern themselves, requires and fosters above all other regimes the psychological dimension of humor. As a system of order dependent upon persuasion and freely given cooperation, politics must sublimate man's innate aggressiveness, even while it permits his competition for office and the competition of his conflicting interests for social preferment. Politics abstains from force and violence; humor mocks social warfare and allievates its pressures.

Social authority in a political regime is freely accepted, critically examined, and often challenged. Its sources and institutions are subject to the same competition and criticism as the rest of politics. Yet, all authority breeds resentment and, at times, occasions the need for strong reaction in the best of us. Humor dispels the resentments and permits reaction against authority without weakening it.

The voluntary subordination of citizens to social authority is even more strained in their habitual and conscious obedience to customs and laws that mold man-the-animal into

1. Elliot Carlson, "Wanted: A Bit of Campaign Humor," *Wall Street Journal,* Sept. 18, 1972.

man-the-citizen. Humor, like dreaming, gives us a socially tolerable outlet for the "discontents of civilization." A political regime that must forgo force and despotic indoctrination welcomes sexual and scatological humor and comic blasphemy. While the humor accomplishes catharsis, it persuades acceptance of necessary conformity.

Moreover, phallic humor, from Aristophanes' scurrilities against Cleon to the youthful obscenities against President Nixon, conjoins sublimated sexual release with equalitarian leveling. It recalls all men to their common biology and inescapable equality. In a political regime where free governance rests upon the proximate equality of the citizenry, the recall of rulers and ruled alike to their common humanity is crucial.

Last, a political regime is the most fragile of systems of governance, hovering between the tyranny of social conformity and the anarchy of democratic permissiveness. The creative impulse of humor constantly generates alternative logics of political rule and ceaselessly challenges the conventional wisdom of even the sovereign people, and its psychology allows it the amused toleration of the court jester in the court of ever-arbitrary sovereignty. Thus, the critical realism of political humor balances the political regime toward the mean and away from excesses of right or left.

However, with the creativity of humor, its rational nature asserts itself over its psychology. For humor to be politically creative it must be critically realistic. Humor must know and experience an objective reality before it can critically assess it and creatively construct alternatives to it. Yet, are not all the psychological functions of political humor more than subjective and individual responses to external triggers?

The mock aggressiveness of political humor requires for its full satisfaction the humorous appreciation and vicarious participation of the audience in the "kill" of the victim. The ridicule of social authority demands a knowledge of its greatest vulnerability. Even the most visceral of political humor, that which counters civilized repressiveness, as well as the phallic humor of democratic leveling, have a high component of rationality in them. Like all humor, taboo humor builds on the play of words, the use of metaphor and analogy, and the offering of a counter-logic to the conventional wisdom. And, as political humor, it relies on audience participation. In all humor, its creator discovers and utilizes common elements in our humanity, sociability, or partisanship, and he must then effectively communicate his comic discovery to us.

Except possibly at the simplest level, there is no purely "gut" reaction in political humor. Though almost all political humor is reactive in that it originates in our nay-saying to some external agent or circumstance, all political humor is highly rational in its negative response and its positive reception by fellow nay-sayers. The humorist, though possibly reacting emotionally, must rationally construct a comic counteroffensive. Its comedy lies in its camouflage—offensiveness is concealed or cushioned by wordplay, allusions, double meanings, puzzle. Consequently, though the humor presupposes emotional kinship in its audience, its camouflage requires their rational activity. In fact, a good part of the pleasurable release of tension afforded by humor comes from the success in reasoning beneath the camouflage.

We have seen that over two thousand years ago Alcibiades described Socrates' irony in this way: "Anyone listening to Socrates for the first time would find his arguments simply laughable; he wraps them up in just the kind of expressions you'd expect of such an insufferable satyr." However, "if you open up his arguments, and really get into the skin of them, you'll find that they're the only arguments in the world that have any sense at all."[2]

The satyr-Socrates personifies political humor, and his irony is the paradigm of comic rationality He is not the supreme political humorist; that honor is reserved for Lincoln, the political man. But Socrates and his humor are su-

2. Plato, "Symposium," p. 572 (221d-22a6).

premely politically comical, for they achieve the ultimate partnership in negativity and rationality.

Socrates is totally negative politically because his reason, prompted by his spirit, has shown him the true Republic, the commonwealth of the soul. It is a world without contradiction—the unity of man and the good. Socrates' quest is the negation of contradiction; his humor is response and adaptation to that contradiction. This essay finds that the essence of political humor is the contradictoriness of man and life. As rationality too begins in the perception of contradiction, the rationality of political humor is solidly based.

The humor of politics is not extraneous to it, but intrinsic to politics itself as the most civilized social activity in the development of rational man. In its true sense as the governing activities of men in a pluralistic society, politics is the agonistic arena for the existential contradictions of man. In respect to man's origins, politics is the least natural of modes of governing; in the sense of man's nature as his potential, politics is the most "becoming" of modes of governing.

Politics, existing on the borderland of man's being and his becoming, is the realm of contradiction. In it man's rationality struggles against his passions, not as their slave, but as their ruler. His egotistic self strives against his social self. His social sense inspires him toward a unity of justice while his drive for self preservation and assertion dictates a hierarchy of power. Hedonistic sloth counters the search for knowledge. Animal appetite counters enlightened rationality. Even reason divides itself as calculation subverts right rationality.

And, over the realm of contradiction, humor reigns triumphant. Its rationality ceaselessly exposes the divisions of the realm of politics. We learn from humor the distinction between the remediable and the irreconcilable. In its final grace, humor confers the political attitude that welcomes the pluralistic freedom of contradictory existence over the sterile unity of perfection.

The Dramatic Production of the Political Regime

Humor is intrinsic to politics, not because politics is a kind of cosmic joke played on confused mankind, but because it is a form of drama produced by man's rationality. Despite the constant chorus of lament from pessimists and perfectionists, the drama of politics is not tragic. It is a comic production with the catharsis of humor built into it, and, like the ancient comedies, it mocks tragedy. In comparison with the drama of all other governments, the political drama is thoroughly a happy one. The actors in their political roles have a guarantee against the tragedies of great heroics or high martyrdom. The audience, in participating in the theatrics, have a guarantee of minimal satisfaction through their ultimate power over the script and the players, not to mention the emotional enjoyment of their own roles.

The analogy of drama to politics has often been recognized. We have seen that the comic sages from Artemus Ward to Will Rogers compared politics to show business. The journalist-satirists constantly parody politics as show business. Even the politicians in their humor reveal a consciousness of playing roles on a public stage. Political scientists and game theorists speak of political scenarios, and one of them (James K. Rosenau) writes a book titled *The Dramas of Politics*, using the analogy to instruct students in political research.

American playwright Arthur Miller covered the Democratic Convention in the 1972 presidential election and wrote a column for the *New York Times*, "Politics As Theater." In it he said: "This last time in Miami I was struck by something which has been observed since politics began—that an election campaign is not only like theater, it is theater. What we are doing now is trying to cast the part of President." Miller goes on to deplore the theatrics, the lack of issue-orientation, and the casting for the presidential play.[3]

3. Arthur Miller, "Politics As Theater," *New York Times*, Nov. 4, 1972, p. C33.

He fails to comment on the virtues of politics as drama and the dramatic restraints placed upon issues and candidates.

In another *New York Times* article Maurice Cranston, a British political scholar, comments favorably on "Politics as Theater of Reality." He writes:

> What is it that people who take up politics actually do? First of all they talk. For surely if politics is an art, it is one of the performing arts, and not one of the creative ones; Plato noticed this when he compared the politician to the flute player.
>
> But the flute player isn't right either. As a performer, the politician is theatrical, not musical: the world of politics is undoubtedly a stage, and every politician is an actor on it. It seems to me a pity that the word "theatrical" should have become a pejorative one, as it undoubtedly has, and it might be worth pausing to consider why.

Cranston continues that the strongest expression of distaste for the theater is Rousseau's. He relates the distaste to Rousseau's radical democratic beliefs and his rejection of representative government for resembling the fraudulence of dramatic art. Cranston adds:

> Politicians, in a sense, do more important work than actors; but why does Rousseau insist so much on the moral distinction between the two? I think perhaps the explanation is that Rousseau had such strong feelings about the disjunction between appearance and reality. He regarded appearance as the domain of deception and therefore as bad; and reality as the province of truth, and therefore as good. The theater was bad because it is an admitted temple of illusions. The political forum, on the other hand, was good, for it was there that men assumed the full reality of citizens. Appearance and reality he conceived to be antithetical; so he could never fully understand the life of politics, where appearance is almost as important as reality: is even indeed a part of it. [4]

4. Maurice Cranston, "Politics as Theater of Reality," *New York Times*, Aug. 13, 1972.

Of course, for Rousseau the true politician is the states-man of a pure democracy, which is, in turn, the political forum for the full reality of citizens. But Cranston's major thrust is well taken. Representative politics resembles the theater because it is a world of appearances, and politics is a performing art, the major skill of which is talk. Cranston does not go into the comedy of the confusion over the dis-juncture of appearance and reality, but certainly the pattern of political humor reveals it.

Moreover, the dogmatic rejection of political theatrics as the deception of appearances in opposition to a truth of re-ality characterizes the most bitter strain of negative political humor. In fact, if political comedy is taken as the bench-mark, Plato with his myth of the cave in the *Republic* serves the more clearly to illustrate politics as drama and its consequent rejection of appearance over reality.

It will be remembered that in the myth of the cave the chained prisoners, representing the citizens of society, are given a show of the shadows on the wall. From these shadows they form their opinions and have their knowledge of reality. The shadows on the wall are created by a kind of puppet show going on behind them that they cannot see. Behind them is a parapet behind which is a fire. People walk and move on the parapet, carrying various objects, and their shadows are cast by the fire onto the wall in front of the prisoners. The way to the truth is upward, away from the prisoners of society, past the parapet and its fire, and up out of the cave into the light of day, and finally, to the sun itself as the ultimate truth.

Plato rejects the conventions and knowledge of society as the deceptions of a shadow show. He opposes these appear-ances to an ultimate truth of reality, and he condemns the drama of politics totally. However, we have seen that in re-jecting the drama of politics, he creates a comic counter-drama to it. Thereby Plato recognizes the reality of appear-ance, and himself bows to the paradox of comedy.

Thus, I would go beyond Cranston and say—as Plato rec-ognized in the comedy of Socrates—that in politics appear-ance is reality, not just a part of it. Politics is drama, but as a dramatic production of a society, politics exists within society and is subject to its reality. And society, the producer of the political drama, is itself part of a larger reality to which it is subject.

The conflict between these levels of reality is one subject of political humor. But finally, as with Plato and Rousseau, the belief that there is an all-embracing reality that politics should embody is at the heart of the most negative political humor. Here are the ultimate contradictions upon which the comic drama of politics rests: appearance versus reality, convention versus nature, expediency versus truth, politics versus statesmanship, and so on.

I deny the ultimate contradiction, even as I admit all the contradictoriness that is the substance of the comic drama of politics. Convention is man's nature, and the political drama constitutes the highest rationality in man's conventional achievements. Let us examine the meaning and conventional construction of politics as drama.

The Oxford Dictionary states that the term *drama* is derived from the Latin for play, and from the Greek for deed, action, or play, especially tragedy. It is also a verb for action in the Greek, meaning to do, to act, to perform. Two examples are given for drama that bear directly on politics: drama is a composition in prose or verse, adapted to be acted upon a stage in which a story is related by means of dialogue and action. It is represented with accompanying gestures, costumes, and scenery as in real life. Second, drama can be a series of actions or course of events having a unity and leading to a final catastrophe or consummation.

At its root drama is deed or action, but it comes to be used, not as an isolated action or deed, but as a series of actions or course of events, unified by some relationship between the actions or events. As theater, drama is the presentation of a story in a manner that mimics real life. Yet, mimicry is only of elements of real life, for drama as story presents a compactness and purposefulness, a sense of meaningfulness, that real life lacks because of its chance and contingency.

Here indeed lies the distinction between political action

and action in the everyday sense. The framework of the political regime provides a stage or arena for man's actions that gives them a meaning and a continuity larger than man's individual and self-contained actions can ever possess. As someone has said, businessmen don't make history, they make business. History is the record of the story of an organized society. Politics is the dramatization of that story in the making.

Not all societies have a history, and even fewer societies have a political regime. Man exists under the sun and always in society, but how he organizes that society is a matter of convention.[5] In John Wild's words, his society or culture constitutes his life-world as distinguished from the objective universe. Man's "life-world" is not an objective given, but a socially created life-space or stage made up of all his artifacts, creations, and their organization, especially his language, which give meaning and direction to his movements and thought.

Man moves and thinks primarily for survival as a part of the objective life-cycle of all things. In organized society he begins to act and reason—to undertake deeds and employ words—beyond himself and his moment of existence. Human life has a purpose other than mere living, and man is given an understanding of his place in that purpose which transforms him from just another animal behaving under necessity to a man-animal acting in freedom. For man has created a culture that is partly free of the necessity of the objective universe. In fact, one's culture in its consciousness and collective power can affect the objective universe. Appearance can become reality.

Yet, contradictions that come to haunt and humor the drama of politics are already apparent. Man, a social animal, is still first and foremost the man-animal; sheer living precedes cultural learning. The life-world, despite its crea-

5. For the concepts that underlie this interpretation of politics as drama a great debt is owed to the thinking of Hannah Arendt, Karl Jaspers, and John Wild. The idea of politics as comic drama is the author's responsibility, but particularly relevant to it are Arendt's *The Human Condition* (Chicago: The University of Chicago Press, 1958), and Wild's *Existence and the World of Freedom* (Englewood Cliffs, N.J.: Prentice-Hall, Inc., 1963).

tion of a space for freedom, remains under the constraints of the objective universe. And, most paradoxically for our comic drama, man's freedom for action is a freedom within his society. He is free only within the chains of the conventions that alone give his living meaning and power beyond objective necessity. The freedom of aloneness or pure individuality is the stark terror of total enslavement to a pitiless universe.

In his beautiful *The Tree of Culture*, Ralph Linton tersely summarizes man's cultural evolution: "We are, in fact, anthropoid apes trying to live like termites, and, as any philosophical observer can attest, not doing too well at it." Shortly thereafter he compounds the contradiction with "in plain English, man is an ape with a brain too active for his own good."[6] These are existential contradictions, but all of man's speech, reason, and culture seek to deny or overcome them. Thereby they become the stuff of political humor.

All culture is a kind of drama staged by society, but until society develops a civilization and history, the full drama of politics is not possible. A preliterate society lacks the cumulative consciousness of itself for staging a purposeful story of itself through its learning and institutions; its history changes the mere behavior of its members into deeds for posterity. Objective necessity still bears too heavily on a pre-literate society.

A civilization, or city-centered culture, seems to be a necessary condition for the emergence of a political regime. Its allowing leisure to at least some members, through its economic surfeit, fosters the development of social rationality and a literate culture, including history. A civilization, because of its economic base, may develop social heterogeneity. The consequent pluralism can loosen the domination of custom and permit the conscious writing of, and acting in, a script for the social drama.

6. Ralph Linton, *The Tree of Culture* (New York: Alfred A. Knopf, Inc., 1955), pp. 11, 51. This brilliant and highly readable work is an anthropological approach to the understanding of society and culture which fully complements the philosophical one. Additionally, it bears the blessing of humor.

That writing and acting develop a sense of history. The script of the social drama can be called, in Aristotle's meaning, a civilization's constitution. Its ethic and purpose, however, narrowly confined to a few actors, generate a continuity of words and actions. The measured continuity provides a story line for society, its history. Script and story line, constitution and history, increase the "artistic" rationality of man over his social drama.

The full drama of man's acting in the life-world is staged only when a civilization develops a political regime. Such a regime can be viewed as a natural goal of man's rational freedom, but it is never complete, nor is it historically or naturally necessary. The drama of politics is a production of man's nature and circumstances as well as his corporate rationality, itself subject to chance. Contradictory possibilities mount, and along with them, the comic potential of politics.

The fully political regime casts the optimum number of actors in its drama of freedom. It thereby increases the sum total of free men, even as it complicates the rational freedom of the society in staging its drama outside of necessity. Dramatically, though, the quality of the political regime is immeasurably enhanced over that of its competitors.

The larger the number of political actors, the greater the scope of their conflicting interests and competitive role-playing. Thus, the greater is the need for the skills of politics: compromise, conciliation, persuasion, and, above all, talk. These skills are dramatic skills; they do not emphasize hard decisions, actions over words, substance over form. On the contrary, their rationale might be stated in those hoary show-business maxims "The play's the thing," and "The show must go on." More important than any single interest at issue at any time are the interests of all in keeping the resolution of issues political.

The political resolution of issues in no way resembles a scientific solution of a problem or discovery of an objective truth. The resolution proceeds rhetorically, not positivistically. It may involve indefinite postponement; it usually requires watering down the substance of an issue, obscuring the chief points at issue, raising patriotic or other deceptive irrelevancies, misleading the contestants, and, finally, passing off minor gains or slight losses as major victories. No wonder ridicule and invective prevail in political humor.

Nevertheless, the peace and unity of a pluralistic society are deeply indebted to its drama of politics. Without the drama and its ritual and rules, quarrelsome, aggressive, self-interested man could never be contained and contented in a society of many interests. Somehow the show of politics reconciles men to less than their full interests and recalls them to the larger social interest; the talk and mock warfare of the political actors mute the issues and diffuse the energies; and the political humor permits the release of aggressions and tensions harmlessly.

The other side of the coin of political invective is the equally dramatic idealism of the public stage. The theater of politics brings out the rhetorical best in its politician-actors. They must play to their audience-actors, and the rules of participatory theater, with its multi-interests and its shibboleth of the public interest, require continuing pledges of allegiance to the general will and constant avowals of disinterestedness.

To proclaim his championing of a special interest for a partisan purpose would be self-defeating for a politician. In the absence of a clear and powerful majority backing a special interest, a politician who callously speaks directly in favor of a special interest courts and stimulates the opposition of all other interests. Indeed, a public display of an acknowledged private interest would be "impolite"—unpolitic. Running counter to the public ethic, it might repulse even members of the favored interest group.

To make public an opinion on an issue is to politicize that opinion by staking a claim to the favorable resolution of that issue with the public authorities. The claim remains self-interested, but ceases to be privately exclusive. For the partisan claim to have maximum public influence, it is framed in the dramatic script of the public interest. In a pluralistic political regime, the special interest must seek sympathetic audience from wider interest groups, not the least of which is the general interest of the concerned public. The dramatic appeal may be tactical, and more rhetorical camouflage than social altruism, but it moderates and molds partisan opinions toward a wider, viable consensus.

The publicizing of partisan opinions does something even more important in the drama of politics. In their stage costumes as public claims, insisting on special treatment but consistent with the public interest, they permit the political actor to play the role of broker and to *ad lib* toward a higher synthesis. As interested partisans on the public stage, politicians present them as better than they are in hopes that the audience will accept them as better than they are; and by the alchemy of the dramatic art of politics, they become better than they are. The public personality is actually a *persona* (Latin, signifying the mask worn by an actor), which modifies the actor's private character.

Finally, the politician in his role as a public broker of an issue must represent the less directly affected interest groups in his constituency. Note that the "re-presenting" on the public stage is itself a form of acting; an original presentation is interpreted by the political actor and repeated for the public audience. For the political actor to fail in this wider re-presentation is for him to invite an even greater issue in the participatory theater of politics, which might threaten his starring role. Thus, in his interpretation the politician must fit the special interests into his estimation of the latent interests of his other constituency.

The politician's personal opinion necessarily will intrude into this dramatic interpretation of the public interest, but it includes a special value of the political art. The politician is a public performer on history's stage, and he desires the honor and glory attendant upon the appearance of greatness. Facts permitting, and other values being equal, he will seek to resolve a political issue toward the greater glory of his public leadership over his private partisanship.

In this dialectic of partisan claims and counterclaims, the drama of politics involves far more than the resolution of issues. Above all, in order to maintain a peaceful and productive pluralism, politics must be staged as a form of psychodrama. Participation in politics at all levels, from citizen-audience to starring role, provides an emotional experience. This psychodrama renders tolerable the strains of living peacefully amid the clash of our truth with others' heresies, our rightful claims with others' fraudulent ones, our self-assertion against others' vicious aggressions, our liberty against others' license.

Politics as psychodrama becomes comedy itself when viewed dispassionately or from a historic vantage point. Seemingly great rhetorical battles of good against evil are being waged. The politicians flail one another mercilessly with the strongest invective. They forecast the direst calamities and promise the most sublime reforms. The John Birchers expose the most vile and traitorous conspiracies. The socialists and communists find the capitalist snake at the root of all evil and promise the new Garden of Eden. The capitalists celebrate the best of all possible worlds and kiss the ring on its unseen hand (Adam Smith).

The average citizens, not to be outdone in "the participatory political theatre of comic exaggerations," raucously proclaim their belief that the battle of Armageddon is being fought between the donkey and the elephant. They shout that the country will go fascist or communist, depending on the election. They bestow hero worship on political leaders of their own persuasion, and revile as common criminals the opposition leaders.

Do our political actors really believe all of this? Not "really"! They believe it dramatically and act upon it politically, and they enjoy it immensely. If they believed it literally and thought that the phenomena to which they verbally subscribed existed as cause-effect relationships in the objective reality of things, they could not abide them. Yet, the political actors passively accept adverse elections, obey the political authorities whom they moralistically denounce, and continue to associate and even fraternize offstage with their partisan enemies.

Politics is important, and in it crucial decisions are taken, but the politics of the system whereby decisions are made and government acts is highly complex and not in the direct relationship to the people that democratic ideals picture. The popular politics of the public stage is cast within a very narrow compass; its stakes are small; its personalities are startlingly similar; and its issues are often symbolic. Only because of a broad moral consensus, very minor political risks, and deep predictability about governmental actions, can we casually participate and passively accept the chances and confusions of democratic politics.

Nevertheless, the drama of politics gives us the thrill of gambling our lives and destinies. We feel that we fight the good fight for moral America and mankind, that we heroically defend our own and courageously assault our enemies. We feel the better for it and may well be better for it. We certainly become more politically active, and through participation in the drama, we become more committed to its political foundation. A political theorist has said that in politics we agree to disagree. Perhaps it might be said that, in the comic drama of politics, we disagree with verbal violence so that we may agree elsewhere. The political psychodrama concentrates and purges our frustrations and aggressions; its purpose is not political action but social conciliation.

The verbal violence of politics as well as its platitudinous rhetoric are at the heart of the dramatic art. Lewin, in *A Treasury of American Humor*, writes, "the abuse of language and meaning lies close to the heart of whatever is funny, or outrageous, in politics. Cant phrases, ambiguous clichés, soothing euphemisms, and meaningless slogans take root more readily and flourish more abundantly here than in any other garden, or weedpatch, or our civilization." Appropriately for an anthology of political humor, Lewin then reverses the thrust of his logic and suggests the functions of political language. He says that our traditional politics calls for rhetorical hyperbole, continual commitments without contracts, the obscuring of obligations. Finally, our advertising culture makes exaggeration and deception the norms of public statements.[7]

Political humor is replete with the parody and ridicule of the speech and language of politics. And, again, the humor dwells on the contradiction between appearance and reality. The talk of politics is said to be for dramatic effect, not factual communication. Let us concede that the primary purpose of political talk is dramatic effect, not the communication of facts. However, dramatic effect is for the sake of political action that is not the same as fact but can not be contrary to it, if the action is to be successful.

Our confusions over the functions of language in the drama of politics are part and parcel of our misunderstanding of politics. Like our belief that politics should mirror an ultimate reality of a harmonious universe, we wish to hold political language to the single standard of denoting objective fact or expressing final truth. We ignore or deny the vast difference between opinions and their compromises as the stuff of politics, and facts and final truths as the reality of an objective universe.

The art of political talk has traditionally been termed rhetoric. Rhetoric, in turn, is defined as the art of using language to persuade or influence others, or the art of expressive speech or discourse. The purpose of political talk is not to convey information. The issues of politics do not center upon the misunderstanding of objective facts; they center upon conflicts of special interests and clashes of differing values. The conflicting interests must be compromised, not rewarded or rejected by some objective standard. Clashing values can only be encompassed within a common and deeper feeling, or synthesized into a more basic value.

In both instances political talk requires a far more complex skill than the mere utterance of precise verbal representations for objective phenomena. Its language requires ambiguity and flexibility, if it is to allow leeway for compromise and permit the various parties to feel some satisfac-

7. Lewin, p. 209.

tion. Its language may have to confuse and obscure the issues at stake, if they are too sharply drawn for peaceful compromise. Its language and the expressiveness of it may have to arouse emotions counter to the logic of the words themselves or to the interests at issue. Patriotism, fellowship, or other prejudices may have to be called forth by the expressive powers of the political speech, if the special interests of rationally calculating men in a pluralistic society are to be kept reconciled to one another in an uneasy unity.

George Orwell in a brilliant essay, "Politics and the English Language," attributed the decline of a language to political and economic causes. He wrote that the characteristics of a decaying language are a lack of imagination in the use of cliches and stale metaphors, imprecision and vagueness, pretentiousness, and meaningless words. For him, political language is "largely the defense of the indefensible," used to name things without calling up mental pictures of them, verbally inflated to bury the facts, blur the outlines, and cover up the details of issues. In our time, "politics is a mass of lies, evasions, folly, hatred and schizophrenia," and Orwell concluded that if one jeers at particular abuses loudly enough, he may aid his own thought and score against the abuses.

Orwell is right, and yet he is myopically wrong. The error is not in his thought, but in the contradictions of politics. Language in politics does become literally "contradictions," speech that opposes itself, or statements that assert or contain within them opposed meanings. Political language must serve at least two clearly different purposes, which may be in direct opposition; one purpose cannot be achieved without nullifying the other.

Orwell saw that language is a function of politics, and it is indeed the extremist politics and warfare that have caused the specific abuses of which he complains. But he denies the political function of language; its only purpose, he believes, should be clarity of thought for effective action through the exact verbal representation of things as they are. But even the language of a peaceful and moderate politics would never satisfy him, for he fails to comprehend politics and its language.

Stale metaphors, clichés, and pretentious language are the speech of the public stage. They are not informational but attitudinal. They emotionally conciliate and reassure the audience, or they excite its members with collective verbal symbols of stimulation. It is not the objective referents of the words to which political speech addresses itself, but the subjective prejudices that it seeks to activate. Stale metaphors, clichés, glittering generalities, and smear words are the triggers to the stereotyped thinking of popular politics (Walter Lippmann, *Public Opinion*).

When effective action in the objective universe must be based on stereotypes, political catastrophe may result. But the politics of the public stage is not the politics of executive action. There is a necessary relationship between the two that can prove debasing, but our system of government has built-in checks against any direct influence. Utopians wish the merger of public stage and executive action, but in the meantime the language of the political drama stabilizes politics, preventing active extremism and allowing for peaceful compromise. Thereby, the political drama gives leeway for realistic political action.

Orwell recommended a direct speech to break through the deceptions of political language. In his *1984*, the heroine resorts to crude, earthy speech to pierce the thought control in the newspeak and doublethink of a totalitarian regime. However, informational language has not countered thought-control language. Rather, the emotional impact of biologically basic speech has countered the more conceptually abstract speech of society, and rebellious thought may result. Orwell has utilized the political dramatics of speech to oppose the language corruption of a detested regime.

If *1984* is not a *tragic* novel of totalitarian terror, its very elements of language, politics, and sex could constitute a comic caricature of rhetoric and the drama of politics. In it, Orewell verges on comic invective against political language. Thus, he describes "doublethink," the mental process of "newspeak," as reality control, and he explains:

Doublethink means the power of holding two contradictory beliefs in one's mind simultaneously, and accepting both of them. The Party intellectual knows in which direction his memories must be altered; he therefore knows that he is playing tricks with reality; but by the exercise of *doublethink* he also satisfies himself that reality is not violated. The process has to be conscious, or it would not be carried out with sufficient precision, but it also has to be unconscious, or it would bring with it a feeling of falsity and hence of guilt. *Doublethink* lies at the very heart of Ingsoc, since the essential act of the Party is to use conscious deception while retaining the firmness of purpose that goes with complete honesty. To tell deliberate lies while genuinely believing in them, to forget any fact that has become inconvenient, and then, when it becomes necessary again, to draw it back from oblivion for just so long as it is needed, to deny the existence of objective reality and all the while to take account of the reality which one denies—all this is indispensably necessary. Even in using the word *doublethink* it is necessary to exercise *doublethink*. For by using the word one admits that one is tampering with reality; by a fresh act of *doublethink* one erases this knowledge; and so on indefinitely, with the lie always one leap ahead of the truth. Ultimately, it is by means of *doublethink* that the Party has been able—and may, for all we know, continue to be able for thousands of years—to arrest the course of history.[8]

As in all comic caricature, there is truth in Orwell's denunciation, and, like the best political humor, it becomes a kind of critical rationality. Unfortunately, Orwell does not see that the contradictoriness of "doublethink" is a contradiction in political existence itself. He does not see that there is no course of history, but that history records the dramas of men as attempts to arrest the course of the objective universe. And those dramatic attempts, forcing the

8. George Orwell, *1984* (New York: The New American Library, Inc., Signet Classic, 1949, 1961), pp. 176-77.

conventional beyond nature despite the naturalness of man's conventions, are doomed to—or blessed with—the comedy of contradiction.

Herbert Marcuse, the pop prophet of the youth revolt of the 1960s, updated Orwell's analysis of political language in his *One-Dimensional Man*, giving it a more theoretical, and also Marxian, foundation. He too has critical virtues, but his assumptions lead to the same weaknesses as Orwell's. Moreover, in his *An Essay of Liberation*, he applies his theory as apologetics to the political obscenities of the youth revolt and the black militants and comes forth with political comedy:

> The familiar "obscenities" in the language of the black and white radicals must be seen in this context of a method- ical subversion of the linguistic universe of the Establish- ment. "Obscenities" are not officially co-opted and sanctioned by the spoken and written professions of the powers that be; their usage thus breaks the false ideological language and invalidates its definitions. But only in the political context of the Great Refusal do obscenities perform this function. If, for example, the highest executives of the nation or of the state are called, not President X or Gover- nor Y but pig X or pig Y, and if what they say in campaign speeches is rendered as "oink, oink," this offensive designa- tion is used to deprive them of the aura of public servants or leaders who have only the common interest in mind. They are "redefined" as that which they really are in the eyes of the radicals. And if they are addressed as men who have perpetrated the unspeakable Oedipal crime, they are indicted on the counts of their own morality: the order they enforce with such violence was born in their sense of guilt. They slept with the mother without having slain the father, a deed less reprehensible but more contemptible than that of Oedipus.[9]

"The unspeakable Oedipal crime" is only unspeakable for the good Marxist professor. For him "motherfucker" is not

9. Herbert Marcuse, *An Essay on Liberation* (Boston: Beacon Press, 1969), p. 35.

a dramatic term used for shock value in the theater of political revolt; it is a symbolic representation of the dreaded crime of incest. For his youthful adherents in their "guerilla theatre" or "street theatre," the term was shouted easily and *ad nauseam* for its shock value or dramatic effect. They instinctively understood the reality of political appearances in relation to social authority, and they sought to impair or change the latter by counterappearance.

In sum, in politics words must precede, indeed surround, action. Words and talk are the chief stock of the drama of politics, and all of their contradictoriness constitute much of its comedy. Still, the political action is rational and realistic for all of that. The talk prevents violence and permits reflection, allowing conciliation and compromise as rational responses to the tenuous and conventional reality of politics.

The Play of Politics

The inflated prose of Marcuse is something more than a comical rationale for revolutionary rhetoric. As a part of a "political" manifesto, his prose displays the wordplay of politics and all of its humorous potential. Though somewhat heavily Teutonic for the more direct and bawdy American tastes, the quoted passage is replete with words, phrases, and titles that are pawns in a game of words, a play within the play: "Establishment," "the powers that be," "the Great Refusal," "pig X or pig Y" and their "oink, oink," "the unspeakable Oedipal crime," and the clever symmetry and pleasurable sound of "slept with the mother" paired with "slain the father," and "less reprehensible" paired with "more contemptible."

If one can free himself of the dreaded sobriety of ideological thinking for a moment, a new appreciation of politics is possible. Political wordplay as a humorous game in itself is characteristic of the play within which it takes place—the play or drama of politics. The facet of play or drama that I now wish to emphasize is that of activity or movement. Play as an activity is engaged in, not for an extraneous end or goal, but for the very pleasure of the action—for the fun of it. Though play and the fun of it are not the equivalent of humor and comedy, the latter are often playful. In turn, the sheer play of politics and its language are a constant source of political humor.

Marcuse and most contemporary political partisans are not consciously aware of "playing at politics." Their ideological affliction imposes on them the role of tragic heroes. Comically, though, the pleasure of "playing" the role often overcomes the seeming tragedy in its realistic futility. At the same time, the role-playing becomes a target of comic invective and parody (e.g., this author's attempts in Marcuse's direction). Despite the surface sobriety, I would maintain that the playfulness is subconsciously present. For if "by their fruits ye shall know them," then only the play of politics makes understandable the vast gap between the appearances of partisan militancy and ideological fanaticism on the one hand, and political peace and stability on the other.

Reflect on a speech that you have made or heard, a letter or paper that you have written, poetry or quotations that you like. There is present a fascination with the words themselves apart from any representation of an outer reality. We enjoy the sounds, the relationship of the words to each other, the movement of the words as we reverse them, pair them, and change their meanings, and we enjoy the exercise of our intellects as we decipher or construct a puzzle of the words. Much political invective is enjoyed, not for its aggressiveness, but for its word playfulness.

Johan Huizinga, in his classic *Homo Ludens*, writes:

In the making of speech and language the spirit is constantly "sparking" between matter and mind, as it were, playing with this wondrous nominative faculty. Behind every abstract expression there lie the boldest of metaphors, and every metaphor is a play upon words.

Thus, in giving expression to life man creates a second, poetic world alongside the world of nature.[10]

Huizinga finds playfulness among animals other than man, but in man play becomes a founding principle of his culture; that is, the organized ways of behavior of men in society are a staged drama for his amusement as much as a rational response to reality. Then, in the very linguistic origins of man's culture there is a contradiction—a nonpurposive playfulness as opposed to a rationalism that can cope with reality.

No more for us than for Huizinga is this contradictoriness to be eliminated. To be exact, the play and its comic facets are to be cultivated; they constitute the hope of man's humanity against his determinism and mechanistic rationalization. As the realm of politics creates a sphere of freedom for man's actions beyond objective necessity, within politics its playfulness is its greatest freedom and promise of peacefulness. Huizinga states:

From the point of view of a world wholly determined by the operation of blind forces, play would be altogether superfluous. Play only becomes possible, thinkable and understandable when an influx of *mind* breaks down the absolute determinism of the cosmos. The very existence of play continually confirms the supra-logical nature of the human situation.[11]

In the last several centuries the seriousness of politics has diminished its play. However, those factors which characterize politics as play persist. They are its nonseriousness; a playground (or stage) set off from the rest of life; the voluntary activities of play, which are "unreal"; a high competitiveness for rewards of glory, marked by chance and tension. Huizinga adds that most play is quite ceremonial and

10. Johan Huizinga, *Homo Ludens* (Boston: Beacon Press, 1938, 1967), p. 4.
11. *Ibid.*, p. 3. I do not agree with Huizinga that play is irrational. Much of it is unrational; some of it serves rationality without being itself rational; but, as with some comic play, there is an alternate logic or a critical rationality involved.

bound by rules. However, play is often associated with joking, jesting, mocking, and trifling, and sometimes play permits a fraudulent outwitting of others as a part of the contest. Though the nonseriousness of play is not identical with humor, the term that is used for play in almost all of the Romance languages is "a derivative of *jocus*, which extended its specific sense of joking and jesting to 'play' in general" (p. 36).

Huizinga refers to another kind of medieval play of particular relevance to politics. In Old High German, *gelp* was a ceremony of mutual bragging and execration, and the term came to be applied later to clamour, mockery, and scorn. The French equivalent is *gab*, which means mockery and derision (p. 70).

Obviously, a great deal of the talk of politics is a kind of ceremonial gabbing, but the characteristics of nonseriousness and unreality do not seem to be political. Certainly fraudulent outwitting is not accepted as a part of the play of politics. But let us remember that the focus of this study is not the entire domain of politics. The humor and comedy of politics are concentrated in the campaigning and competition of politics, especially in the language, speeches, debates, and the show of representation.

Here is the public stage, the playground; on it there is a lack of seriousness, an "unreality," or a reality that must be understood on its own terms. When the most political of actions are recognized as play, then the extravagance, exaggerations, distortions, and even fraudulent outwitting become acceptable, even commendable. As playfulness in themselves, they are the very sustenance of political humor and comedy. Huizinga writes that long before the team play of the two-party system had developed, "electioneering in America had developed into a kind of national sport." He continues:

Nomination by majority vote, i.e., by the loudest clamour, was inaugurated in the election of 1860 which brought Lincoln to power. The emotionality of American politics lies deep in the origins of the American nation itself: Americans have ever remained true to the rough and tumble of pioneer life. There is a great deal that is endearing in American politics, something naive and spontaneous, for which we look in vain in the dragooning and drillings, or worse, of the contemporary European scene. (pp. 207-8)

The play of politics is humorously enjoyable in itself, but Huizinga also refers to its comic functionality. He points out that the play eases tensions that could be unendurable or dangerous, "for it is the decay of humour that kills" (p. 208). Political play and its comedy have another function; they counteract the ideological fanaticism of contemporary politics. The dogmatism of ideology is fully serious, but imposing it would destroy the flexibility of politics whereby the pluralism of society is accommodated.

And the pluralism guarantees a sympathetic audience for the political ridicule or invective against others' ideological politics. Again, most people are superficially ideological in their politics, and playfulness contradicts their notions of political propriety. Hence the play itself can become a source of comic ridicule.

The Contradictory Nature of Politics

Thus, another contradiction in man himself comes to center in politics. Man at play, *homo ludens*, creates the political drama to express himself, compete sportingly with his fellows, and act freely for the fun of it. Ideological man strives to use politics to bring heaven to earth. His vision of the final truth would end the drama of politics. That drama accommodates the plurality of society and the ambiguities of man; the heavenly drama of ideology would re-present a final truth and conform man to it.

Politics can not be a drama for the staging of high moral actions and great decisions of earth-shaking consequences. We may seek to project the appearance of such and play to its roles, but the political drama founded on a pluralist soci-

ety burlesques us. The Alphonse of our revealed truth col-
lides with the Gaston of another's vision of truth, and the
pratfall of compromise results.

Ours is not a moral community for the perfection of
homogeneous men. The pluralist society is impersonal,
pledged to individual freedom, and in pursuit of economic
affluence. Its basic moral understandings are loose and essentially operational. Within this basic morality, pluralist
politics is necessarily accommodating to the underlying social structure and conciliatory to the interests-at-issue that
support politics-as-usual. Change occurs through politics,
but as slowly as can be managed, and seldom before it has
been recognized and accepted in the larger society.

If we can not read these passages without feeling repelled
by their seeming cynicism, let us ask how the drama of
politics could be otherwise in a pluralist society. A revolution could change the structure and powers of society, but a
revolution is not politics. And the postrevolutionary governing system would have to be other than political. Why,
then, are we repelled by the statement that the truths of
politics are expedient, opportunistic, relative, and tenuous?

For the same reason that we feel inspired and depressed
by Plato, fascinated and repelled by Machiavelli! We are
torn within our being by our nature as our actuality and by
our nature as our potentiality. We must live with ourselves
in our basic natures—our biological origins and temporal
situation; we must survive within a given reality that affords
rather narrow leeway for change. But man the learning
animal is the most malleable of all creatures; to live within
himself as he is, and with his reality as given, is for man
and his reality to be worse than they might be. Thus, we
must live against ourselves and our reality, toward our potential natures and ideals of reality, knowing that neither
will ever be what they possibly could be, but that hopefully
they will be better than they are.

Politics is the agon of man striving against himself to be
more than he is. Its ideal represents the best that man
could be, living in freedom and cooperating voluntarily with

his fellows in an association of mutual benefit. Its reality necessarily allows man less than ideal freedom, freedom of self-service and low appetite, freedom of moral and mental mediocrity, freedom of power politics and class domination. Within politics the highest aspirations conflict with the most sordid machinations, and often each is enlisted in support of the other.

The confusion and contrariety in man, his actions, and his institutions could be destructive—a fatal flaw in a tragic drama of man's Sisyphean attempts at perfection. But the existential contradictoriness is not tragic. Rather, it is a social manifestation of man's genus and genius. Unfinished man, cultural man, the learning animal, *zoon politikon*, is blessed and burdened with his freedom. And the constant contradiction is the human comedy, laughably happy because the spark of freedom ever dampened ever flares anew. No contradictoriness, no differences in men or between them. Man without differences would be man without freedom to be other than what he is or other than what his fellows are.

The contradiction within us and the contradictions between us are the highest expression of the "multiverse" of creation.[12] They express unlimited possibilities in the chances of action, for the margin of man's freedom lies in the clash of opposing tendencies. And in the dialectic of politics there converge both the contrariety of man and the multiverse. Thereby, the chances of freedom in conscious action are multiplied. As Hannah Arendt writes, "Thus action, seen from the viewpoint of the automatic processes which seem to determine the world, looks like a miracle. In the language of natural science, it is 'the infinite improbability which occurs regularly.' "[13]

Rationality distinguishes human action from objectively determined behavior. When we act in full thought of what we do, we control our actions and will their purposes. In

12. William James, *A Pluralistic Universe* (New York: Longmans, Green, and Co., 1909).
13. Arendt, p. 222.

the conflict of opposing tendencies we are most likely to
have a consciousness of external determination, an awareness of alternative possibilities, and the opportunity to
choose between them, according to our own values and interests.

But in the contradictoriness that is man, his reason too
can come to be a form of inhuman determinism. The an-
cients distinguished a "right reason" from man's reason in
general. They meant a reason in man illuminated by natural
law. Without our plunging into those metaphysical depths,
we can still distinguish between reason as enlightened self-
interest and reason as shrewdness or calculation. The
former takes into account long-range consequences, underlying values, and the private as a part of the social good.
The latter, calculating reason, is but a slave of the passions
in their immediate and appetitive sense. Though to identify
passions with appetite and to ignore noble passion and social sympathies is to oversimplify a very complex relationship, the main point is merely that a reason that lacks moral
consciousness is but a superior instrument of animal behavior. In some men, rationality is not the foundation of
human action; it is only a dangerous increase in man's animal appetite.

A second form of deterministic rationality grows out of
calculating reason, but in its social and idealistic dimension
it is almost qualitatively different and much more of a
threat to freedom. It can be termed technological rationality,[14] though it has affinities to many gnostic heresies and to
modern scientism. Essentially, technological rationality is
man's projection on the objective universe of a scheme or

14. Jacques Ellul, *The Technological Society* (New York: Random House, Inc.,
Vintage Books, 1954, 1967). Elleul maintains that all of modern civilization is
being encompassed and determined by technical thought, which has ceased to
be a mere system for the application of scientific, philosophic, or moral language. It has become self-justifying, and self-aggrandizing, always seeking and
imposing the one best way. However, its basic motivation is economic. Thus,
it does stem from man's appetitive urges. See also Bernard Crick, "A Defense
of Politics Against Technology," *In Defense of Politics* (Baltimore: Penguin
Books, 1962, 1964), chap. 5. Crick simply explains the total antithesis of technical thinking to politics and the disastrous consequences of the one for the
other.

system devised by his thought. The logic of the system is intended to answer all questions and solve all problems of man's life-world. Technicism is the belief that a system can be instituted to provide the correct answer—objective truth, or the one best way for all the problems of man.

Technological rationality is a seductive form of thought that proceeds from basic assumptions of unity and efficiency along a prescribed method to inexorable conclusions. Man himself objectifies a system of thought, and through its persuasive logic, or for material or psychological rewards, imposes it on other men and their relations to each other and to things. Thereby, man is chained by his own mind into a rational uniformity and determinateness as relentlessly as by an objective universe. Man may freely choose technocracy, but its technique then becomes determinative for man and against his freedom.

There is a final and supreme contradiction within democratic politics, and it permeates its political humor from its psychological roots to its critical realism. A democratic political regime establishes a popularly based and politcally accountable system of government pledged to the common welfare. Yet, at least in the United States, the people are profoundly anti-political and anti-government. Their negative humor strikingly corroborates a dislike and distrust evident throughout American history and politics. Occasionally they will follow a popular leader or demagogue, but most often the latter is running for government by running against it. [15]

The people, oblivious of all the democratic romanticists from Rousseau through Jefferson, instinctively sense that in politics and government it can never be "we," but will always be "they" (and as the popular saying goes "them as has, gits"). If the people can never be the political rulers, then democracy, self-government, popular sovereignty, "government of the people, by the people, and for the people" represent an ultimate contradiction of rhetoric to

15. A 1964 witticism was that presidential candidate Barry Goldwater was running against the presidency.

reality. The achievement of democratic politics in human freedom is undeniably great, but when it comes to the taxes and laws of government, the ruled are still subject to the rulers. Possibly, due to the democratic ethos, people in a democracy are the most conscious and resentful of their minimal subjection.

The logic of comic rationality seizes upon all contradictions, and in the clash of democratic rhetoric with governing reality it has a field day. Not all political humor can be called rational, but that which is a conscious response to the reality of politics is generally negative and never dogmatic. Thus, political humor grasps a contradiction of politics and comically exposes it in some way. However, which side political humor will strike against is never certain. For instance, in the case of the people against their politics, the humor will take a negative stance, but it may be pro-people or anti-people. Of course, the biases of the humorist-protagonist influence the initial response, but that political humor which becomes a part of the common stock does seem to have a pattern, that of striking against defect or excess. Since political humor is negative, the genuine humorist will find the claim or stance that deviates most from a basic norm the best target for comic counteraggression. To the extent that deviation is perceived by the audience as a threat or claim of superiority, they will identify with the comic retaliation. Then the political situation determines the negative response.

Yet, there are recurring constants in political excesses, and there is corresponding stock humor for them. For example, we have seen the comic reaction to the public piety of presidential candidate Governor George Romney: "What bothers me about Romney running for the presidency is that he only wants to use it for a stepping stone." Or, the burgeoning power of the American presidency that has brought on the Watergate joke: "Nixon is testing the divine right of the presidency by trying to walk over Watergate."

Comic rationality is nondogmatic, but in its negative response to political excess it serves to restore equilibrium to politics. For that matter, even the least rational kind of political humor, namely political invective, usually maintains balance in politics. Most typically, the comic insult points to defect or disproportion in its target. Though its motive may be mere malice or emotional reaction, to be successful it must focus upon a weakness apparent to the audience and implicitly contrast it to a commonly accepted norm. Thereby, politicians and politics are exposed in all the weakness of their human contrariety, and both are kept within the limits of our common equality.

We have seen that the cathartic effect of political humor also serves social stability, and thus there is an innate conservatism resulting from the comic drama of politics.[16] However, comic rationality in its critical realism can move for progressive change toward the values and purposes of a political system. It can do so when it implicitly reveals a standard or norm in anti-political humor, for to ridicule or caricature something is to call to mind its defective contrast to something of the same order but better. To a great extent, the successful reception of the humor depends on its audience's agreement on the standard. Then comic rationality reminds of common values; it does not declare revolutionary standard of politics. However, in a period of political change, it may rely on developing values over traditional values when the former are becoming widely acknowledged.

One difficulty with this conservatism is the negativity of comic rationality in politics. The implicit standard is very often an adumbration of Plato's *Republic*—a social unity founded on final truth in which politics has been superseded. A utopian standard can not express comic rationality. In this instance the standard of perfection constantly calls politics to account for its mortal corruptibility. Though the goal is impossible (and, in fulfillment, undesirable), it calls

16. Leszek Kolakowski, *Toward a Marxist Humanism* (New York: Grove Press, Inc., 1968). In his first chapter, "The Priest and the Jester," Kolakowski maintains that all social thought veers between two poles, the dogmatic and the comically critical. Well and good, but he finds that Marxist thought is of the latter type, anti-dogmatic and of the jester—a prime philosophic joke.

politics to a social unity and human equality, the ideal of which is essential to the solidarity of the body politic. As long as comic rationality is quick to ridicule political millennialism and its true believers, social balance is served. The rationality is writ large: Aristophanes versus Socrates.

The Comic Dialectic of Politics

Because comic rationality builds on the inherent contradictions of politics, it can be understood as a kind of dialectical reasoning in politics.*[17] The significance of understanding political humor as dialectical is that, if valid, it parallels the reasoning most natural to politics as a system of governing. Thereby, the sense of political humor again is demonstrated to be rooted in political life itself and to be a key element in its continuing health. In fact, to say that political humor is indigenous to actual politics is to assert the first claim for its dialectical kinship.

As we have seen abundantly, all forms of political humor are responses to real-life situations. Moreover, the very response is an indication of the presence of political strife. The comic response can be considered as a form of argument or a counterclaim in that strife, and, in many instances the humor, is partisan in a political issue. It would seem then that the comic rationality cannot be dialectical,

*The dialectical reasoning of politics is its give and take, which constitute a kind of corporate rationality and achieve a communal resolution of social issues. Partisans with special interests at issue make claims against each other and to the larger society, each seeking victory. But their claims are moderated, first by their implicit recognition of common social membership, and second, by their framing the claims in terms of the public interest in order to gain the support of the general community. In turn, the resolution of the issue by the public authorities proceeds from the general interest toward a compromise, which takes into account the partial justice of the special interests and attempts to give some satisfaction to all. The resolution of the political dialectic, then, is not truth, but a social sharing in a compromise that maintains community.

17. Cf. Leo Strauss, "On Classical Political Philosophy," *Social Research* (Feb. 1945). Also Leo Strauss, *What is Political Philosophy?* (Glencoe: The Free Press, 1959), pp. 78-94. Strauss explains the method of classical political philosophy, and from it I draw the model for the dialectical reasoning of politics.

let alone arbitrate an issue or provide for its impartial resolution. The partisanship of most political humor would
seem to disqualify it as dialectical reasoning. It does not
rise above civil strife in order to heal or understand it, but,
as comic aggression, is a factor in the strife. How can it
then maintain political community, mending its factional
wounds by calling forth its fundamental values?

But comic aggression is not the partisan aggressiveness
that divides political community. The very essence of political humor is that it is, at the same time, partisan and disin-
terested, factious and communal. If this contrary duality is
so, then comic rationality is supremely political; it politics
while insuring the political resolution of social conflict.

The partisanship of most political humor is self-evident,
though it need not take sides in a political issue. Political
humor may well ridicule or otherwise be against the entire
political context of an issue. However, comic partisanship is
not a direct challenge or conflict with another claimant for
political preference in the settlement of an issue. The comic
partisan is once-removed from the immediate fray in that
his claim is presented in the guise of humor. Thus, its overt
aggressiveness is sublimated into a peaceful mode that
pacifies the opponent while it covertly appeals to the audience on the grounds of commonly shared interests and values. The very nature of political humor as a communicative
art requires its transcending of special interest in an issue
and embracing a general interest of its audience. In the
very act of challenging his opponent, then, the comic partisan by his humor declares for peace with him, calls upon
the community of feeling, and reminds the audience of
their moral commonalty. To a lesser degree this is true
even of personal political invective, due to its leveling or
equalizing effect.

The ability to sublimate one's political aggressiveness and
rationalize it into a comic assault presupposes a certain detachment, even though fear inspired. The element of disinterestedness permits the comic partisan to grasp the weakness of his opponent, and conversely his strengths, to relate

them to the general interests, and to present implicitly in the political humor a guide to the resolution of the conflict. The comic aggressor is a partisan in a political issue, but just as his aggression is sublimated into a peaceful comic response that improves community goodwill, so also his partisanship transcends itself into the essence of political reciprocity—compromise.

Implicit in any comic partisanship is the compromising attitude. To retreat from the full and direct claim of one's interests or beliefs in a conflict to the peaceful and socialized comic claim is to be willing "to settle for half a loaf." Political humor not only solicits the audience for their common interest, but it advances its comic partisan claim in the context of that interest in order to make the audience its ally.

The comic claim is compromising in another way as well. To view something humorously is generally to cease to regard it as an enemy. That at which one can laugh is no longer fully threatening, and the very pleasure of the humor gives one some appreciation of its source. To laugh at someone in political humor is a step toward community with him.

Obviously, the dialectic of comic rationality is not explicit; neither is the humorist necessarily conscious of his reasoning. It is enough to say that there is a social sense in man that cultivates humor for the sake of community, and that successful political humor requires knowledge and reasoned construction. Its dialectic, rooted in the contradictions and actual clashes of politics, goes beyond them to create a politic attitude. In the classic case of Abraham Lincoln, the humorist-statesman does employ humor consciously and dialectically, but often the comic dialectic exists in the interplay of political humor: now anti-political, then anti-utopian; now anti-politician, then anti-people. However, the "anti" of political humor is always comically mellowed and compromising in its very response.

Finally, political humor that displays comic rationality parallels the classical dialectic of politics in its highest ex-

pression. It does so in the learning that humor affords political men of goodwill. The best humor is always something
of a puzzle in its camouflaged criticism, implicit standards,
and negativism. Its appreciation requires mental participation by the audience, and its lessons are not hortatory, but
self-learned. We come to our own conclusions through the
mix of our mind and the humorous materials. Because the
audience must participate mentally in the humor, it enters
into a community of comic political fellowship. When an
audience is comically receptive initially, it latently possesses
tolerant fellowship. It is open to the compromises of the
political give and take as it gropes toward the lesson of balance between man's moral potentiality and his existential
contradictoriness.

Comic Democracy and Democratic Politics

Winston Churchill observed that democracy is the worst
of all possible governments except for every other one.
Here, perhaps, is the ultimate contradiction of politics.
Democracy as the freest and most extended form of politics
allows the most people with the least qualifications the
greatest opportunity for participating in their own social
governance. Thereby, democracy sets in motion those con-
trarieties that are termed by some "the great issues of politics": the rule of the best versus the rule of the many, freedom versus equality, direct democracy versus representative democracy, and so on.

Democratic government cannot be classed dramatically as
a tragedy, unless one has faith in an infallible elite or a divinely inspired philosopher-king. There is nothing in the
annals of democracy to match the tragedies staged by Hitler
and Stalin. The blunders of politics may rise to the level of
grand farce. In American democracy the records of the
worst political leaders and the politics of their administra-
tions present high comedy, and political humorists have
fully exploited their opportunities.

Humorists may artfully refine the comedy of democratic politics, but the comedy is, at first hand, natural to the politics. One cannot read Francis Russell's political biography of Warren G Harding, *The Shadow of Blooming Grove*, without recognizing the spontaneous humor of democracy. The contemporary accounts of Richard Nixon's "seventh crisis," "the Watergate conspiracy," still enflame partisan passions, but the blundering and illegality are comical, not heinous criminal acts. In short, democratic politics, in its extension of franchise, increases the confusions of man's contradictoriness; it does not necessarily lead to a tragic tyranny of the majority.

The concomitance of political comedy and democratic politics is natural and functional. In his *Poetics*, Aristotle remarked on the rise of comic drama in Megara along with the emergence of democracy.[18] Whether the statement is historically accurate or not, it is hard to conceive of politically or socially relevant comic drama being permitted in a nondemocratically inclined political regime. Humor is natural to man's reasoning and is often directed against civilization and social authority, but the artful cultivation and public expression of it require the freedom and tolerance of democratic politics. Otherwise, governments will react to the negativism and critical realism of political humor as immoral or traitorous.

The functional relation of humor and comedy to democratic politics is due to its political nature. The contradictoriness of man comes to its peak in democratic politics; comic logic and thought build on contradictions. But, most important, sustaining democratic politics requires maintaining man's contradictoriness in tolerable compromise. Of all living creatures, man is biologically dual in nature and pluralist in society. Resolve unilaterally the conflicts and contradictions that spring from this existential fact and you end man's evolutionary and political freedom.

Political humor thrives on contradiction by ridiculing it; thereby, paradoxically, comic ridicule maintains political

18. Lane Cooper, p. 172.

contradictoriness. For comic ridicule generally focuses on the side of the opposed pair that threatens, through defect or excess, the continuance of the contradiction. When humor focuses on politics itself, its ridicule acts to prevent politics from ending itself by moving in a direction that would resolve a more fundamental contradiction in man. Moreover, political humor is always cathartic and, often, rationally constructive. Thus, humor fosters the political attitude of "live and let live."

In conclusion, the democratic nature of political humor is as clear as the demand for democracy in politics. As man is social, so does he speak and think; so also does he laugh. The distinctive manliness of his laughter is due to his distinctive sociability. His highest humor is of his language and reason, and is found in his politics. In politics, humor achieves the most universal communicability, speaking understandably to all men about matters of deepest concern, and in its own manner of reason and community. In politics, humor exults in our differences while ever reminding us in comic pithiness of our biological oneness; the humor of sex and toilet is the great equalizer of democracy. Moreover, if banal humor is the bane of the power hungry, then blasphemous humor is the antidote to the poison of pulpit politics. Aristophanic ridicule of the God-mad preserves the freedom of earthy politics.

The beast-driven and the God-man cannot abide with the political paradox of freedom in equality. Earthy men and their political humor cherish the paradox. Comically aggressive now against one side, then against the other, they laughingly patrol the borders of humanity against defect and excess.

Selected Bibliography

Aristophanes. *The Eleven Comedies*. New York: Tudor Publishing Co., 1912, 1936.

——. *The Complete Plays of Aristophanes*. Edited by Moses Hadas. New York: Bantam Books, Inc., 1962.

Bergson, Henri. "Laughter," Meredith, George, "An Essay on Comedy," in *Comedy*. New York: Doubleday and Co., Anchor Books, 1956. The most valuable feature of this book is a supplementary essay and appended bibliography by Wylie Sypher.

Blair, Walter. *Horse Sense in American Humor*. Chicago: University of Chicago Press, 1942.

Cooper, Lane. *An Aristotelian Theory of Comedy*. New York: Harcourt, Brace and Co., 1922.

Cornford, F. M. *The Origins of Attic Comedy*. New York: Doubleday and Co., Anchor Books, 1914, 1961.

Cox, Samuel S. *Why We Laugh*. New York: Benjamin Blom, Inc., 1876, 1969.

Feibleman, James K. *In Praise of Comedy*. New York: Horizon Press, 1939, 1970.

Freud, Sigmund. *Wit and Its Relation to the Unconscious* in *The Basic Writings of Sigmund Freud*. Edited and translated by A. A. Brill. New York: Random House, The Modern Library, 1938.

Goldstein, Jeffrey and McGhee, Paul, eds. *The Psychology of Humor*. New York: Academic Press, 1972. A very technical discussion, but it contains a valuable bibliographic essay, "Early Conceptions of Humor: Varieties & Issues," by Patricia Keith Spiegel.

Greene, William Chase. "The Spirit of Comedy in Plato." *Harvard Studies in Classical Philology*. Cambridge: Harvard University Press, 1920.

Harris, Leon A. *The Fine Art of Political Wit*. (New York: Dutton and Co., 1964.

Highet, Gilbert. *The Anatomy of Satire*. Princeton: Princeton University Press, 1962.

Huizinga, Johan. *Homo Ludens*. Boston: Beacon Press, 1938, 1967.

Kerr, Walter. *Tragedy and Comedy*. New York: Simon and Schuster, A Clarion Book, 1967.

Klein, Jacob. *A Commentary on Plato's* Meno. Chapel Hill: The University of North Carolina Press, 1965. A valuable bibliography of the comedy and drama in the Platonic dialogues.

Koestler, Arthur. *The Act of Creation*. New York: Dell Publishing Co., Laurel ed., 1964, 1973. I consider Koestler's Part One, "The Jester," to be the single most valuable essay on the general theory of humor.

Lewin, Leonard C., ed. *A Treasury of American Political Humor*. New York: Delacorte Press, 1964.

Murray, Gilbert. *Aristophanes*. London: Oxford Press, 1933.

Sandburg, Carl. *Abraham Lincoln: The War Years*. 4 vols. New York: Harcourt, Brace and Co., 1936. The best essay and study on Lincoln's humor is in vol. 3, chap. 56, "Lincoln's Laughter and His Religion."

Strauss, Leo. *Socrates and Aristophanes*. New York: Basic Books, 1966.

Tandy, Jennette. *Crackerbox Philosophers in American Humor and Satire*. New York: Columbia University Press, 1925.

Thomson, J. A. K. *Irony: An Historical Introduction*. Cambridge: Harvard University Press, 1927.

INDEX

337